Ricky Tomlinson was born in September 1939 and was brought up in Liverpool, where he now lives with his wife Rita.

'There are many memoirs . . . rushed out to capitalise on even the most momentary blaze of public attention. Of an altogether higher standard, Ricky Tomlinson relates an amazing life: a childhood marked by privation but rich in colour; a strong political idealism forged in early adulthood; jailed on conspiracy charges and hailed as a political prisoner; then fame as a TV actor in *Brookside* and *The Royle Family* . . . This wonderful memoir is studded with magnificent detail, Tomlinson stepping nimbly between nostalgia and clear-eyed self-examination' *The Times*

'If there is a better written, less pretentious book by an actor, then I have yet to read it. Undoubtedly the show business book of the year' *Independent on Sunday*

'Ricky comes up trumps . . . the book thrums with energy . . . beautifully constructed' *Sunday Times*

'Deliciously indiscreet . . . what elevates this book from most showbiz biographies are the chapters about Tomlinson's six-week trial and subsequent imprisonment as one of the Shrewsbury two' *Sunday Express*

'His life has been as messy as any reader could hope' *Evening Standard*

'A rollicking autobiography . . . Ricky is now a star for life, and his book throbs with astonishment at the fact' Paul Foot, *Oldie*

'Ricky Tomlinson is an amazing actor – one of the very few that can make me both laugh and cry. He is also one of the most genuine, warm-hearted and sincere people I know. But I would never tell him that. Is he a scouser?' Caroline Aherne

'Ricky Tomlinson is a rarity in this business, a real person, a genuine talent, and one of the best actors I have ever worked with' Robert Carlyle

'Actors are born, not made. Ricky was born an actor, but what makes him shine is his heart – open, generous, fun-filled and bigger than the mouth of the Mersey' Roland Joffe

'Ricky Tomlinson is a fine actor. His work – and comedy – springs from a life that has seen hardship and struggle and many changes in fortune . . . he has always known which side he is on, as those who have experienced his generosity and loyalty will testify' Ken Loach

'I love Ricky. It's not for his looks, that's for sure. And it's not for his talent, huge as it is. It is for this: his wonderful humanity' Jimmy McGovern

Visit Ricky Tomlinson's website: www.rickytomlinson.com

RICKY

RICKY TOMLINSON

timewarner
paperbacks

A *Time Warner* Paperback

First published in Great Britain in 2003 by Time Warner Books
First published by Time Warner Paperbacks 2004
Reprinted in 2004 (three times)

A CIP catalogue record for this book
is available from the British Library.

ISBN 0 7515 3403 X

Typeset in Caslon by M Rules
Printed and bound in Great Britain by
Clays Ltd, St Ives plc

Time Warner Paperbacks
An imprint of
Time Warner Book Group UK
Brettenham House
Lancaster Place
London WC2E 7EN

www.twbg.co.uk

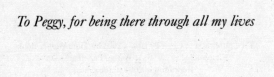

To Peggy, for being there through all my lives

Contents

They hang us now in Shrewsbury jail:
The whistles blow forlorn,
And trains all night groan on the rail
To men that die at morn.

There sleeps in Shrewsbury jail to-night,
Or wakes, as may betide,
A better lad, if things went right,
Than most that sleep outside.

A.E. HOUSMAN, 'A Shropshire Lad'

Introduction

As a youngster of about thirteen I toyed with the idea of being a writer. I didn't know the name of a single famous author, but I loved reading spy stories and stuff about the supernatural by Denis Wheatley. Becoming a writer was unheard of for someone with my background. Even reading was a dangerous pastime. Get caught with a book and my brother Albert was likely to clip me round the ear and say, 'Who have we got here then? Bloody Einstein!'

Operating in secret, I used to write bits of poetry and short stories. I couldn't risk showing anyone so instead I ripped them up in case anyone found them and started taking the piss.

One day I wrote a story called 'Mulberry Mansions'. I must have been about sixteen by then. I took it over to Lenny Johnson's house because he had sisters who could type.

Brenda Johnson took the story from me and came round to the house the next day with it neatly typed and double spaced.

'This story,' she said. 'You haven't got the rest of it, have you? I want to know what happens.'

I was made up, but I still didn't finish it. By then I had started playing the banjo and chasing after girls who did more than just type.

It took me another fifteen years before I wrote seriously again. By then I was in prison scribbling a diary on toilet paper that I smuggled out to my solicitor's office. Writing was like a safety valve and a way of passing the long hours in solitary.

This time it is different again. They say you should never use an autobiography to settle old scores. Why not? A lot of lies have been written about me in the newspapers and it hurts. It doesn't hurt as much now that my Mam has died, but I still want to make amends.

I know that I'm going to get stick over this book, but there you go. It can't be helped. And some readers might think I'm a terrible liar when they read what follows, but everything I've written here is true. Enough lies have been told about me, without me adding to them.

I don't care how badly I come out of these pages. I have done things in my life that I'm not proud of. I have made mistakes and said things I wish I could take back. I have fallen out with people who didn't deserve it and lost touch with others I would desperately like to find.

At the same time, I have to make one concession. I don't think it's fair if I hurt people who have done nothing wrong. Why should I reveal their secrets or private moments? I guess I'm thinking in particular of all the wonderful women that I've known. Most of them are now mums and grandmums and I don't want to embarrass them. That's why I've decided to change a few names to protect the innocent.

So where do I start? With a bit of the present and a bit of the past because the thread between them is thinner than a prison blanket.

1

You'll Never Walk Alone

Monday 14 May 2002

I can't find my black shoes. A man can't go to a funeral without black shoes. I mean, what else are they for? Weddings, christenings, film premieres and funerals – that's about the sum total. Maybe Rita knows where they are.

She has gone to the dry cleaners to pick up my suit. I hope I fit into the bloody trousers. For months she's been badgering me about losing weight – a few less bacon butties and pints of Sainsbury's Mild. That's why there isn't a biscuit in the place unless you count those rice crackers that taste like cardboard.

The funeral is at one o'clock. I know I'm going to cry. I always do. Ever since I was a boy and right into adulthood I have been a sucker for winning goals in Cup matches, underdogs winning Olympic medals and triumphs over adversity.

I'll never forget that 400-metre semi-final at the Barcelona Games when Derek Redmond collapsed on the track with a torn hamstring. He kept getting to his feet and hobbling down the track when everyone else had finished. Then this old guy jumps the fence, pushes aside security guards and goes to help him. It was his Dad. How could anyone not be moved?

Englishmen aren't supposed to have any emotion. Italians and the Spanish ooze it, but we're supposed to have this stiff upper lip and keep everything under control. My arse!

Mam always hated me swearing. Then again, if a grown man can't shed a few tears over his mother dying there is something wrong with the world. Mam deserves buckets of them. Let them fill the Mersey and the Irish Sea.

I still can't quite believe that she's gone. For eighty-six years she seemed indestructible; like one of the mythical Liver Birds perched high above the river, Mam watched over our family and kept us together.

Last Christmas she sat in this very chair, looking out over the water, watching me feed the swans from the balcony. We have seven of them now, including five little 'uns, along with two cormorants and some Canada geese. Listen to me. I sound like David bloody Attenborough.

Not that long ago, the Mersey was so polluted that you didn't see many birds unless they were covered in oil. And nobody went fishing for anything you could eat. A lot about Liverpool has come back to life in the last ten years, but it still carries the scars.

Margaret Thatcher was far more successful than the Luftwaffe *at destroying this place – closing down the docks, shutting up factories, hammering the working classes. A generation of Scousers will dance on her grave one day. Mam won't be there, but hopefully I will.*

Rita cooked a lovely Christmas dinner. Mam sat at one end of the table wearing a Christmas hat with a small glass of wine in front of her.

'Do you want another roast potato, Peg?'

'Just a small one.'

'How about some more parsnips and sprouts?'

'Just a spoonful.'

She finished up with a pile of food on her plate that Red Rum couldn't have jumped over. It made me laugh.

Every time she went to get up I panicked. I was frightened of her slipping on the runners in the hall with her walking stick.

'Take it easy. I'm not going to break,' she told me, when I held her too tightly.

After dinner she sat back in my armchair and watched the sun going down on the water. At about nine o'clock she was nodding off with a cup of tea on the table beside her, alongside a little bit of Christmas cake.

'C'mon, Mam, time for bed.'

She went reluctantly. She wanted to make the day last because she didn't know how many more Christmases she'd see. She shuffled into the back bedroom and got herself ready for bed before calling Rita to come and tuck her in. She loved having a fuss made over her. And why not? She made a fuss over me for long enough.

I'll tell you the saddest moment for me. We were watching the TV news together and there was a story about a ninety-six-year-old woman who was battered about the head by thieves, who broke in and stole her pension.

Mam turned to me and said, 'Rick, I am so glad I'm going out of this world and not coming into it.'

She meant it. The world had changed. Until a few years ago I had never heard of a pensioner getting attacked or of 'no go' areas where emergency services wouldn't answer calls because of fears for their safety. Mam survived a terrible war and spent thirty years a widow, but she still wouldn't swap any of those years for the present. It's enough to make you weep.

Adolf Hitler did his best to overshadow my arrival. There I was, snug and cosy, with nothing better to do than head-butt Mam's bladder five times a night, when he decided to invade Poland. It's amazing what some people will do to compensate for having only one ball.

Peggy Tomlinson was nine months pregnant when she

was evacuated from Liverpool in case of bombing. A lot of kids were sent away in the early days of the war, billeted on farms or with relatives who lived in the country. Mam left behind my brother, Albert, aged two, and my Dad who had a priority job as a baker and couldn't go with her.

I was born at a place called Burleigh House in Bispham, Blackpool, on 26 September 1939 (war had been declared on 3 September). I've always pictured it as one of those rambling seaside boarding houses with a rose garden and deckchairs on the lawn. It was only forty miles by train from Liverpool, yet it was another twenty years before I travelled that far again.

I was a big lump – nine and a half pounds, with blond, very curly hair that was so fine people used to think I was bald. Mam had me christened Eric, but only a handful of people have ever called me that. To everyone else I was Rick.

Mam stayed in Blackpool for three days before she packed her things, ignored the warnings, and went back to Liverpool.

'We're all in this together,' she told Dad, as she criss-crossed the windows with sticky tape and dyed flour sacks to make blackout curtains.

Despite my size at birth, I proved to be a sickly little bastard, going back and forth to hospital for 'failing to thrive'. Mam used to come four times a day to feed me, trudging through the snow to Belmont Road Hospital, half a mile away.

'Sometimes mine were the only footsteps in the snow,' she said later.

Eventually, they discovered that I had asthma – a disease as baffling to the experts then as it is today. Hot days were the worst, when there seemed to be no air. I fought for every breath, dragging it into my lungs in wheezing gulps. Wide-eyed with fear, I felt as though I was slowly suffocating.

One of my earliest memories – I must have been about four or five – is of Mam lying next to me, whispering, 'Just take it easy. Breathe in. Deep breaths. Relax.'

She would put a cool flannel on my forehead and stay with me until the panic had gone.

The doctors gave me exercises to develop my lungs. Dad would put a blanket over our little square dining table and put a table-tennis ball in the centre.

'Come on, Rick, blow the ball off the table,' he'd say, handing me a drinking straw. I did this for an hour every day, while other kids were outside playing.

Of a Saturday Mam would give me an old-fashioned penny and send me to Hughes's Chemist in Heyworth Street to get weighed. The pharmacist wrote down my weight on a piece of paper. For a while they talked about sending me away to a convalescent home 'over the water' in the Wirral, where the air was less polluted, but clean air is no substitute for a family. In the end I stayed put, growing up at 37 Lance Street – a two-up-two-down about three-quarters of a mile from Liverpool's football ground in a working-class area of Everton full of terraces with back entries and outside lavatories.

Mam and Dad had the front bedroom overlooking the street, while Albert and me shared a double bed in the back room. Our David came along eighteen months later and Ronny didn't arrive until 1948 when I was almost nine.

Downstairs, at the back of the house, was a kitchen with a black fire-grate in the corner, a sink, a cooker, a dining table and four chairs. This was the heart of the house – where we ate our meals, settled our arguments and learned the sort of lessons that all parents teach their children.

The front room was known as the parlour or 'the best room' with a three-piece suite, a sideboard and radiogram.

Mam had hung nice net curtains on the windows and Dad put good lino on the floor. None of us were allowed to play in there. It was reserved for visitors and special occasions like Christmas.

The toilet was outside in the small rear yard, which meant a trek by candlelight at night and ripping off squares of the *Liverpool Echo* to wipe your arse. None of us had ever seen proper toilet paper.

Once a week on Saturday night, the 'bungalow bath' was taken off the wall outside and placed in front of the fire. Albert got to go first, being the eldest, and then we each took turns.

I dreaded bath night because I hated water and cleaning behind my ears. Mam scrubbed us with Derback soap, which killed anything in our hair, and then threw a big towel around us to stop us shivering. Kneeling behind us in front of the fire, with a newspaper on her knee, she combed our hair for nits with a horrible metal-toothed comb that left tramlines in your scalp.

'Ow! Mam. No, ye hurtin'.'

'Ah'm not havin' people talk about me.'

A letter from the nit nurse was the cause of great shame.

My Dad, Albert Edward Tomlinson, looked a bit like George Raft, the big Hollywood star of the thirties. Slightly built, with dark eyes and black hair slicked back with a comb, he was a snappy dresser and a good dancer when given the opportunity – which was rarely.

For twenty-seven years (from the age of fourteen) he worked nights as a baker. This would have been enough to put paid to many marriages, but I guess that's a testament to how much they meant to each other.

'Don't make a noise, your Dad's in bed,' Mam would warn

us during the day. And then at about seven each evening, she'd say, 'Give your Dad a shout. It's time for his tea.'

He woke and I watched him strip down to his old-fashioned white vest. He had a wash in a basin of cold water and put on his work clothes. I remember being shocked when I caught him with his teeth out. I had no idea.

Downstairs Mam had set a plate of chips and an egg on the table, alongside a copy of the *Liverpool Echo*. We lads hovered around him like gulls, scavenging chips. Mam used to scold him for feeding us, but my Dad ate virtually nothing. He seemed to survive on tea and toast or the cheese and crackers that Mam saved for him special.

'I'm goin' in a minute, Peg,' he'd say.

'Got time for another cup of tea?' she'd ask.

'Just a half a cup, thanks.'

This would crack me up. 'Which half do you want, Dad, the top or the bottom?' I'd say.

If the tea was too hot and he was running late, he poured it into his saucer and slurped it up. Mam went bonkers. She liked to think we were a bit better than that.

I know they loved each other. You could see it in dozens of little ways. 'Get out of your father's chair,' she'd say, when he was due downstairs. And when he left for work, she'd put a scarf on him and tuck it into his jacket. That was the closest they ever came to a public display of affection, apart from the Christmas I saw him kiss her on the cheek.

I loved my Dad. I loved him when I didn't even know what the word meant. I used to get excited waiting for him to come home. I would see him coming or I'd hear the latch lift on the back door. Then I'd bury my head under his arm which smelled of flour and warm bread.

Dad worked at a little bakery on Heyworth Street called Kelly's. He was a hand-baker not a machinist – a skilled craftsman. The ovens were in the cellar and it was hotter than hell down there and the air was always thick with flour.

Some people gave Dad some stick because he wasn't away fighting – the white feather and all that. This hurt him because he would have gone if he'd been allowed. Bakers were considered essential workers and he had to supply the local hospitals and schools. When the air raid sirens sounded everyone else could scurry for the shelters, but Dad had to keep baking. A bombed city would still need bread in the morning.

The sirens seemed to go off constantly and there were shelters built in almost every street. These consisted of four walls with a nine-inch slab of concrete on the top and doors at either end. Bunks ran down either side but nobody ever slept.

There were half a dozen shelters in Lance Street. When Mam was heavily pregnant with David it was hard for her to get all of us out of bed and into the shelter. The sirens would sound and Albert had to make his own way down the stairs in the pitch black, while Mam held tightly on to my hand. She came down the stairs on her bum one step at a time. If the bombers were already overhead, she panicked and bundled us under the stairs, lying on top of us.

I remember Mr Hart, who lived over the road, coming to get us. He was registered blind, which meant he had less trouble getting around in the dark. Mam held me, while Albert kept hold of her dress as Mr Hart led us to safety.

After David was born it became even more difficult. Some nights Mam was too exhausted to care. She gathered us into bed, wrapping us in her arms, saying, 'If we go, we'll all go together.' We lay under the blankets, listening to the explosions and the bells of the fire engines.

I was too young to realise the danger we were in or to

understand death or war. Our soldiers were glamorous in their uniforms, while the Germans made good villains. We were always playing war games in the streets, mowing down the Nazis with our wooden tommy guns and souveniring shrapnel from the bomb sites.

The local coppers would often drop by the bakery of an evening for a pot of tea and a fresh barm cake (bap). Policemen in those days still walked the beat and kept young troublemakers in line with a good clip around the ear and 'on yer way'. The Panda cars changed all that. The police lost their presence on the streets and a lot of the community respect they enjoyed.

Two policemen arrived at the bakery one night and told Dad that Lance Street had gone up. He was off in a flash. It was only six hundred yards to home, but they were the longest yards of his life. As he came down Heyworth Street he saw the smoke and flames. He didn't know whether it was our house. He knew it was close.

A house diagonally behind us and two down had taken a direct hit. The flames were bigger than any bonfire. Dad found us huddled under the stairs and took us to the shelter.

Whole blocks were flattened where Granny Tomlinson lived in Robsart Street. Her parlour house became a makeshift morgue as she helped wash down the bodies and get them ready for burial. This wasn't her job, but circumstances alter cases, particularly in wartime.

Nobody called Gran by her married name. She was forever known as Fanny Hunter and was the sort of character that Charles Dickens might have created. She was the family matriarch and such was the power of her personality that my father was more often called Albie Hunter than Albie Tomlinson.

Fanny was small and stocky, with her hair pulled back from

her face. I never saw it hanging out or looking glamorous. Everyone deferred to her, even our family GP, Dr McCabe, who sought her advice on various ailments involving children. The moment she walked in his surgery he pulled a bottle of whisky from his bottom drawer and poured her a shot.

'What do you think of this one, Fanny?' he'd ask, describing the symptoms.

I was in awe of my grandmother. We used to visit her every Sunday and her house was always full of people. She had a sister living next door and various daughters and sons-in-law, along with their offspring, lived in the adjoining houses. Fanny fed them all on a single gas ring and a big black fire-grate, where a large kettle steamed and potatoes cooked at the side. She also went to the washhouse two or three times a day with a bundle of dirty clothes and sheets on her head. Afterwards she did the ironing with an old flat iron heated on the gas ring.

Times were tough and often families struggled to put food on the table. Fanny would pawn Grandad Tomo's suit for a few shillings and lend the money to the wives to buy bread, potatoes and milk. She didn't charge anyone interest. Come Friday, when the loans had been repaid, she got the suit back so Grandad Tomo could wear it on Sunday.

My father was the first grandson in more than a generation and he was spoilt rotten by aunts, great aunts and female cousins. They bought him brown and white patent leather shoes and little jackets with matching hats. My Uncle Ritchie came along later, which probably saved Dad from being completely ruined.

(Uncle Ritchie fought in the war as a Chindit – one of the so-called 'Forgotten Army' who fought deep behind enemy lines in the jungles of Burma. The Ministry of Defence sent a telegram to the house to say that he had died in action. A

few weeks later they sent another telegram sa~~y~~
been a mistake. Would you believe it, a third teleg~~r~~
saying that he'd definitely been killed. They were all wrong.
He came home from Burma, fathered three lads and lived to
be fifty-one.)

My grandfather was known as Black Dick and 'the little
shoe shine boy' because of his dark skin. These nicknames
weren't coined as insults and were as much a product of his
job – mixing the black pitch to repair roads – as his colour. As
a kid I used to think it was his job that made his skin so dark.

According to my Aunt Dooney, all of his brothers and
sisters were white, which only adds to the mystery. Whatever
the explanation, race and colour were never an issue in those
days. Our next-door neighbour Mrs Gossen was West Indian,
with wonderful crinkly hair that had just started to go grey. If
we ever came home and Mam and Dad were both out, we'd
go over to Mrs Gossen's and she made us a cup of tea and a
jam sandwich.

On the other side of us lived Mrs Rowan, who had tattoos,
one collapsed nostril, and a bit of a reputation. I didn't see
Mrs Gossen as a black woman and Mrs Rowan as being
white. They were just our neighbours.

Far more than race, it was religion that divided people in
Liverpool. As a young woman Fanny Hunter worked in a
tobacco factory – the only Protestant on a floor full of
Catholics. According to the family legend – told to me by
Dad – someone was hired to kill Fanny or at least make sure
she didn't come back to work.

The knife sliced through her clothing but missed her vital
organs. Before her attacker could land a second blow, Fanny
launched herself at him, pummelling him with her fists and
feet. Nobody ever threatened her again.

Religious intolerance was part of the fabric of my childhood, ingrained into youngsters in a thousand little ways. Catholics were different. It was us against them.

On the sides of the terraces around Robsart Street there were huge drawings of William of Orange and the Battle of the Boyne. 'No Surrender' declared the banners. And on 12 July the bands would assemble there, along with hundreds of people dressed in purple and orange. They marched down Netherfield Road singing Orange Order songs, playing quietly as they passed the hospital and then striking up again.

When the march reached William Henry Street, a Catholic stronghold, the Catholics would stand at the top of the street and hurl stones, bottles and abuse.

'Fuck off, you Protestant bastards,' they cried, and their kids would hurl bags of pepper into the eyes of the marchers, many of whom were only kids themselves.

Fanny Hunter didn't march on 12 July, but joined the celebrations afterwards on the train to Southport and by the seaside. Once or twice, if I was off school, she took me along.

Religion didn't seem to figure as large in Mam and Dad's thinking. Live and let live seemed to be their attitude. You take the Taggarts, a Catholic family who lived about three or four doors from us. They had four lads and a daughter called Pattie. I remember them losing a son, a toddler, who died when a coal cart drove over him.

My Dad was very fond of Pattie, perhaps because he had no daughters of his own. When she was about six years old she came down with TB meningitis – a rare and generally fatal disease. She lost her hair, her hearing and some of her speech. Nobody expected her to live.

Dad had a mate who was going to Lourdes and he asked him to bring back a bottle of the holy water. It was a Catholic shrine but that didn't enter his thinking. I took the holy water to the Taggarts and every night they put a few drops on

Pattie's head. Slowly she began to get better until she was out of danger, albeit profoundly deaf. To this day the Taggarts will tell you that she was cured by the holy water. Religion and faith were two different things to Dad.

Mam was working as a waitress in Brown's café when she met Dad. Although not a great beauty, she was dead attractive with brown hair and dark eyes. She and her girlfriends all looked like Veronica Lake clones, with their hair brushed to one side and their lips painted bright red. Apparently, Dad looked very handsome in his suit and best shoes. They fell in love over a cup of tea and a biscuit.

I think my Mam liked to think her family was a little bit more refined than the Tomlinsons. For one thing they lived in a slightly nicer street and had a parlour house with a proper hallway, rather than having a front door that opened directly into the 'best room'. Gran Wilson was also not the sort to get involved in knife fights at work.

My grandad, Billy Wilson, was a carter with a team of horses that hauled wheat, maize, sugar, wool, cotton and other produce to and from the docks. In those days almost every pub had two doors opening on to the same street. They reckon this was because of the carters, who would leave their horses walking along the road, dash in one door, down a pint and head out the other in time to meet the cart. It takes a serious thirst to do that.

Grandad 'Willow' used to pride himself on winning the best horse at the May Day competitions. He spent hours scrubbing, grooming and polishing, hanging the horse tack off the stairs.

Grandad also bred dogs, which he sold to rich people who would come to the house in Rolls-Royces and Bentleys. It was the only time I ever saw real toffs.

The dogs were rare breeds like Chihuahuas and Pekinese. He used to put the newborn puppies in the oven to keep them warm and, if the breed called for it, he bit off their tails with his teeth, which he said was the kindest way of docking them. The Chihuahuas were the size of mice when they were born. Gran used to sometimes tuck the puppies inside her shawl against her breasts, while she was doing the housework.

Years later, after Grandad died, she came to live next door to us, but by then Granny Willow had gone a bit senile and used to flush her money down the toilet and ramble on about people from her past. I had left home by then, but I still dropped by for a cup of tea and some of Mam's cooking.

No one was rich and no one was poor in Lance Street. We were all in the same leaky boat – struggling to make ends meet. With a husband and three kids to look after, Mam couldn't afford to stop working. She was cleaning two pubs and working in a washhouse.

At night she used to cut up old coats and make fireside mats out of bits of sacking. These were given away to friends or swapped with neighbours. She also dyed our clothes or altered them to make them last a bit longer because we couldn't afford new ones. In the kitchen she weaved the same sort of magic, even at the height of the food shortages and rationing. None of the meals were fancy, but there was always plenty of bread and potatoes.

When Albert started school, she sent me and David to a nursery. On the first day, at home time, David wandered around crying, 'I want my Eric. I want my Eric.' They couldn't find me anywhere.

They opened the lid of a toybox and found me trapped

inside. The darkness and fear had triggered an asthma attack. 'I won't be naughty any more,' I cried. 'Please. I'll be good.'

Our David still ribs me about saving my life. That's what brothers are like.

The winters were bloody freezing in those days. Pipes would burst or the cistern in the lavatory would freeze solid. Ashes and salt had to be scattered on the footpaths to stop people slipping over.

By the time the coalman came through the streets, nine times out of ten we were usually down to nothing but dust and fragments. In a really bad winter I used to pull my trusty steering cart down to the coal yard in Roscommon Street where they sold coaldust briquettes. You could wait up to three hours to get a couple of the bricks made of compressed coal dust and cement. They were shite, but at least they burned. And if we were really lucky, the gasworks sometimes sold bags of coke for a couple of coppers.

On the coldest nights Dad would come home from the bakery and set the fire before we woke. God love him. By the time we came downstairs the kitchen would be warm and a big pot of tea and fresh barm cakes were waiting on the table. Then he went back to work for a few more hours.

During the day he slept and did chores around the house. His only vice was a little flutter on the horses of a Saturday.

'Don't tell your Mam,' he'd say, as he checked out the form guide. I don't think Mam really minded. It was only ever a couple of two shilling doubles.

Dad wrote his instructions on a piece of paper and wrapped the money inside. Then he sent me to a back entry near the top of Heyworth Street where an illegal bookie had his pitch.

The bookie gave each of his regular customers a *nom de plume* like 'Bertie the Baker', which he wrote in a ledger, along with the bet and the odds.

Dad checked the 'Stop Press' of the *Liverpool Echo* for the results of the races and then sent me to collect his winnings.

'Anything for Bertie the Baker?' I'd ask the bookie.

'Yeah, half a crown. Here you go, son.'

'But me Dad said it was three and thruppence.'

'I got it written down here. It's only half a crown.'

I stood my ground. 'No, it was definitely three and three. That's what me Dad said.'

We argued and he swore under his breath. Passers-by began to stop and stare. I wouldn't budge. Eventually, he paid out to avoid the unwanted attention.

It took me years to discover that Dad made a habit of scamming the bookie. He knew exactly how much money he was owed – half a crown – but he still tried it on and managed to get away with it more times than not.

His other great fiddle was claiming to have put down a bet during pitch-and-toss schools. A popular form of gambling in pubs, two coins were thrown in the air and people gambled on the result. Two heads meant a win, two tails a loss and a head and a tail meant a re-throw. A 'belt man' collected the bets and paid out the winnings.

Dad would always have his hand out for his share, even though he'd never had a bet. Some poor sod would start screaming about being jibbed as the belt man shook his head and said, 'No, it's all paid out.'

By then we'd be off home, having caused bloody murder.

Dad didn't drink as such. A couple of pints would be enough. At weddings, engagements or if Liverpool had won through to the Cup Final, he would take Mam down to the Garrick, a little pub on the corner of Lance Street. Mam would have a port and lemon and Dad a bottle of Brown or a light ale.

I used to climb up on the windowsill and look inside. The women were all squashed around tables and the men stood at the bar. Dad would bring us crisps and a bottle of lemonade and Mam would scold him. She didn't approve of kids hanging around in pub doorways.

Because he drank so little, Dad's mates would always ask him to mind the kitty when they went to the pub. Dad would act as though this was a real chore, but in truth I knew exactly what he was doing. He always skimmed a little off the top so he could buy himself ten Woodbines.

Invariably, he started singing, usually Bing Crosby medleys and cowboy songs. I don't know if he had a good voice, but I was always made up when he sang to us at bedtime.

Like most lads my age, I was a bit of a tearaway, and the neighbours would often complain about things I'd done.

Dad would stand in the doorway and call me home. As I ducked inside he took a swing at the back of my head, but I was always too quick for him. The other lads were the same.

At night when we shared the double bed and told ghost stories, David would shout down the stairs, 'Maam. They're frightnin' me.'

'You boys stop scaring your brother.'

Of course, we kept going.

'Maam, they're still frightnin' me.'

'Albert.' (We always knew she was serious when she called him Albert.) 'If you don't be quiet I'll send your father up.'

We pushed it right to the limit and then some.

'Right, I've warned you,' Dad yelled, taking a stair rod and storming up into our room. He swung open the door and went whack, whack, whack on the bed.

We were moaning and groaning. 'No, Dad. No. We're sorry.'

He went back downstairs and I heard Mam say, 'It's about time. They've been askin' for that all day.'

Under the blankets I whispered to Albert. 'He missed me.'

'He missed me, too.'

'He never hit me either,' echoed David.

For ten years he missed. Three boys in the one bed and he couldn't hit one of us. He was wonderful.

2

'Comedy isn't as Hard as Boxing'

I know what you did with the frogs, Mam. I spent years trying to work it out, but eventually Dad gave the game away. All those frogs disappearing . . . I should have known something was up. You said they went off to the countryside. You made it sound like there was some holiday camp for frogs.

I still remember how we got that aquarium. You decided you wanted to keep the coal under cover in the back yard. Granny Wilson had this huge metal sea chest which would do the job perfectly.

You sent me and Albert to collect it, with Dad to supervise. I must have been about twelve and Albert fourteen. We carried this chest home, banging on the side and singing at the top of our lungs. Dad walked ahead of us, not wanting to be seen with us, I suppose.

We started making fun of him and winding him up. Dad got a bit of a gob on and clipped us around the ear. 'Yer snotty-nosed bastards,' he said.

Albert and me fell about laughing. Dad very rarely swore and we'd never heard him use the word 'bastard' before. We took off, running up the street, still carrying this chest. Dad chased after us like a man possessed and caught us about two or three yards from home.

'Don't tell yer Mam,' he said, looking panic-stricken. 'Yer both promise me. Don't tell her I swore.'

That coal chest sat out back for years, until it outlived its usefulness. Then I turned it into an aquarium and filled it with loads of frogspawn collected from Kirkby. First I had tadpoles and then pet frogs. It was brilliant.

Strangely, they began disappearing.

'Mam, me frogs are gone,' I said.

'Well, they've probably gone off to the countryside.'

'How?'

'They hopped.'

'OK.'

So I went and got another jar of frogspawn but the same thing happened again . . . and again.

I must have been in my twenties when Dad told me what really happened. You made him put the frogs down the toilet because they made you squeamish.

Everyone knew everyone in Lance Street. No doors were ever locked. You just knocked and walked in. The street was just wide enough for two cars to pass although I can't remember ever seeing two cars in the street at the same time.

There were around sixty houses and most had children. I can name virtually every family. The Flemmings had seven boys and the Muskers seven girls. Then there were the Taggarts, Moores, Bains and Jennings . . .

In the long twilights we played catch and chase games on the street like 'Tick' and 'Alalio'. Most of the boys had wooden tommy guns or sometimes the real thing, with the firing pin removed. These had been bought for a couple of coppers after the war when fellas would come round the streets with handcarts selling old rifles.

By far the most terrifying game was played along the entries, which ran between the houses. The passages were three feet wide, flanked by high brick walls slick with moss.

It was a test of bravery to balance on one wall and then hurl yourself across the gap, hopefully landing on the other side on your stomach. We called this 'belly banding'.

The bigger kids could jump from wall to wall in one long stride and would have races leaping from one to the other. One slip could mean a broken neck.

One of my favourite tricks was to tie black cotton to a doorknocker in the street and then trail it across the road to a hiding place in one of the entries.

I tugged the cotton.

'Knock. Knock.'

Mrs Stringer, a fifties version of Hyacinth Bucket, opened the door, looked up and down the street and then closed it again.

I waited half a second.

'Knock. Knock.'

The trick was to see how many times I could do it before she caught on and snapped the cotton. No matter what door I targeted and how well I hid, the reaction was always the same.

'I know it's you Ricky Tomo, you little shite. I'm gonna tell your Mam.'

Every street had its own little gang, safeguarding territory and feeling self-important. Mostly it was just posturing, but occasionally we got into scraps. Nothing serious. A bloody nose at worst. Although small for my age, I knew how to handle myself. Coming from Liverpool and having three brothers teaches you to learn to punch above your weight or talk your way out of trouble.

Later on, when I became a teenager, even the other side of the road became a dividing line. It was only twenty feet across, from door to door, but we still managed to create a rivalry that was almost tribal. It was the same at school. Everything became a contest, whether pissing highest up a wall or playing soccer at recess.

For years after the war there were dozens of bombed-out houses in Liverpool, which looked like missing or broken teeth. We called them 'bombdies' and were always being warned not to go near them. At the end of Lance Street there was a bombed-out shop called Scots, which had sections of floor missing and a collapsed roof. We created a great hideout by scavenging a table and chairs, along with candles. We even lit a fire and made cups of tea that were full of cinders and bits of floating wood.

I climbed over the wall one day and found a suitcase full of clothes in the shop. My imagination ran wild. I thought of German spies and Gestapo agents infiltrating the neighbourhood. I could be a hero. Maybe they'd give me a medal.

I dragged the suitcase home.

'Where did you get it?' asked Mam.

I had to tell her. 'In the old shop on the corner.'

She gave me an earful about bombdies being dangerous and then sent me upstairs.

'But what about the German spy?'

'Don't be so daft. I don't know where you get such ideas.'

I watched through a crack in the door as she opened the case and examined the contents. Dresses and blouses? What would a German spy be doing with them? I thought.

The suitcase belonged to a girl in our street, Bessie Highfield. She and her boyfriend were planning to elope that night but I had messed everything up by finding the suitcase. For a long while I worried that I had ruined someone's happiness, but Bessie eventually married the boy and they lived in Lance Street for years.

*

Every 5 November the pride of Lance Street was at stake. A huge bonfire blocked the road, built from wood that had been stockpiled for weeks. Floorboards were ripped out of bombdies and packing crates were broken down. Anything we couldn't scrounge we stole, organising raids on neighbouring streets.

A favourite trick was pinching lavatory doors and 'Liverpool pans' (toilet seats), which were basically a big sheet of plywood with a hole through the centre. While we'd be off pinching someone else's, they'd be pinching ours.

The bonfires were so huge they blistered the paint on the nearest houses. Dad usually bought a little box of fireworks. Nothing fancy: just a few Roman candles and Catherine wheels. We were always trying to sneak off with the penny thunderclaps, which were great for putting into people's letterboxes and terrorising the neighbourhood pets.

As the fire burned down we cooked potatoes in the coals and tossed them from hand to hand until they cooled. And around midnight, as people drifted away, young bucks would challenge each other to jump over the embers. Someone always fell in and turned up next day in bandages.

Mam and the other mothers would be up early, sweeping up the ashes with a hand shovel and a bucket. The asphalt would be pitted and scarred beneath the bonfire and became a permanent reminder of the night.

Christmas was the other big celebration. Despite their finances, Mam and Dad still managed to surprise us. I got a pair of football boots one year and walked up and down the street, listening to the sound of the studs on the pavement. Another time Albert got roller skates and Ronny a pedal racing car, which Dad bought on credit and took five years to pay off.

On really special occasions like Christmas we set up a table in the front parlour – the best room. Dad even brought home a bottle of non-alcoholic wine and poured us each a glass. Somehow Mam managed to get tipsy from just the excitement. As I said – that's the only time I ever saw them kiss. Dad gave Mam a peck on the cheek and she looked at him with a kind of adoration that I knew must have been love.

Once wartime rationing had been lifted we used to have wonderful Sunday roasts with all the trimmings, including thick rounds of docker doorsteps (bread), still warm from the ovens, to soak up the gravy.

My first school, Heyworth Street Primary, at the bottom of Lance Street, was only two hundred yards from home. Most of the other kids had boots or clogs or no shoes at all, but I had to wear special leather shoes with wedge heels because of my flat feet.

In my family you had to be at death's door to get a day off school. Mam wouldn't accept any excuses and knew every trick in the book when it came to faking illness. Our David went through his entire schooling never being late or missing a class.

One particular teacher left a big impression on me because she read stories to us like *Black Beauty* and *Treasure Island*. I could picture scenes so vividly that I became lost in these adventures. I'd be Jim Hawkins hiding in that apple barrel, listening to Long John Silver plotting murder.

When I was a little bit older, Mr Drew, my English teacher, encouraged me to make use of my imagination.

'Tomlinson, get up and describe that scene,' he said, pointing to a picture of the pampas and the gauchos in Argentina. I started talking about the bulls and the horsemen, creating a story that had heroes and villains, romance and danger.

I found it very easy to lose myself like this. It happened when I listened to radio plays like *Dick Barton*, *Special Agent* and *Journey into Space*. I loved the wonderful sound effects of rocket ships landing on strange planets and the air hissing from doors as they opened.

There were never books around our house, so I joined the library by St George's Church and used to borrow penny thrillers and comics like *Wizard* and *Hotspur*. My favourite sections were the serials such as 'Roy of the Rovers' and 'Alf Tupper, Tough of the Track'. Alf worked in a welding shop under some railway arches and was a super athlete. He had no proper running shoes and lived on a diet of fish and chips, yet he could run like the wind. I covered every yard with him, until he breasted the tape and fell exhausted to the track.

My other escape was the cinema where it cost only a couple of coppers to go to a Saturday matinee at the Everton Picture Palace. As well as the main feature there were normally a couple of shorts and a Pathé Newsreel about the aftermath of the war. The Germans were booed and the British Tommies were cheered.

As the light from the projector shone on to the screen we threw bits of orange peel into the air, which looked like falling stars as they fell through the light. The usher – a war veteran – would hobble down the aisle, saying, 'Oh aye, who's throwing that bloody peel? Yer out on your ear if I catch you.'

Liverpool seemed to be full of fellas like that – a legion of injured heroes who became doormen, ushers and lift attendants, or worked on the market stalls.

From the moment the credits rolled and the landscape flashed up showing wide open plains, I groaned, 'Bloody hell, not another Western.' I hated cowboy films, but my mates loved them. They'd come out afterwards 'shooting' people with their fingers and smacking their arses as they 'rode' home.

Sometimes I'd sneak around the corner and see a romance or a comedy, but I couldn't tell anyone. As with my writing, the lads wouldn't have understood.

That's how I discovered the Old Mother Riley films. Arthur Lucan and his wife Kitty McShane were the biggest box-office stars of their day. Lucan would dress up in a frock and play Old Mother Riley, a gossipy Irish washerwoman, while Kitty played the headstrong daughter. I laughed until tears ran down my cheeks.

Inspired by these films, I convinced a mate of mine, Davey Steele, that we should put on a show for the neighbourhood kids and charge them a penny at the door. I walked the streets banging on a metal drum to publicise the show, while Davey hung a sack for the curtain in the loft over his garage. The audience were literally packed to the rafters as I donned one of Mam's frocks and did my own version of Old Mother Riley.

This was my first experience of acting – unless you count trying to con my little brothers into doing chores for me. From memory it wasn't a bravura performance, but none of the kids asked for their money back. Most of them were included in the show, which proved a clever ploy. I've been improvising ever since.

At the Lytton Cinema on Everton Road you could see a movie for empty jam jars, which had a deposit on them. One of us would get a ticket and go inside, where he opened the back door for the rest of us. We couldn't all sneak in at once – it would have been too obvious – so each of us had to wait until someone in the cinema went to the toilet. Then we ambled back into the auditorium, without arousing suspicion. The ushers must have known, but they never kicked off.

As we grew older, Mam and Dad would take the whole

family to the Hippodrome or the Majestic to see the latest movies. We caught a bus or a tram into town and then waited in the queue for the first house to come out. There were always buskers and bands playing outside. Some wore bits and pieces of military uniforms, with nothing ever quite matching; and one or two would be missing an arm, or a leg, or have an exaggerated limp.

They often had a sign saying 'Ex-Servicemen's Band' and I always imagined they were war heroes who had fallen on hard times. Maybe they were. Then again, they could have been desperate old chancers in borrowed uniforms, with one arm or a leg tied up behind them.

I remember seeing an escapologist perform on a bombsite covered in cinders. His whole body was wrapped in chains, padlocked together, and he stepped inside a big kitbag that was locked with another chain.

He started rolling around on the ground, wriggling and kicking up cinders. This seemed to go on for ages until we heard him groan. Finally this plaintive voice from inside the sack said, 'Can you get me out? I've swallowed the friggin' key.'

Another fella, who made a living going around the pubs, knew only one song on his ukulele, 'Oh, Salome'. He used to stand in the pub doorway, his foot propping it open, and sing until someone paid him to go away.

Years later I was to meet dozens of people like 'Salome' – amateur entertainers with a one-song/act repertoire, who performed for drinks, coppers or simply for fun. By then I was playing the pubs and clubs, meeting a legion of irrepressible characters that treated life like a stage.

At a quarter to eleven every morning, Dad would come to the railings at school with a bag of balm cakes. He would have cut them in half and put a smudge of margarine inside.

There were only two bakers at Kelly's, Dad and his mate John Sumner. Both of them went on strike at one point because they were fed up with working nights for starvation wages in a dim, unventilated basement. The two of them were so conscientious they continued baking for hospitals and nursing homes, but wouldn't make any bread for the shop upstairs.

Within a few days Dad had begun to worry about the neighbourhood kids. What if they had no bread for breakfast or school? So he spent all night making barm cakes, which he posted in paper bags through people's letterboxes. He was supposed to be on strike, but he couldn't help himself.

I don't think Dad knew much about politics and I doubt if he cared. The only time I ever saw him cry was when George VI died.

'The old King's dead,' he said, blinking back the tears, as he sat on the chaise longue in the parlour. I didn't know what to say.

In those days you either voted for the Labour candidate or the (Conservative) Protestant candidate and in our area the Protestant won every time. I can still remember his name – George Carmichael.

At election time kids were often paid to stand outside the polling booths and collect the how-to-vote cards after people had used them. This acted as a type of exit poll, giving people some idea of how votes were being cast.

Albert spent one election day collecting cards for the Labour Party and earned half a crown. There was murder afterwards. He had to go and see Fanny Hunter and apologise. The Labour Party was seen as the enemy because it was too closely associated with the Catholics.

Grandad Wilson was out-and-out Conservative and totally opposed to welfare, which included the dole, hardship

allowances and food parcels. He used to openly berate p
queuing for welfare, calling them parasites and freeloaders.

It seemed to me that political parties were like football teams. You supported the same team as your Dad and he supported the same team as his Dad and so on. I wasn't given a choice, but that didn't matter. Most people didn't have time to debate the strengths and weaknesses of the various parties and their policies. They were too busy trying to put food on the table.

Apart from my Dad, all the heroes of my youth were football players. My all-time favourite was Billy Liddell, who played outside left for Liverpool. He could run like the wind and he could hit a bloody ball from anywhere.

I went to Anfield almost from the time I could walk, riding on Dad's shoulders through the sea of red. If he couldn't afford the shilling, he used to lift me over the turnstiles and only pay for himself. The turnstile man didn't seem to mind. Later I began going to the boys' pen while Dad stood in The Kop, separated by an iron railing fence where he could keep an eye on me.

There was a real buzz in the air before the big games. Wrapped in scarves and wearing red rosettes on our coats, we carried big wooden rattles that spun into a deafening roar.

This was in the days before The Kop choir became famous and Gerry Marsden's 'You'll Never Walk Alone'. Before every match a fella would jump the fence and stroll on to the pitch wearing a red and white top hat. He had this marvellous routine where he blew up a balloon and placed it on the penalty spot, preparing to take the kick. The crowd loved it.

One of my greatest regrets is that Dad never got to see Liverpool win the FA Cup. He went to Wembley a few times, but Liverpool lost each time.

*

Sport played a big part in our lives. During the winter (on the 'dark nights' as we called them) Albert and me would go to St Saviour's boys' club to box, play table tennis and have relay races. I was built like a whippet and could run like the wind, but they stopped me boxing when they discovered I had asthma. They also stopped me swimming and to this day I still can't swim a stroke.

At least they let me play football. Every Friday until I was about fourteen I visited the Children's Hospital in Myrtle Street where Dr McCauley, an asthma specialist with a dreadful stutter, gave me an injection of ephedrine that was supposed to stop me having an attack when I played football on the weekend. He once designated the task to a trainee nurse who used my arse as a pincushion, which explains my morbid dread of needles and injections.

There was no such thing as a 'friendly' football game. Even playing in Lance Street, with a couple of coats as goals, when you took a penalty it was the equivalent of taking one for England. Everything stopped. Adults stood in doorways or stopped everything to watch.

'Who do you think you are, Billy Liddell?' women would shout.

Or the Everton supporters would say, 'Who do you think you are, Dixie Dean?'

This fierce competitive streak has never left me. Years later, as young men, we'd play cricket using dustbins for stumps and you'd swear we were playing for the bloody Ashes. It was *that* serious.

Dad loved his football and turned out for pub teams well into his forties. These Sunday morning games were played on bombsites cleared of rubble and covered with cinders. There were proper goal posts and nets, but no markings or painted penalty areas.

Dad played in goal and his knees and elbows were always cut to ribbons as he threw himself about. Similarly, the tackling was brutal and the odd fight broke out, but these were some of the best games of football I've ever witnessed.

Just like Dad, I started off as a right half and later went into goal. And I even played for a couple of pub teams when I left school, with Dad watching from the bench, with a bucket of freezing water and a sponge at his feet. The old magic sponge is still the greatest reviver in sport, especially when shoved down the shorts.

Caked in mud after the game, I was too old to bath in front of the fire, so I was sent to the 'Wash All Overs', a public bathhouse in Netherfield Road. The bathhouse had about a dozen cubicles each wide enough for a bath and a chair. The walls were about six foot six high and you could see over the top if you stood on the edge of the tub.

The fella running the place would clear the queue by getting the younger lads to share. Undressing with a mate one day, we took off our vests and trousers, hanging them on the hanger behind the door. He was about to step in the tub.

'Eh! Take your socks off.'

He looked up at me. 'I 'ave got 'em off.'

His feet were that dirty!

We sat facing each other, having a scrub, when a minute later the manager banged on the door.

'C'mon, time's up. Get outa there.'

'But we only just got in.'

'Aye, but you're just getting out.'

There was no such thing as a leisurely soak.

In just the same way, every haircut was the same – short back and sides. Our barber, Jimmy Lynch, had a shop about four doors away from the school. Jimmy called everyone 'townie'.

'All right, townie?'

'Yeah.'

'How's it going?'

'Good.'

There were two chairs in the shop, but Jimmy normally worked alone. Smaller kids had to sit on a plank across the armrests to lift them up. Jimmy was always forgetting whose hair he was cutting.

'You out tonight, townie?' he'd ask some kid in short pants.

'No.'

'Anything for the weekend?'

The poor kid had no idea what he was talking about.

By the time I understood what he meant, I couldn't go to Jimmy for my 'weekend supplies'. He knew Dad and my brothers. Instead I found a chemist as far away from Lance Street as possible.

Working-class kids had very few avenues to better themselves and the eleven-plus was one of them. This exam was supposed to sort the wheat from the chaff; to weed out the best and brightest, while setting the rest on a more practical career path.

Kids that did well could go to a college or the institute in Liverpool. They could become professionals and perhaps even climb the social ladder.

On the morning of the exam Mam made a big fuss over me, straightening my tie and polishing my shoes.

'Don't you make a show of me,' she said, which was one of her favourite sayings. It meant that I was supposed to do her proud.

Without the commotion and excitement, perhaps I would have been fine. Instead, I suffered an asthma attack and struggled to concentrate. My exam results were disappointing but this didn't seem to matter. There was no tradition of academic achievement in my family. Nobody had ever been educated past the age of fourteen.

Not long after the exam I moved to Venice Street School. I had no idea what I wanted to be. My only talent seemed to be my ability to tell a story. Whenever my art teacher Mr Jackson had to leave the classroom, he'd say, 'Right, Tomlinson, tell them a story.'

I kept a class of twelve-year-olds on the edge of their seats with stories of bank robberies, gangsters or German spies, each with a reluctant anti-hero, who triumphed in the end.

I was never lost for words. Storytelling came naturally. Although I didn't realise it then, these were my first performances. They were like mini one-man shows, each requiring a bit of acting, imagination and getting people to suspend belief.

By then Mam and Dad must have had more money and would take us to the Empire Theatre on Saturday evenings. There were always half a dozen acts on the bill and I got to see comics, singers, magicians, fire-eaters, acrobats, jugglers and bands.

A little blackboard on the side of the stage would have the name of each act as they came on. All except for the top of the bill, which was announced on posters outside and advertised in the local paper. Among the highlights was getting to see Old Mother Riley in person, as well as Frank Randall and Big Bill Campbell, an American country-and-western star.

Afterwards, as a special treat, we'd have fish and chips for tea. Dad and I would run ahead to make a fire and put the kettle on before the others got home.

When television arrived I was equally captivated. One afternoon in 1953 I found a wooden box with a twelve-inch grey screen in the corner of the parlour. Up until then, my Aunt Elsie, who lived off Mere Lane, was the only member of the family to have one. I used to trundle round and watch it at her place.

On that first night I watched a football match in grainy black and white. From that moment I was hooked. My favourite shows were things like *Sunday Night at the London Palladium* and a comedy called *The Huggetts.* Then there was *What's My Line?* and *Dixon of Dock Green.*

On the variety shows I always admired the comics. The Americans seemed very slick, but as I grew older I began to appreciate how brilliant the British comics were.

Years later an old comedian called Eddie Archer said to me, 'Comedy is hard, Rick. It must be the hardest job in the world.'

I replied, 'Well, I don't think it's as hard as boxing, Eddie.'

He nodded sagely. 'Yeah, but if you're a boxer at least you can hit them back.'

3

Getting off at Edgehill

Lance Street no longer exists. Nor do the short cuts, hiding places and most of the landmarks from my childhood. Heyworth Primary School is now a recreational park full of drug addicts on the dark nights and there is no Garrick pub or Everton Picture Palace.

All the houses and shops were bulldozed in the sixties when Liverpool City Council decided that the two-up-two-downs were slum housing. Initially they promised to create public parkland, which is why people didn't get paid the full market value for their properties.

They built a bloody great housing estate instead of a park. And some of the bungalows have already been knocked down and replaced. Things aren't built to last any more. Mam always said that and she was right.

At least St George's Church is still there, up on St George's Hill, the highest point in Liverpool and therefore a little bit nearer God. That's where the funeral is going to be.

Not many people realise that St George's Church was the very first cast-iron building anywhere in the world. A guy called Thomas Rickman, who hadn't designed as much as an outhouse in his life, convinced people to trust him as an architect and then dreamt up the idea of using iron for the infrastructure. Maybe that's what they mean by blind faith.

I've never been much of a churchgoer. That's not to say I don't

*believe. I'm interested in religion because I love to question it.
Unfortunately, organised religions are businesses nowadays and the
balance sheet is more important than the people.*

*The new vicar at St George's is a thalidomide sufferer and seems
nice. None of us wants to make a speech, I couldn't get the words out,
so we're going to leave that up to him.*

*When he came round to discuss the service, he wanted to know a
little bit about Mam so we bent his ear for a couple of hours. I tried
to think of some stories and I remembered the one about Albert's first
girlfriend, Audrey Lewis. He must have been about seventeen.*

*Mam asked him dozens of questions about Audrey. Where does she
live? What does her father do? Why don't you bring her back for tea
on Sunday night? Then she made a big fuss, laying out the table in
the parlour, getting cheese and crackers and a couple of fairy cakes.*

*With no girls in the family, we were all a bit uncouth although
Mam wanted to prove otherwise. Straight away she said to Dad,
'You behave yourself. And don't be walking round in your bare feet
or socks.' I was under even stricter instructions.*

*When Audrey arrived she was ushered into the parlour like
royalty. I was already sitting up at the table with a scarf tied under
my chin, pretending to be Albert's little sister.*

*Mam gave me a filthy look and began pouring the tea. She was so
desperate to impress that she kept putting her 'h's in the wrong places.
Meanwhile, I had my hand in the air trying to get her attention.*

Finally, she said, 'What's up with you?'

'Can I leave the table, please?'

'Why?'

'I want to go for a shit.'

*Audrey near choked on a biscuit and our Albert couldn't stop
himself laughing. There was murder, of course. I thought Mam was
going to explode she was so angry. I don't suppose that's the sort of
story a vicar can tell at a funeral, which is a shame.*

*

Nobody ever sat me down and gave me the talk about birds and bees. Like most of my generation, the knowledge was passed on from older brothers and collecting small details from encyclopedias, graffiti and the rumours you hear behind bike sheds.

One summer in the early 1950s I went on holiday with the church to Great Hucklow in Wales with kids from all over the place. We stayed in Nissan huts with bunks down either side and had to fill our own mattresses with straw.

If I were to pinpoint a single moment when I began to notice girls, it would be on this holiday. Which ones had bumps on their chests? Which ones didn't? Who had the nicest curves and the prettiest smile? Up until then I knew they were different, but only because they smelled nicer and didn't fight so much.

My entire life changed. I had a mission. The nightly games in Lance Street reflected this. Suddenly the aim was to catch a girl and kiss her, instead of running the other way.

We didn't have dates as such. Instead we found a dark corner and hoped to steal a kiss or perhaps a little more. That's when I made my next important discovery. The other lads were trying to impress girls by boasting or fighting, but I had more success making them laugh and feel good about themselves.

I told them how pretty they looked and how nice they smelled. I talked about the moon and the stars. Most of these girls weren't used to being complimented because it had never happened before.

I was still only young – maybe eleven or twelve – but that didn't stop me. I adored girls. They were the gear. I couldn't sleep, eat or work without thinking about them.

There must have been twenty who lived in Lance Street, including my mates' sisters. Mrs Musker across the road had seven daughters. I remember for the Coronation she asked Albert to help nail up the bunting across the street.

'Oh, be careful, Albie,' she told him, as he climbed the ladder. 'You could be my son-in-law one day.'

It was probably a good thing that I didn't have a sister. There would have been loads of trouble if anyone had come sniffing around her. You judge everyone by your own standards and I was a complete rogue.

Another family living in the street had a niece, Jenny, who visited two or three times a week. Although only thirteen she had the biggest pair of knockers I had ever seen in my life. We chatted and laughed. I told her how nice she looked. We kissed a little and then some more.

Mates would ask me, 'How far did you get?'

'Inside her blouse.'

'You got bare tit?'

'Yeah.'

'You lucky bastard! I wouldn't wash me hand for a month.'

Soon they were hanging round Jenny like flies round a jam pot. Honest to God, she had the most incredible breasts.

Eventually, as the weeks went by, I grew more adventurous and her resolve weakened. All the old clichés came out:

'Oh, come on. I really love you.'

'You'll tell everybody.'

'No, I won't.'

'Yes, you will.'

'I won't tell a soul.'

'You'll tell all your mates.'

'No, I won't. I love you.'

I did the honours – an old-fashioned 'knee trembler' with Jenny leaning up against a wall, with one leg wrapped around me. Being only thirteen, I told all my mates the next day. It was the biggest thing that had ever happened to me.

Jenny and me kept seeing each other. She was lovely. We didn't use any protection apart from coitus interruptus – known locally as 'Getting off at Edgehill', the last station before Liverpool Lime Street (the end of the line).

She had girlfriends and I had mates who paired off into couples but these partnerships were always breaking up and getting back together again. We often arranged to meet at someone's house if their parents were out working. The front door was kept latched and the back door open in case one of them came home early and we had to make an escape. Turning down the gas lights and closing the curtains, we played games like 'Truth or Dare' and 'Spin the Bottle'. The sexual tension has never been equalled.

Eventually, I broke up with Jenny. I can't remember why. I suspect she found an older boyfriend. A lot of the girls did when they became more confident.

A mate of mine in Lance Street, Brian Craig, lived next door to a young couple. The wife's sister Joyce had come to live with them. She was often home during the day and the husband worked night shifts.

He was a smashing bloke, who used to invite Brian and me to play darts with him. We were mucking around one day when he suggested we play strip poker with darts. Joyce scolded him and giggled. Brian and me got instant erections.

Whoever hit the lowest number with the darts had to take off a piece of clothing. Joyce was a lousy darts player. She lost a few times and took off her shoes and her stockings. Brian and me were doing the mental arithmetic. If she lost again, it would have to be her skirt or her blouse.

Next thing she said, 'I won't be a minute.'

I looked at Brian. We both thought the same thing. She was going upstairs to put on more clothes.

She came back down again and we each threw the darts.

Joyce lost. She slowly unbuttoned her blouse and, honest to God, my jaw dropped. Instead of putting clothes on she had taken her bra off! We were staring at a full-grown woman's breasts.

Suddenly, the husband interrupted. 'Right you fellas, hop off now.'

He shooed us out of the house and I've a pretty good idea why. He wanted to see even more of his wife's sister and I got the impression that Joyce was happy to oblige.

I guess you could call it a 'Mrs Robinson' moment, although Joyce was hardly Anne Bancroft and I didn't have much in common with Dustin Hoffman.

In those days an exam called the thirteen-plus was available to students who they thought should have or could have passed the eleven-plus. It was like a second chance.

This time I had no problems and was given three choices to further my education – Engineering College, Building College and Commercial College. The latter appealed to me because it taught English, typing and shorthand, but I knew I couldn't be a writer without being labelled a 'nancy boy'. Instead I chose to learn a building trade and enrolled in Walton Technical College, a bus-ride away. Dressed in my school blazer, flannels and a cap, I was always getting into rows because lads would call me a 'college pudding'.

Of a morning we did normal school lessons like English and maths, but in the afternoon we learned how to lay bricks and plaster, as well as having metalwork and woodwork classes.

They made me a prefect in my third year and I got to wear two little bits of gold braid on my cap to let everyone know. It didn't mean very much to me, but Mam was pleased as punch.

Having well-turned fifteen, I took my intermediate City and Guilds exams. Then I had to make up my mind what I wanted to do with my life. A part of me still dreamed of being a writer, but I knew it was a fanciful idea. Out of all the building trades, the one I liked the most was plastering.

The teacher in the plastering shop was named Adams and was related to the firm of Adams Bros, a highly regarded plastering firm in Liverpool. He gave me a letter of recommendation and sent me down to the company for an interview as an apprentice.

Adams Bros took me on when I turned sixteen. It meant taking classes at night and working on building sites during the day. As an apprentice, I had to make the tea, run errands and fetch the chips or cakes at dinnertime. I also had to help unload the wagon when it arrived with bags of plaster and sheets of plasterboard. Still being on the small side, I almost bent double under the hundredweight bags of plaster and cement, but I wouldn't let the labourers see me struggling.

Adams Bros specialised in fibrous plasterwork as well as granite and monolithic flooring. We did mostly commercial work for schools, churches and offices whereas other companies plastered the housing estates. Known as 'house walloping', this was looked down upon by some of the tradesmen I worked with.

I passed my City and Guilds exams at seventeen, but still had four years to go before I finished my apprenticeship. I was given the opportunity to keep studying and perhaps become an architect, draughtsman or clerk of the works: white collar jobs. I didn't take up the offer.

It wasn't that I had my heart set on being a plasterer. I always thought I'd finish up doing something else, but like most lads my age I thought the future was a long way off, and having a good time seemed a good enough ambition. The

Grafton, a famous local ballroom, had a Saturday afternoon tea dance. For a shilling you got a cup of tea, two biscuits and the chance to hold a girl close during the slow numbers.

The ballroom era was ending and rock 'n' roll had arrived, but the Grafton was slow to embrace the change and the bouncers would drag anyone caught jiving off the dance floor.

A proper big band provided the music, with bandmasters like Johnny Hilton and support acts such as the Billy Ellis Trio, which had a blind piano player and a double bass player with a broken nose.

Girls would stand on one side of the dance floor and boys on the other. No-man's-land lay in between. The walk back seemed twice as long if a girl refused to dance with you.

I had a system. I picked my target and approached at an angle, popping the question while still a few paces away. If she said no, I could simply carry on walking as though heading for the toilet.

Rock 'n' roll eventually took over and Saturdays at the Grafton became jive night. All the guys had hairstyles like Tony Curtis with a DA (duck's arse) at the back, and wore button-up Italian suits, drape coats, tight trousers and beetle-crusher shoes.

In 1957 Marty Robbins had a hit song called 'A White Sports Coat (And a Pink Carnation)'. I got myself a white coat and black slacks, with black shoes. When I walked into the Grafton I thought I was the bee's knees.

The Grafton was famous for the fights as well as the dancing. The bouncers were quick to pounce on troublemakers and what started inside would finish outside, with a crowd watching the contest.

I'm not naturally a fighter, but, as I said before, circumstances alter cases. In Liverpool, you either stood up for yourself or risked becoming a professional victim.

Heading to the movies one night with a gang of mates, I exchanged words with a guy called Alan Smith. We got into one of those 'don't-tell-me-what-to-do' conversations which led to pushing and shoving. Fists came next, but like most street fights it didn't last more than a minute or two. We traded blows, wrestled and rolled on the ground.

What happened next still lives with me. I can remember the blow that finished it off. I had Alan on the ground with his head pressed against the bitumen. I couldn't swing my fist at him sideways so I raised it like a hammer and hit him in the face.

'Woah! That's it. I'm done,' he said, looking pale. He stood up and we shook hands. Then we went off to the movies.

Confrontations like this were pretty common. We could be fighting one minute and best friends the next. Every street had a gang and every school was seen as a rival. People supported different football teams, or practised different religions. And it didn't matter what the fight was over or who started it. If one of your mates got a smack then it was all in. No questions asked.

Just before my seventeenth birthday I was plastering at a pub called Lulu's in Heyworth Street, owned by a woman who had a mouth like a docker and a husband known as Fat George, for obvious reasons.

While working in the toilets, I heard a wonderful plink, plonk, plink sound coming from the bar. I put down my tools and went to investigate. A fella sat on a stool in the corner, picking at the strings of a banjo. People were soon singing and tapping their feet.

That evening I told Mam all about it.

'Do you want a banjo?' she asked. 'Your birthday's coming up.'

'No, it'll be too expensive.'

I didn't want her wasting her money on a five-minute fad.

Mam went looking in second-hand music shops and found a battered banjo for two quid. I was made up. The lessons cost one and six and my teacher, Mrs Scobble, didn't know much about the banjo (she played the piano) but understood the theory.

I found out later that the instrument that I'd heard at Lulu's wasn't a banjo, but a long-armed ukulele. The man playing it, Georgie Sheridan, was a brilliant musician, although a bit of an ale tank, and later became a great mate.

Another of Mrs Scobble's students, Wilf Murphy, was about six feet tall, with very blond hair and real musician's fingers and hands. He called himself Wilf Neilson and was a much better banjo player than me. He picked at the strings playing the melody, while I played 'side' (strummed the chords).

The two of us decided to start a band. We had half a dozen American folk songs and Lonnie Donegan numbers, which proved to be more than enough. To compliment the banjos, we recruited two guitarists, Brian Craig (who had shared my 'Mrs Robinson' moment) and Alan Jennings, another lad from Lance Street, who had a shock of red hair and pale skin. We called ourselves The Guitanjos.

The motivation for the band had nothing to do with dreams of stardom or wealth. We wanted to pull birds and in my experience there were two sure-fire ways of doing this – being a good dancer, or playing in a band.

Even Brian Craig, who had a glass eye (the legacy of childhood measles) and was going bald at sixteen, pulled the most amazing looking girls when they heard him sing and play guitar.

Meanwhile, Mam and Dad had decided to buy a place in

Elmore Street, which was just next to Lance Street. The ceiling had come down and it needed work, but they agreed a price and we moved in. A builder fixed up the ceilings and I did the plastering. We built a proper bathroom with an indoor toilet.

The house had four bedrooms, a parlour room, a lounge and a long, thin kitchen. It also had a shop at the front, which became a games room and somewhere for The Guitanjos to rehearse.

Although only two years older than me, Albert had always seemed much more grown up. He went into the Army at seventeen and finished up in Cyprus. These were dangerous times, with terrorist bombings and campaigns to get the British bases out.

Mam was worried sick and used to sit by the radiogram listening for the latest news. I'd watch her from the doorway and occasionally hear a gentle sob. I wanted to say, 'It's all right, Mam, he'll be OK', but I didn't know how to reassure her.

Every letter that arrived from Albert was reason to celebrate. And when he came home, dressed in his uniform, he suddenly seemed like a man, while I was still a boy. Dad took him out around to Fanny Hunter's and then to the Penrhyn Street pub to show him off.

Dad was proud of all his lads. David was still at Venice Street School and Ronny had only just started primary. Being the youngest he was doted upon and spoilt rotten, especially by Dad. The two of them were mates.

Albert left the Army and went to work on the docks. He used to tell me stories about the rats in the warehouses that were so big that guys would put collars on them and lead them around. To this day I don't know if he was winding me up.

Albert had his twenty-first birthday at Elmore Street and he married Pat soon afterwards. He didn't move far. Mam helped him buy a house about eight doors down and he lived there until the compulsory purchase order arrived and the bulldozers followed.

Although I worked during the week, the banjo and the band were much more exciting. Deciding to branch out, we went along to a Sunday afternoon audition at a local club called Ozzie Wade's. This was where all the concert secretaries from the social clubs and working men's clubs would gather to hear new bands and comics. Each act was given ten minutes.

The Guitanjos were hardly what you'd call 'polished', but we did have a certain style. I came on stage wearing a grass skirt and a bra filled out with rubber balls. After singing 'Lilly of Laguna', I told a few gags and bounced the balls on stage. Miraculously, we finished up with six bookings.

Our first gig was at the Knowsley Labour Club and the audience seemed to like us. Brian was the main vocalist, but I did a bit of singing and a few comedy turns, while Wilf had a banjo solo.

The social clubs would book a handful of acts for each night. Usually this included one or two comics, a singer and a band. It was a huge business and there were dozens of acts doing the circuit.

Albert often came along to watch us, but David and Ronny were still too young. I thought I was a real jack-the-lad, playing in pubs and clubs, when I couldn't even drink legally.

Girls like Mavis Downer would come knocking on the pub door, asking for me. She was only fifteen, well built for her age, and more emotionally mature than I was. Normally, we'd make do with a knee trembler behind the pub, but now and again her parents would be out and I could do the honours at her place.

This went on for more than a year and [...] sixteen. I was in the pub one day, drinking wi[...] brothers from George's Hill.

One of them said to me, 'I'm getting married [...]'

'Congratulations. Who's the lucky girl?'

'Mavis Downer.'

He was waiting for me to say something.

'You know that I've been with her?'

'Yeah.'

Enough had been said. It was never mentioned again.

More than forty years later I was doing a public appearance in Netherley, when I met Mavis again, along with a young girl who was her granddaughter.

'Do you know there was a time when I was really sweet on your grandmother?' I told the lass. Mavis blushed and her smile lit up the room.

She had been married to the same fella for all those years and they had a string of grandkids. I love happy endings.

4

Hobo Rick

Our Ronny has organised the funeral, right down to what Mam is wearing. He even found her favourite pair of shoes. Being the youngest he's always been close to Mam. When the rest of us had left home, he was still there keeping her and Dad company.

We're all meeting at Mam's bungalow in Queens Road. The gardens are looking really nice, thanks to Ronny. She used to love that garden. Sometimes in the summer she sat outside, but mostly she just looked from the kitchen window.

The place is chock-a-block with neighbours, friends and family, come to pay their last respects. Some of them I haven't seen in years. Mam wasn't a drinker, but I know she won't mind us offering everyone a tipple. We've got every bottle of spirits under the sun, as well as cans of lager and mild. People just help themselves.

The front lawn is covered in wreathes, flowers and bouquets. Pride of place is a huge wreath with the word 'MAM' spelt out in flowers. Dennis, the funeral director, is going to put it by the window of the hearse so people can see it on the drive to the church.

Dennis directs everyone into the cars, taking off his bowler hat when he nods towards the coffin. When everyone is ready, he does a slow march in front of the hearse in his black suit, black tie and black bowler hat. He carries on until we reach the end of Queens Road and turn the corner. Then he gets in the hearse next to the driver and we drive slowly towards St George's Church.

I start thinking about the fuss they made over the Queen Mother dying. Never washed a shitty nappy in her life; never cooked a meal; had people doting and waiting on her at the taxpayer's expense. Yet people queued for days to see her coffin in the Palace of Westminster.

I can appreciate the Royal Family's sadness. She was a mother and a grandmother. But so was Mam – and she worked a damn sight harder and suffered through more.

Admittedly, I didn't make things any easier – always getting into fights and scrapes. I spent half my life in pubs and clubs. I'll never forget when I first came home with a motorbike. Mam almost had a heart attack.

I was plastering for Adams Bros and working with the boss's son, Derrick Adams. He used to go scrambling every weekend on this motorbike and come roaring into work on Monday with his bike covered in mud.

He taught me how to ride in my lunch hour around the building site, dodging cement mixers and scaffolding. We were working on a big printing place in Liverpool and Alf the foreman had a small motorbike. The lads dared me to take it for a spin around the site and I took up the challenge. Everything was going fine until I hit a patch of sand and the front wheel went out from under me. I wrapped the bike around the scaffolding. Alf gave me a bollocking, which I deserved, and thankfully there wasn't much damage. It taught me a lesson about being careful.

One day I knocked off work early and went into town with Derrick. I bought a little Triumph Tiger Cub, which was only 200cc. He drove it back to the site and we made a set of 'L' plates out of old cement bags.

That night I drove home. As I turned into Lance Street I saw Mam standing on the doorstep.

'What are you doing on that?'

'I bought it.'

'You didn't.'

'I did.'

'Well, if you fall off that bike, Ricky Tomo, and break your legs, don't come running to me.'

I didn't think it was funny at the time, but it breaks me up now. She was always saying stuff like that.

'You'll smile on the other side of your face', whatever that means, and 'Have you seen the inside of your ears?'

When she got really angry she'd turn into a ventriloquist and speak without moving her lips, muttering, 'Do you know who I am?'

As if I was likely to forget!

Some people spend a whole lifetime searching for love and come up empty-handed. That's why I regard myself as being so lucky. By my reckoning, I've been in love four times and I wouldn't swap the memories for anything, even the painful ones.

My first real love was a girl called Margie King, who was a few years older than me and had already been married and divorced while still in her early twenties. She had a young daughter, Tina, and a boyfriend, Peter Miller, who I would have trusted with my life.

That was the hardest thing about being in love with Margie. She was a mate's girl and therefore off-limits. She was even living with Peter's family.

I knew it was love because I felt physically sick every time I was apart from her and ten feet tall when I stood next to her. She wasn't particularly pretty or glamorous, but she had a wonderful smile and the best personality of any girl who went to the Grafton.

It may be hard to believe, but I was pretty fancy on my feet back then (and still enjoy a turn on the dance floor today). Margie could dance like an angel and people would clear the dance floor to watch us. We were like the Ginger Rogers and Fred Astaire of the Grafton, spinning and turning, separating and coming together as though choreographed.

One Friday night, Peter said to me, 'Are you walking home, Rick?'

'Yeah.'

'Will you take Margie? Make sure she gets home?'

'Sure.'

I don't know why Peter couldn't walk her home, but I guess he trusted me. Peter's house was just off Netherfield Road, about a mile from Lance Street. There were no buses or trams at that hour, but I didn't mind the walk – not when it meant spending time with Margie.

This became a regular thing. After the first few times Margie began putting her arm in mine as we walked. Sometimes I found excuses to see her during the week and even plucked up the courage to steal a kiss before she pushed me away.

Margie must have noticed the difference between me and Peter. I was always writing her bits of poetry and telling her I loved her. That wasn't really Peter's style.

Deciding how far to push my luck was a delicate matter. Too far and Margie would slap me in the face. Then again, I knew Peter would smack me much harder if he found out. What to do? I loved her.

Margie knew I had fallen hard and she treated me like a lovesick puppy.

'I don't think I'll go to the dance next week,' she'd say, teasing me.

'Why? Why?'

'Might do something different. Just for a change.'

'You can't do that.'

'Why not?'

'You . . . you just can't.'

She could see the hurt on my face.

'Oh, OK. I guess I might go.'

The fact that Margie was living with Peter and his folks made things even more complicated. I used to go round to their house and Peter's mum was really nice to me. She was always saying to Peter, 'Why can't you be more like Rick?'

This went on for months until it came to a head one night. I don't think Margie told Peter. Maybe he worked things out for himself. I wasn't sleeping with her. It had never gone past kissing and fumbling.

This particular night, I walked Margie home, kissed her goodnight and set off home in the early hours of the morning. We were still living in Lance Street. Less than a hundred yards from home, I spotted Peter standing at the bottom of Elmore Street. I knew he had to be waiting for me.

Discretion being the better of valour, I slipped up Hamilton Road and down our street, avoiding any confrontation. I sat in the kitchen wondering what to do. Peter had a reputation as a scrapper. I'd seen him in action. He was big, fit and genuinely hard.

I thought of all the reasons I shouldn't go out and face him. I was sure to get a hiding. It was David versus Goliath. All the same, I couldn't leave him out there. I respected him too much.

I put my coat back on and walked down the street. At that moment (even though I hated Westerns) I knew exactly how Gary Cooper felt in *High Noon*.

'Are you waiting for me, Peter?'

'Yeah. You know why, don't you Rick?'

'Yeah.'

He battered me senseless, but at the same time I knew he could have hit me a lot harder and for a lot longer. He was fast and strong. I threw a few punches and landed one of them, but it was really no contest. I finished up trapped in a recess where the bins were kept.

He landed the last blow, pulled down his sleeves and said, 'OK, Rick, I'll see you tomorrow.'

'OK, Peter.'

And that was it! I watched as he walked away up Heyworth Street. He was probably hurting as much as me, but not from a few punches. It was a different kind of hurt. He had done what he had to do to save his reputation. We were two working-class lads settling a score.

Peter is probably embarrassed about it now, but he shouldn't be. I deserved a beating. And he could have really hurt me but he didn't. The worst of it was a black eye and a bit of bruising.

The following Saturday, I went straight from work to Peter's house.

'Hi, Rick. Sit down. Have a cup of tea,' his mum said.

My left eye was completely closed, but she didn't say a thing. She must have known, but everyone acted as though nothing had happened.

I didn't walk Margie home again, but you could tell sometimes by the way we looked at each other that we both knew.

Margie and Peter eventually split up and we all got on with our lives. As far as I know Margie married again and it didn't work out. I met her about ten years later and we took up for a little while. The magic was still there and a part of me will always cherish her.

My apprenticeship lasted six years and I loved the camaraderie of the building sites. I learned to skim ceilings and walls, as well as laying sand, cement, tiles, granite and monolithic floors.

Albert had left the docks and come to work with me on the building sites as a labourer. Without any formal training he was ten times the plasterer that I would ever be. He picked everything up so quickly and turned himself into a first-rate builder.

Adams Bros handled big contracts like the Manchester Airport Hotel and the Carrington Power Station. Some of these jobs took years, which meant a regular income – something you could rarely guarantee in the building game.

The big sites had all the trades – joiners, pipe fitters, electricians and plasterers. A lot of the labourers were Irish and they were huge, but I didn't have a lot to do with them.

In our little gang we had big Joe Seward, the driver, Barney Snagg, who had boxed professionally, Ruben Bennett, the strongest man I ever met in my life, and Georgie Schofield, another ex-boxer, who could catch a fly out of the air he was so quick.

We worked hard from morning till night, never moaning and always having a laugh. And the lads looked after Albert and respected him, calling him 'the gentleman'.

It was so cold one morning on the site that the water had frozen. We couldn't mix cement so Barney came up with the idea of getting a drum full of ice and putting it next to the brazier to thaw.

He started mixing the cement when this huge Irish fella came along, dipped his bucket into the water and took some without saying a word.

Barney said to him, 'That's OK, lad, but don't take any more. I need that water.'

The guy said nothing. A little while later he came back and took another bucket.

'I told you to fuck off!' said Barney. 'No more water.'

The Irish fella laughed at him.

The next time he came back, Barney put his shovel in the sand, threw one punch and knocked him unconscious. This guy was twice his size. Suddenly it was all in. Barney had four Irishmen surrounding him, all of them over six foot. By the time Georgie and Ruben arrived it was all over. He had flattened the lot of them without breaking into a sweat.

I had a real soft spot for Ruben, who was known as 'the sand man' because of his prodigious strength. Some jobs had no hoist lift so we had to carry sand to the upper floors in a plasterer's hod, which is about three times the size of a bricklayer's hod.

Ruben would carry from morning to night, never complaining. Adams Bros used to send him on jobs when they needed sand on the top floors or when they were cement-screeding the roof. Ruben's party piece was to get this huge hod, three times bigger than any other, and fill it with sand. He used to challenge all the hard cases to see if they could lift it.

Lads sweated and strained and finally gave up. Then Ruben would get underneath, brace it against his shoulder and carry it to the roof.

He wasn't the brightest pebble on the beach, Ruben, and he hated letting on that he couldn't read or write. During the tea breaks he'd pretend to be looking at the newspaper, but have it upside down.

'Do us a favour, Ruben, can I borrow your paper?' I'd say, glancing at a page. Then I'd hand it back to him the right way up. We all knew he couldn't read, but I didn't want to see him embarrassed in front of strangers.

I had never had strong political views, but I guess I followed my father as a royalist and a Tory. At Walton Tech, my mate

came from Toxteth, a poor area in south Liverpool,
member of the Young Communist League. So was
Jimmy.

John was always trying to talk me into joining. He argued
that the rich were getting richer and the working class was
being kept in its place. It sounded convincing and I could see
evidence of this on the building sites. No employer ever gave
a pay rise out of the goodness of his heart. Nor did he spend
money on improving conditions or safety unless forced to do
so. Factories weren't built to create employment. They were
built to make money.

At the time that John was trying to woo me to the
Communist cause, trouble flared in Hungary. Soviet tanks
and troops ruthlessly crushed an uprising of students and
workers who were demonstrating over Soviet occupation.
Thousands were killed or imprisoned.

This ended my brief flirtation with Communism, but
Jimmy Rand went on to become well known in left-wing
politics. I don't know what happened to John. A few years
ago, I was on a film shoot at a magnificent house near
Birmingham – a huge baronial hall like something from
Brideshead Revisited. The lady of the house came up to
me one day and said, 'You're from Liverpool aren't you,
Rick?'

'Yeah.'

'So am I.'

'Oh, where abouts?'

She told me the street.

'I had a mate who used to live in that street – a lad called
John Rand.'

'I'm his sister.'

I couldn't believe it. She was living in this massive house.
Turned out that she had married an ordinary guy, who

invented something that had made him extremely wealthy and now she lived in absolute luxury.

'Sometimes it makes me feel guilty,' she admitted.

'Why? It's your good fortune.'

'I suppose. My husband doesn't know it, but every Friday I go out with a pile of ten pound notes and I give them away to *Big Issue* sellers or anyone else who needs a hand.'

'Does it make you feel better?'

She shrugged and didn't answer.

The site convener on the Carrington job was a fella called Joe Lief, from the Transport and General Workers' Union (TGWU). Each of the different trades had their own union reps. For the joiners it was Alan Abrahams, who was known as 'the Red Jew'. I don't even know if Alan was Jewish, but he was a tremendous shop steward who could explain the issues without rabble-rousing.

Thanks to Alan the joiners managed to negotiate a bonus because of problems on the site and long hours. All the other trades followed suit and negotiated the same deal except for the plasterers.

We were working just as hard, if not harder, but were bloody hopeless at getting organised and showing solidarity. The joiners were on the job from practically the first day until the job finished. Plasterers and painters were always last on site, which made it harder to negotiate.

No one would volunteer to become our shop steward and I found myself in the job even though still an apprentice. I went to the site meetings and put our case. The employers agreed and gave us an extra shilling an hour.

We also negotiated for a minibus to take workers to and from the Carrington site. The weather had been atrocious and there was no public transport.

A couple of weeks later the firm moved me. It was a typical tactic by the employers. Identify the ringleaders and get rid of them, thus avoiding any future problems.

Any of the other trades wouldn't have tolerated such an obvious attack on the union. One of the cast-iron rules on the job is the shop steward is the last man to go. But the plasterers didn't kick up a fuss.

Although I missed working with Georgie, Ruben and Barney, I still bumped into them occasionally in various pubs. Albert was working with them and I went along for a drink or they came to hear me play.

For a while I worked on the Catholic Cathedral in Liverpool, which the locals had nicknamed Paddy's Wigwam because it looks like a giant tepee. Sometimes I'd finish up with more plaster on my overalls than I had on the walls. Mam said she knew when I was home by the big white footsteps leading into the house.

The rule with doing floors is you start laying at eight in the morning and you carry on until about midday before stopping. Then you spend the rest of the day trowelling the water back into the floor as it rises so the surface doesn't crack.

I was working with Derrick Adams, the boss's son, who was superbly fit and would sometimes carry on laying floor until four in the afternoon. This meant we were there trowelling until two or three the next morning. Sometimes I'd get home to Elmore Street and literally climb the stairs on my hands and knees I was so tired. I had to soak my hands in warm water to get the fingers to open. A few hours later I'd be back at work.

One of our jobs was working on the Grafton, which was being refurbished. I rode my motorbike home each lunchtime and had just enough time for a cup of tea, a sandwich and a bit of fooling around with my latest girlfriend before getting back to the plastering.

The foreman Terry Johnson was a mad Liverpool fan and he heard a rumour one afternoon of a plane crash in Europe involving Manchester United. The team was on its way home from Belgrade where it had qualified for the semi-finals of the 1958 European Cup by beating Red Star the previous day.

'Go find out if it's true, Rick.'

The front of the Grafton was cordoned off with corrugated iron to stop people wandering in. I climbed a ladder and peered over the top.

'Is that right about Man United?' I asked a passer-by.

'Yeah.'

'What happened?'

'Plane went down on take-off from Munich. They say it was snowing. Twenty-three people are dead, including eight players. A lot of the others are injured.'

As a diehard Liverpool supporter, I had wished all sorts of misfortune on Man United over the years, but nothing like this. Some of the finest footballers of their generation died that day.

Although I enjoyed the friendship and knockabout humour of the building sites, I still felt as though something was missing. There had to be more to life than laying floors and plastering walls and ceilings.

Walking home from Anfield one day, mourning a Liverpool loss, I began daydreaming about being an actor. I couldn't picture myself in the context of being famous or rich. I just thought, 'I want to be one.'

Nobody in my family had anything to do with the theatre or music or show business. I didn't even know there was a difference between film actors and stage actors or how to become either one of them. Yet at the same time something told me that it was going to happen.

A few days later I came across an advert in the newspaper for a local drama group that was holding auditions for a new production. Again, I didn't have a clue what this entailed, but I hurried home from work, had a quick wash and turned up at Rushworth and Draper's Theatre.

A couple of middle-class guys in black polo neck sweaters were sitting behind a table.

'Have you done any theatre work?' one of them asked.

'No.'

'Well, just read this for us.'

He gave me a script and I read the page in a monotone, with my head down.

'Don't call us, we'll call you' was the gist of the response.

Instead of abandoning the idea, I went along to the Bootle Drama Society, which met once a week at a local school. The atmosphere was less intimidating and it felt more welcoming. We sat round a table and began working through a play that everyone else obviously knew. I waited for my lines to come up.

Suddenly, I heard this deep, sonorous theatrical voice. I looked up and discovered it had come from this skinny teenager with glasses on the end of his nose. Wow!

The only other person that sticks in my mind was this tall, reed-thin woman, in a red velvet dress, who had a Persian cat on a lead. She was like a character out of an Oscar Wilde play.

I didn't go again. I told myself that I couldn't afford the time because of working all over the place in Crewe, Manchester and Wales. In truth it frightened me how little I knew.

*

By the early sixties the band had a new name: Hobo Rick and the City Slickers. The name 'Hobo' came about because I often arrived late at gigs still covered in plaster and crap from the building sites. Meanwhile, all the other lads were dressed in red-and-black striped blazers, white shirts, bow ties and straw boaters. After a while it became part of my image. The lads were fine about the new name. Whatever few quid we earned was always split equally between us.

There was nothing very slick or sophisticated about the shows. Anyone could get up and do a spot and each venue had its own atmosphere and cast of wonderful characters. There were singers, drunks, raconteurs, gigolos, gangsters and joke-tellers.

Among them was Georgie Platt who used to do Elvis impersonations. Every introduction began the same way: 'This is for the greatest man who ever lived,' he'd say, 'Elvis Presley.' Not only did he sound like 'The King', I'm convinced he thought he really *was*.

Crosby the sand dancer would toss sand on the floor and shuffle between the tables, while the most bizarre 'performer' was 'The Claw' who had this green withered false hand, which he would stick up his sleeve and suddenly produce as he went round collecting the glasses.

My favourite was Paddy Moyster, the ugliest man in the world. Paddy was a lovely Irishman and a docker, who had this incredible mug.

'You're bloody ugly,' I said to him once.

'Yeah, I know, but it's only for work,' he replied.

Some of the pubs became as much a part of my life as the houses of my childhood. Places like the Thirlmere – the best little pub in Liverpool – where lots of Everton footballers used to drink.

The Thirlmere had its own sporting teams and one of the

most eagerly awaited fixtures was a cricket match against the local fire brigade. The firemen even provided a trophy – a piece of polished wood with a fireman's axe stuck in the top and a small plaque engraved with each year's winner.

They were fit bastards and had a fella called Peter Skinley who could bowl like lightning. The match took up most of Sunday and afterwards we headed back to the Thirlmere for a singsong and sandwiches before the presentation.

Unfortunately, when the firemen were on duty they had to get back to the station. One of them pulled me aside: 'Listen, Rick, at about nine o'clock send someone outside to ring the alarm.'

(Most streets had fire alarms because very few people had telephones in those days.)

My little sidekick, Paddy Rush, was only five-two with glasses perched on the end of his nose. Paddy had been one of the Catholic kids who threw pepper bombs at Protestants who marched on 12 July, but I didn't hold it against him. At nine o'clock he slipped outside, smashed the glass and pulled the lever of the fire alarm. Inside we were singing away. Five minutes later I heard the siren. The fire engine pulled up out front, met by Paddy.

There was an old narky guy who sat permanently in the corner of the Thirlmere, never smiling and always complaining. He sucked on a pipe and lived inside a permanent cloud of tobacco smoke.

Next minute the door burst open and Paddy came rushing in wearing a fireman's hat and a coat that dragged on the floor it was so big on him.

'Where's the fire?' he yelled.

He seized a soda siphon, charged across the bar and hit this guy between the eyes with a stream of soda. The place just erupted with laughter.

The Halfway House was a pub in Scotland Road and among the regulars was Cilla Black's old man, John White. Everyone called him 'the black and white minstrel' for obvious reasons.

John was a docker and a real gentleman, always dressed smartly, with brightly polished shoes. Once or twice Cilla popped in to see him and I thought she had loads of personality and a lot of bottle.

Over the road was a place called the Honky Tonk, which had another rogue's gallery of locals, including Jogger Morley who was five foot nothing and an ex-pro boxer. Jogger had this massive Alsatian that was damn near as big as him and whenever he ordered a pint of beer he bought a half for the dog, which he poured into a tray.

The pubs shut at ten o'clock and it was still light on summer evenings. As Jogger walked home one night a cute little poodle ran out on to the pavement and Jogger gave it a pat. This made the Alsatian jealous and it nipped him on the arse.

Jogger turned and punched the dog on the nose, dropping it like a stone.

'You bastard, I've been drinking with you all night and this is how you repay me.'

The Mediterranean pub had a different crowd again. The most memorable was Joe Murray, a mad Everton supporter, who had the best Irish jig (wig) I have ever seen in my life. It must have been stitched into his head.

Joe was a 'businessman' and the police always took a great deal of interest in his activities. He would come into the pub, flush with loot from his latest business deal, and toss money into the air or thrust it into the hands of pensioners.

Joe drove this great big American car, which everyone recognised, including the police. As he was heading home from the Mediterranean one night with a few mates, the police pulled the car over. An officer walked up to his window. Joe wound it down.

'Been drinking have you, Mr Murray?'

'Yeah, I've had a real good drink tonight.'

'Have you now. More than the two pints?'

'Oh yeah, I must have had at least eight or nine pints.'

'Did you have any shorts?'

'A few chasers – a Scotch or two.'

'Do you think you're fit to drive home, Mr Murray?'

'Definitely not. I must be way over the limit.'

This copper was getting really excited about nailing Joe, but couldn't understand why he was so relaxed.

'I'm a very lucky man,' Joe explained.

'What makes you think you're so lucky?'

'Well, I'm lucky to have a mate who can drive me home. This is an American car, officer, and I'm sitting in the passenger seat.'

The Britannia pub in Stanley Road was Albert's local. The manager, Tom McCain, must have been a hundred and forty years old because of all the stuff he'd done in his life. No matter where you said you'd been and what you'd done, Tom had been there first and done it for longer.

Mention the Army and Tom would say, 'Oh, I spent five years in the Paras.'

Or the Merchant Navy: 'Yeah, when I worked on the freighters in the Far East . . .' Basically, Tom had seen more, pissed higher, fallen further, shagged longer, run faster and gambled bigger than anyone he ever met.

Despite his stories, or perhaps because of them, Tom was a brilliant landlord. He had a Staffordshire bull terrier, Butch, who had lots of different tricks. A crowd of Norwegian sailors came in one day and were impressed by this dog.

'Come here, Butch,' said Tom, throwing a packet of crisps on the floor. 'Open it.'

Butch ripped the crisps open.

'Salt,' said Tom, and the dog used his nose to nudge crisps out of the way until he came to the little blue sachet of salt inside. The Norwegians applauded.

For his next trick, Butch wandered outside and came back with half a brick in his mouth. He walked past the bar and disappeared down the steps into the cellar.

'What's he doing?' asked one of the sailors.

'Building himself another kennel,' said Tom, without batting an eyelid.

Gigging my way around Liverpool taught me more about people and life than all my years at school. I was happiest in the pub. People knew me. I was Hobo Rick. Nothing else created the same excitement or sense of belonging.

Like a lot of young people I don't think I fully appreciated the magic of the late fifties. I was too busy playing music, chasing girls and holding down a job. Only later, looking back, did I begin to realise how much freedom I enjoyed compared to my parents.

People often let nostalgia colour what really happened, but I don't think anyone can deny we were part of something special. It was a wonderful time to be alive. You could walk the streets day or night, any time, anywhere and never be in danger.

By the time the swinging sixties arrived I was a married man with a wife. I had long hair and a beard, but I was never a child of the sixties. Only the middle classes could afford to buy old VW vans, paint them psychedelic colours and do the rounds of the rock festivals, spreading peace and harmony. Most working-class kids had jobs or were helping out at home.

Television, fashion, music, films, technology, the Pill . . .
the world was changing more rapidly than I could keep up
with. And Liverpool played a huge role as the birthplace of
the Merseybeat.

It might sound sacrilegious, but I was never a great fan of
The Beatles. I thought there were loads of better bands in
Liverpool like Ian and the Zodiacs, Derry and the Seniors
and The Big Three.

I'm not taking anything away from the Fab Four, but I'm
always quick to correct people who imagine they were
working-class heroes in Liverpool. Lennon and McCartney
were middle-class, well-educated boys. They were dead
sharp and they knew where they were going.

Although I didn't get to hear The Beatles play live, I
watched a lot of other local bands and some of them should
have gone all the way. One of the best was Rory Storm and
the Hurricanes, with a young Ringo Starr on drums. One of
the other lads was an apprentice joiner who had worked with
me on the Grafton job.

I saw them playing at Butlins one summer when I went on
a week's holiday with a few mates. After they finished the
concert, Ringo came over and said, 'Can you do us a favour,
Rick? We're getting a bit of hassle from this gang of Scots
fellas. We're going to have a straightener tomorrow.'

'Yeah, we'll give you a hand.'

Ringo was only small and none of the other guys in the
band could really handle themselves. The next afternoon I
turned up with my mates, but the Scots fellas didn't show.
Ringo was still grateful for the back-up.

'There's a talent competition this afternoon,' he said. 'Why
don't one of you lads get up and sing?'

'What do we sing?'

'It doesn't matter.'

Davey Smith volunteered and did a rock 'n' roll number with Rory and the band backing him. Then I realised that Rory and Ringo were judging the competition. Davey won first prize – a tin of full-strength Capstan cigarettes. I didn't smoke, but appreciated the gesture.

5

Donnie,
the Walton Road Gooser

There are so many people waiting at the church, they spill outside and stand in groups, shaking hands and nodding in greeting. Nobody has made them come. They're here because they want to be here.

The hearse parks near the main entrance and the back doors swing open. As I brace one shoulder under the coffin, I catch a glimpse of our Ronny. I've been worrying about how he's going to handle the funeral. Sod's law, I'm breaking my heart and he hasn't shed a tear. That's OK. Everyone grieves differently.

Our David is standing next to Ronny. He's almost a head taller than me, but now it's buried in a handkerchief as he blows his nose. His wife Lee is behind him. She reaches over and squeezes his hand.

As we walk into the church I recognise some of the faces and sympathetic smiles. Some have obviously come straight from work and are wearing black armbands and black ties instead of suits. Joe Murray is among them. He's standing on the opposite side of the road because he's wearing his work clothes and he doesn't wish to be disrespectful. Nowadays he runs a little carpet cleaning business, which is a far cry from the days when he drove that big American car and kept the police on their toes.

Peter Miller is here – forty years after he caught me kissing Margie King. And there are neighbours from Lance Street like the Johnson girls and Davey Steele.

Lots of my show business mates have turned up including Mickey Finn, Johnny Mack, Jimmy Hackett, Tony Parr and Pat McMullen. There are comics, impressionists, actors, musicians . . . At least half a dozen pro singers are among them and they make the hymns sound brilliant.

We chose 'The Old Rugged Cross', one of Mam's favourites, and 'Abide With Me' because Dad loved it so much. Whenever I hear that hymn I think of the time he went to Wembley to see Liverpool play in the Cup Final in 1950. We lost to Arsenal 2-0.

The church is so packed there are people standing at the back. Their voices carry high into the air where light streams through the stained glass windows. Ronny and Albert are sitting on either side of me. Albert's eyes are misting over but he has an amazing stillness, like a statue.

The vicar talks about the different jobs Mam did, cleaning pubs and houses, working in cafés and laundries. He mentions how she worked at Everton football ground and also at Anfield serving teas and pies in the Liverpool canteen. That's where she met Bill Shankly, the legendary manager.

'He's a real gentleman,' she always said. 'We might only be the tea ladies, but he remembers every one of our names and says hello every time he sees us.'

Mam would have loved all this attention; people saying prayers for her and thinking nice thoughts. It's a shame we can't enjoy our own funerals. Seems like a waste of a good party. I know what I'm gonna do. I want a proper jazz band and people singing and dancing like you see in New Orleans. And I'll put enough money behind the bar to last a fortnight. Knowing how thirsty my mates can be, it'll probably only last a week.

*

The second time I fell in love was at a fairground in Wrexham, Wales, in 1961. She was a nice-looking girl, with bright red hair, great legs and freckles on her nose.

I must have been nearing the end of my apprenticeship and Adams Bros had a big contract at the Brymbo Steelworks in Wrexham. I was living in digs during the week and travelling the forty miles back to Liverpool on weekends to play in the band.

Davey Williams, another apprentice, suggested we go to the Wrexham Fair one evening. We were wandering through the carnival when we spied two girls. He made a beeline for the one he fancied.

'What's your name?' he asked.

'Mary Richards.'

Even before I asked her name, I said to the other one, 'What religion are you?'

She looked puzzled. 'What do you mean?'

'What religion are you?'

'Nothing really,' she shrugged.

At least she's not a Catholic, I thought.

This is the truth, honest to God, and it doesn't make me proud. Why did it bother me? What did it matter?

Her name was Marlene Clifton and she was much more prim and proper than any of the girls I had dated. She worked as a machinist in a clothing factory and lived at home with her folks in Queen's Park, Wrexham.

She had six brothers and two sisters, but one of the lads, Cyril, had died as a baby. Every morning Mrs Clifton would yell up the stairs, telling the kids to get ready for school. She'd run through the names – Doreen, Jackie, Ronny, Raymond, Marlene, Shirley, Dennis . . . and Cyril. She never missed him out.

Old Charlie, the Dad, was a fitter down the mines and a

real good grafter. He was only about five foot two tall and a similar distance across, but was incredibly strong and marvellous with his hands. He was always tinkering with an old Jaguar.

Charlie had been a soldier in the war, but developed a reputation for going AWOL and heading back to Wales to see his wife and kids. Eventually, they posted him overseas to stop him absconding.

They were a smashing family. Very working class. In those days Queen's Park was a nice estate almost in the countryside. The Clifton house had a front garden and a path along the side to another big garden at the back where old Charlie had a vegetable garden and a big shed that he'd built himself.

Some time after the war an official from the council turned up and told him the shed had to be pulled down because it had no planning permission.

'I have got permission,' said Charlie.

'Who gave you permission?'

'Winston Churchill.'

'Winston Churchill! What are you bloody talkin' about?'

'Well, I was listening to the radio and Churchill was telling everyone about the food shortages and how times are gonna be bloody hard. "England expects," he said. "We all know food is in short supply, so grow your own cabbages or keep chickens . . ." Well, that's what I done; I built a chicken coop.'

'Are you trying to tell me that bloody big shed is a hen house?'

'Yeah. And if you want to take it up with anyone, take it up with Winston Churchill.'

Needless to say he didn't hear another word from the council.

The first time I went to Marlene's house her five brothers turned up. I guess they were checking me out and also sending me a message not to mess about with their sister.

We dated for nearly two years. Because she lived in Wrexham and I lived in Liverpool we only saw each other on weekends. Marlene would come and see me or I went to Wrexham. The train journey took almost two hours because of the timetables and interchanges. Sometimes I rode my motorbike, but nine times out of ten it would break down just as I reached Queen's Park and I'd have to push it the last hundred yards. Charlie would always manage to fix it for me so I could get home.

Whenever I took Marlene out, he would be waiting on the doorstep at eleven o'clock to make sure I had her home on time. Then he'd allow me inside for a quick cup of tea before saying, 'Right, my lad, off you pop.'

During the week at 7 p.m. Marlene would wait at the public call box near her house. I called her from a public phone in Heyworth Street, by the school. If she didn't hear from me, she knew to be waiting at eight o'clock.

Most of the girls I knew were very forward, but Marlene was quiet and reserved. I don't think she had ever been in a pub until I took her into one. She also wouldn't entertain the possibility of sleeping with me unless we were married. I quite respected her for this, but it didn't stop me trying.

I can't remember when we decided to get engaged, but everyone seemed happy. I was twenty-two years old and had become a fully-fledged City and Guilds plasterer. We married on 22 March 1962 at a church in Wrexham. Dad hired a minibus to transport the family from Liverpool. Albert drove and was also my best man.

All of my brothers were there. Lined up together we all looked so different, despite the brown hair and dark eyes.

David is the tallest and has a wonderful laugh. He had become a sign-writer, but later he had dozens of different jobs and ran various businesses. Our Ronny was still at school and destined to be the brains of the family.

Albert and I were probably closest because we shared a love for the music scene. He had a wonderful voice and could sing right down to the depths of his boots, just like Dean Martin. I swear to God I've seen a girl swoon when listening to him.

Instead of a honeymoon, I put down a £250 deposit on a parlour house in Salop Street, close to Goodison Park, Everton's home ground. It had three bedrooms, a lounge, parlour, back kitchen and a long yard with an outside toilet.

Mam instilled in me the whole idea of buying a place. She wanted her sons to be independent. All that time in Lance Street we had rented and afterwards Mam used to say, 'If we had bought that house we would have owned it years ago.'

In my spare time I re-skimmed all the walls and ceilings balancing on a stepladder because I couldn't afford proper scaffolding. Dad would come down and give me a hand for a couple of hours.

He was no longer working as a baker. Most places had automated the entire process and machines were making the bread. Dad was a hand-baker and a real craftsman, but there wasn't a demand for these skills any more. For a while he worked in a bread factory and then in a storeroom. He was proud of the fact that he had never been out of work.

By the time I put in a bathroom and toilet upstairs we had no money left for furniture. I had left Adams Bros and started working for a little jobber called Davis, who did small contracts like patching walls and skimming ceilings.

Sometimes I came across bits of furniture that were being thrown out including a three-piece lounge suite, which I collected in a handcart and had re-upholstered. Mam and Dad gave us a bedroom suite as a wedding present and Marlene made the curtains and other bits and pieces.

Slowly we made a nice home and it didn't seem empty when we were together. I would rush home from work, excited about seeing her and drag her upstairs to bed. She giggled and complained about cooking the dinner, but the protests were always pretty hollow.

In the building game I could be out of work for three months at a time, which meant I relied heavily on doing gigs with the band, particularly during the lean times. In a sense I had become almost semi-pro with four gigs of a Sunday as well as Friday and Saturday nights.

Apart from playing the banjo and singing a few songs, the rest of the material seemed to happen intuitively. Some of the stuff was fairly blue and I remember doing a church social club, St Peter and Paul's in Kirkby, when the local priest asked the manager, Glynn Jones, if he could have a word.

'What is it, Father?'

'Well, I've been having a lot of complaints from my parishioners about this fella on stage. They're not happy about his language and some of the jokes he's telling.'

'Well, Father,' said Glynn, respectfully. 'You had better have a look at this.'

He took him over to the cash register and pressed the till roll. A figure printed out, showing the takings for the night.

'That's the trouble with some of my parishioners,' said the priest. 'They have no sense of humour.'

At first Marlene came along to watch me play, but she was never very comfortable in pubs and clubs, surrounded by drunks and extroverts. She wasn't a drinker and she didn't find showbiz exciting. Maybe she would have preferred me to be more like Charlie, working regular hours in a normal job.

In order to spend more time at home, I quit plastering and became a salesman in a 'cheque shop' at the bottom of Salop Street. A 'cheque shop' sold household goods, furnishings and clothes on hire purchase, with people paying them off in weekly instalments. Granny Tomlinson had done this for years and even my school uniforms had been bought on the 'never-never'.

My new boss, Mr Dennison, was a sprightly little guy in a three-piece suit, with a thin moustache and his hair slicked back on his head. He always had a newspaper tucked under his arm, like a sergeant major with a stick.

He showed me all the tricks of the trade when it came to selling. Our department handled soft furnishings, carpets and curtains and each week we were expected to meet certain sales quotas.

I remember taking one thousand pounds one week, which put us way above the target. But when the manager came round Mr Dennison told him that we'd only taken six hundred pounds.

'Why did you do that?' I whispered, imagining some sort of scam.

'Because next week we might only sell two hundred pounds' worth of stuff,' he explained. 'You can't guarantee that every week will be the same. This gives us four hundred pounds to make the bad weeks look better.'

We made a great team. Often he'd say, 'Go have your tea break, Rick. You can nip home if you like. Come back in half an hour.'

'What if the manager comes round?'

'I'll tell them you're delivering some carpets.'

The wages of a salesman were even worse than plastering and after six months I decided to leave. The store manager tried to convince me to stay, saying I could have my own department in six months, but I wasn't interested. I went back to what I knew, working on the building sites.

Things were tough and I struggled to get work. I needed a car or van to get to the sites. Finally I plucked up courage and went to see Joe Murray, who had a little car showroom in Scotland Road.

I didn't have a carrot for the deposit, but Joe let me have this little second-hand A40 van on hire purchase. I only made about three payments and Joe waived the rest. He was that type of fella. I've never forgotten his kindness and have looked for ways to make it up to him since.

The van did a lot to improve our finances. After plastering all day Friday, I would drive up to Hanley-in-Stoke and buy seventy quid's worth of cups, saucers and plates from the pottery factories. The wholesaler would always throw in something extra, just for me, which covered the cost of petrol – a nice vase, or a serving plate or a tea service.

It was late by the time I got back in Liverpool. I went straight to Ozzie Wade's, which stayed open until the early hours and was a popular showbiz hangout. Ozzie had been dead for years, but his wife Aida Taylor ran the place. She was only prosecuted once in thirty years for after-hours drinking and the Judge apologised when he fined her and called her 'Lady Bountiful'.

A lot of local entertainers and club acts went to Ozzie Wade's after performing around Liverpool; guys like Ken Dodd, Bert Cook, Sonny Jones and Bill Dean, who I worked with years later in *Brookside*. Dozens of showbiz stars would congregate downstairs and put on impromptu performances. Billy Hutch would play the piano, while Billy Wheeler or Pat McMullen gave us a song. Afterwards, 'Laughing Johnny Mack' told a few gags or one of the other comics did a set. There was a load of piss-taking and good-natured professional rivalry.

At about five in the morning I left the club and drove to Great Homer Street where I set up a stall to sell my cups and saucers. The markets were full of solid, hard-working grafters like Cilla Black's mother, who sold clothes four or five pitches away from mine. The guy next to me flogged vegetables. His gimmick was to get a tray of tomatoes, sprinkle dirt over half of them, and label them 'Home-grown English tomatoes'. He sold them for two bob a pound instead of one and six.

Sometimes I played the banjo to draw a crowd or I took a 'no fishing' sign out of the van and knocked it into the ground in front of a puddle. On a good day I covered my costs and made about eight quid clear profit.

Marlene had started going home of a weekend to see her Mam, who she missed terribly. She would leave on Friday and not come back until Monday. I should have realised that she was lonely in Liverpool. She had left her friends and family behind and moved from a small town to a large city.

Similarly, she had grown up in a house with eight siblings, where the chatter and laughter must have been constant. Now she found herself on her own during the day when I went off to work.

Although she made friends in Salop Street, Marlene had always been quite shy and reserved. I told myself things would be different when she was pregnant. We were trying, but nothing had happened.

As the years ticked by with still no sign of a baby, I think it began to weigh on Marlene. After five years of trying we went to see a doctor and did the tests. The experts told us nothing was wrong. We just had to keep trying.

Slowly Marlene became more withdrawn. She no longer came to see me play and spent longer and longer periods in Wrexham with her family. We no longer talked to each other or spent time together. I didn't understand that being a husband meant more than bringing home a weekly wage packet. No wonder she was lonely.

The Stanley Park Hotel, just next to Everton's football ground, had earned the nickname of 'the Blue House'. Tommy Scully and a band called the Hi-Fi Three were playing there one Sunday when I dropped in for a drink. The boys invited me to join them and I told a few gags and sang a song.

The following evening I was sitting at home at about nine o'clock when Scully hammered on the door.

'You're late.'

'What for?'

'We're on.'

I grabbed my coat and followed him. Soon after that we became known as Hobo Rick and the Hi-Fi Three, with Scully on vocals, Brian Edwards, a docker, on bass and Tony Scoggins (Scoggo) on rhythm guitar. The other lads grew these little Vandyke beards to enhance their image but I kept my scruffy beard.

Scully was often called the white Sammy Davis Jr because he sang just like him and had a lot of the same mannerisms. As a giggle we used to put Sellotape over his nose to make it look punched in like Sammy's.

Scoggo was an ex-seafarer, who had worked as a rigger on the docks and a scaffolder. A big, fit, good-looking lad, with a mass of dark hair that later turned into a shock of white. He and I have been mates for years and we discovered acting at about the same time.

We were always playing practical jokes on each other. I remember going round to his little council house one day and Scoggo began filling up the electric jug to make us a cup of tea.

'You see where that electric point is,' I said. The sink had a double socket just beside it. 'That's dangerous. You're not supposed to have it so close to running water.'

'Oh, it's all right,' said Scoggo, as he kept filling the kettle.

I knew straight away what I was going to do. I quietly got a brown paper bag and blew it up like a balloon.

'I'm serious, Scoggo. That's an accident waiting to happen.'

'Nah, you're all right if you're careful,' he explained.

He reached over and plugged in the jug. At that moment I smashed the bag with my fist. The bang was so loud he thought he'd been electrocuted. The kettle went flying up in the air and hit the ceiling. By then I was rolling on the floor laughing and Scoggo looked at me as if to say, 'You bastard!'

Brian Edwards, the original bass player of the Hi-Fi Three, was tall and slim, with short back and sides and a quiff. Brian was a little quieter than the rest of us, but had a great sense of fun.

In the months that followed, our gigs at the Blue House developed into a cross between improvised theatre, pantomime and organised madness. We did a different sketch every week, each playing a part. Nothing was ever written down or rehearsed. It was off-the-cuff, spur-of-the-moment, seat-of-our-pants stuff and it went down a treat.

Scoggo and I would normally get things rolling and Scully would jump in when he could. Brian stood at the back, roaring with laughter, trying to join us but not knowing what to do.

The Blue House was chock-a-block every weekend, with a crowd of 150 crammed inside and a queue stretching round the corner. The Sunday afternoon show was a lot raunchier, but we cleaned up the material for families of a Monday night.

We always started off with some gags and songs like 'Mack the Knife' and 'More (Than the Greatest Love the World has Known)'. Then after the interval we did the sketch. Often I arrived with absolutely no idea what we were going to do. Someone from the audience would shout an idea and we took up the challenge.

At other times I came up with ideas while plastering or out driving. I began collecting props, perhaps an old Army helmet or a gun or a frying pan. These were tossed into the van and later stored in the cellar of the Blue House.

We did cowboy sketches, marriages, shipwrecks, gunfights, bank robberies . . . you name it.

One of the regulars at the Blue House was Donnie, the worst singer I ever heard in my life. Small and weedy, with uneven teeth, Donnie was a ha'penny short of a full shilling, but a really lovable guy, who couldn't wait to get up on stage and take part in the sketches.

He'd sing and strip off his shirt, flexing his muscles and revealing a vest as black as the hods of hell. All the girls in the audience would scream and treat him like a pop star.

I nicknamed him 'Donnie, the Walton Road Gooser' – a name that became known the length and breadth of the city. The name had nothing to do with pinching women's arses. The term 'goosing' in Liverpool meant 'shagging' and I doubt if Donnie had ever had a woman in his life.

We began taking him round with us from pub to pub, paying him a few quid and buying him drinks. One night we had a gig in Wales and swung by his place to pick him up.

'Have you got your passport with you, Donnie?' I asked.

'No.'

'How are you gonna get into Wales?'

He looked crestfallen.

'Don't worry. We'll smuggle you in.'

As we neared the Mersey Tunnel, I pulled over and Donnie began climbing into the boot. He had no idea we were taking the piss.

Another wonderful character at the Blue House was old Arthur, a local pensioner, who helped us set up every week. Arthur must have been eighty and could have been knocked over by a sneeze. We promoted him to the official pub bouncer and even gave him a special coat. He was made up.

Every week a few of the lads would start a scuffle and I'd say, 'Go and sort that out, Arthur.'

He'd march over and the fellas would start pleading, 'Don't hurt us, Arthur. We'll be good.'

One week we pitched a tent on stage and hid old Arthur in the back. When the show started we chose a girl from the audience and dressed her up in a leopard skin leotard like Jane out of *Tarzan*.

Then we chose a strapping young lad from the audience to become our Tarzan.

'OK, in you go,' I said, shoving them both in the tent. 'I'm sure you know what to do.'

Scoggo walked across the stage carrying a board saying 'Three Months Later'.

Old Arthur emerged from inside, nothing but skin and bone, with a concave chest and a gaunt face. The audience howled.

Another week we married Arthur off to a buxom eighteen-year-old girl in a full bridal gown. Scoggo played the best man and Arthur was decked out in the dicky bow and suit, with a flower in his lapel. I played the vicar and the audience sang 'Here Comes the Bride'.

The following week we did a honeymoon sketch, with a double bed on stage. This young girl wore a flimsy nightgown and Arthur wore his pyjamas and his little round glasses. You should have seen his face. I'm convinced he thought it was real. He tried to get his leg over this girl who started screaming. Scully rushed in with a fire-hose to cool him down.

We were making comedy out of anything and it was exciting and dangerous. Another sketch involved a hospital scene, where a woman from the audience pretended to be pregnant. She had two dolls under her frock – a black one and a white one.

'OK, gentlemen,' I said, as we stood around the operating table in our whites. 'Put on your masks.'

We had Mickey Mouse masks and Donald Duck masks.

I lifted the dress of the 'pregnant woman'.

'Hammer.'

I was passed a huge hammer.

'Chisel.'

'Saw.'

'Wrench.'

This went on until I finished up holding a pneumatic drill.

'Right. Success at last. We've got her drawers off.'

It was corny and slapstick and rude, but some of it was inspired and people would come back week after week for more.

We were a really tight bunch and there were never any fights or disagreements in the band. This is why it came as such a shock when Brian Edwards fell sick. He was diagnosed with brain cancer and was dead within weeks. He was only in his twenties.

Up until then death had never been an issue for me. Yes, I'd lost relatives, but they were old. Brian was a mate. He was my age. One day he was laughing and joking and the next he was gone. It seemed so unfair.

As a tribute to Brian we carried on with the Hi-Fi Three.

Our new bass player, Tommy Bowness, fitted into the band and grew a Vandyke beard like the other lads.

An old fighter called Les Radcliffe and his wife Hilda managed the Blue House. Hilda had been engaged seven times before she married Les. They were good people to deal with, but after about eighteen months the band decided we wanted a change. Our shows had been written up in the *Stage* newspaper and we were getting new offers for better money.

Scully gave me the job of telling Les the bad news.

'It's been great, but the lads are moving,' I said.

Les looked heartbroken. 'No, you can't move. Everybody loves you.' Instead of being truthful about our reasons for moving on, I tried to make up an excuse.

'Look at this place, Les. People can't see properly because of all the partitions. There's no proper stage. The lads are just a bit pissed off, that's all.'

'OK, I'm busy now, but come in tomorrow with Tommy. Let's see if we can sort things out.'

I went to see Scully. 'You should have told him the truth,' he said.

'I know, but I didn't want to hurt his feelings. We'll set him straight tomorrow.'

The next day I arrived at the pub and all the partitions had been knocked down and a team of workmen from the brewery had spent all night refurbishing the place and installing a portable stage. How could we leave him after that? We finished up staying at the Blue House for another year.

As a test of our popularity we decided to do a special one-off gig in a much bigger venue, the Mons Hotel in Liverpool.

A few support acts started the show and we came on for the second half. The Olympics were in the news, so we chose a sporting theme for the sketch. It began with Donnie, dressed up in his shorts and vest, carrying the Olympic flame into the concert room. Scoggo made the 'torch' out of a wire coat hanger, metal foil and a ball of cotton soaked in methylated spirits.

Donnie set off jogging with this burning torch, while we played some suitably stirring music. He did the first circuit and was halfway round again when the torch became red hot and he dropped it, setting fire to the carpet and then the curtains. There was mayhem.

We managed to extinguish the blaze and carry on with the show, but our entire profits for the night were spent compensating the hotel for the damage.

Dad would come and see me perform at the Blue House, but I couldn't get Mam to join him. She said the show was 'too blue'.

'How do you know?'

'That's what the women in the laundry tell me.'

Her friends were coming to see me every week and then recounting all the sketches and jokes.

Although I was busy, I still managed to drop round to Elmore Street once or twice a week to see Mam and Dad. She still fussed over him and seemed to worship the ground he walked on.

One weekend in about 1966 she asked him to unblock a drain in the back yard. He took out a pick and began lifting the heavy concrete slabs, but suddenly felt unwell. On Monday he went to see the doctor and tests were ordered. Within a fortnight he had been diagnosed with lung cancer. It was well advanced and inoperable.

Mam blamed herself.

'Why did I let him dig up them pavers?' she said. 'They were too heavy.'

I kept telling her it had nothing to do with the paving stones. Dad had smoked Woodbines for years and worked in an unventilated basement in a cloud of flour. Mam kept punishing herself. She was already grieving. For thirty years she had cooked his meals, washed his clothes and tucked his scarf into his coat as he left for work. Losing him was too much to bear.

Dad went downhill very quickly and couldn't work any more. Even as he deteriorated I used to love making him laugh. When Albert cut his hair, Dad would say, 'I love our Rick, but I wouldn't let him near me with a pair of scissors.'

He knew I'd give him a Mohican.

I still took him to the Blue House and sat him among the celebrities who came to watch; fellas like Ian St John, the former soccer star, Johnny Cooke, the boxer, and Tony Kaye, the best halfback I ever saw.

When the cancer spread Dad was put into Clatterbridge – a big cancer hospital over the water in the Wirral. For all the jokes and banter, I now realised that he was dying and I didn't know what to do.

Albert found me one day. 'We're all going in to see our Dad today.'

'I can't. There's a gig.'

He looked me straight in the eye and said firmly, 'No. We're *all* going in to see him.'

He fetched me in his little pick-up truck and all four brothers were squeezed in the front.

When we reached the Clatterbridge they wouldn't let us all visit the ward at once, so the others went in first. They each had something for Dad – cigarettes, a football magazine, fruit, that sort of thing. I bought him a penny bar of chocolate because he didn't eat sweets. I knew he'd get the joke.

Dad was standing at the end of the ward dressed in his pyjamas. I put my arms around him and started crying.

'I know, Rick. I know,' he said.

He knew why I hadn't been in to see him ... why I struggled.

'Take me home,' he whispered in my ear.

A few days later we brought him back to Elmore Street. He was too weak to get up and down the stairs so we made up a bed in the parlour. I went to see him every day, along with the other lads. We had card schools and you could hear us laughing up the street.

Dad still tried to cheat. It was even more obvious because his hands weren't as quick. We'd see him slipping a card under the blankets. Albert, David and Ronny would just let it go, but I wouldn't.

'Hang on, Dad.'

'What?'

'I saw what you did. There's a card under the blankets.'

'Where?'

'Under the blankets.'

'There's no card down there.'

'Show me.'

He was totally shameless. 'How did that get there? Must be from the last hand. I'm not very good at shuffling any more.'

We used to take turns staying on the settee of a night to give Mam a break from being up and down to him.

'I want one of me lads with me when I die,' he used to say. I think he was scared of being alone.

For nine months he lingered until he couldn't get out of bed without help and his body wasted away to less than six stone. There had never been much of him, but now he seemed to be disappearing bit by bit.

He would cough his lungs out and spit into a white enamel pan. All sorts of crap came out of his lungs. One day he coughed so hard that his teeth fell into the pan. Normally, I'm a finicky bugger and anything can make me baulk, but I didn't hesitate. I put my hand into this blood and phlegm and retrieved his teeth. Then I washed them and put them back in his mouth. I would have done anything for him.

I was leaving one day and he called me back.

'Will you put on me pink pyjamas for me, lad?' he asked.

'What's wrong with your vest and underpants?'

'I got people coming to visit.'

I had never seen Dad without clothes, but when you're that sick you lose any sense of modesty and allow yourself to be looked after.

As I buttoned his pyjama shirt, he said, 'I don't want to be buried, Rick.'

'But I thought that's what you planned. You always said you wanted to be buried in Anfield Cemetery, facing The Kop.'

'I know, but I've changed me mind. I don't want to be lying there under the snow. It's too cold. Get me cremated instead.'

'OK, Dad. Whatever you want.'

He could barely lift himself off the bed and had to be carried everywhere, but he didn't complain. His doctor visited three times a day to give him morphine injections. At one point it had snowed so heavily we had to push the doctor's car to get it started.

That night we had a gig at the Mediterranean. It was a retirement bash and Albert chose to stay with Dad rather than come along. Dad told him to go out and have a good time.

'What about you?'

'I'm OK. Just make sure you call in and see me on your way home. Don't matter what time it is.'

Albert came to the pub and we had a great night. At about half two in the morning we were still there. Someone bought Albert another pint, but he said he couldn't stay. He had promised Dad.

He caught a cab to Elmore Street and walked past his own house until he reached Mam and Dad's. Mam met him in the hallway.

'Your Dad's been asking for you.'

Albert went into the parlour and sat on the edge of the bed.

'All right, are you?'

Dad lifted himself up and threw his legs out of bed, putting his arm around Albert's shoulder as though comforting him. He hadn't been able to lift his back off the bed for nine months, but suddenly he found the strength. At that same moment he died. He had been waiting for Albert to arrive.

All of us were devastated, none more so than Ronny. He was eighteen years old and had become Dad's best mate since the rest of us had married and left home. They always had a little bet together of a Saturday and watched the football on TV.

Ronny was the sharpest of us all. He won a scholarship and went straight off to the Collegiate. He was also a great footballer and could have gone all the way. Dad never missed watching one of his games.

A professional footballer called Phil Eastam was recruiting for an American league and Ronny had agreed to see one of the scouts. When Dad took poorly Ronny jipped the final interview and trial. After Dad's death he quit a good job at Customs and Excise and spent weeks laying on a couch, sleeping and staring at the television. Mam was beside herself with worry.

Dad died on 28 February 1967, eighteen months after being diagnosed with lung cancer. He was fifty-five years old and had worked all his life. He didn't leave a carrot. Not a penny.

I still miss him.

6

The Wreck of the Hesperus

Apart from the vicar, nobody else makes a speech. None of us need to be told about how hard Mam worked or how ill she'd been. And this isn't about Rick the actor or Albert the singer or David's work with underprivileged kids.

Quite rightly, Ronny gets a mention for all he did for Mam, particularly in the later years when her health began to fail.

Up until three years ago I never regarded Mam as being old. She was always so independent. Because of her legs she became pretty much housebound and eventually needed a walking frame and then a wheelchair. It would take an eternity for her to walk to the front door, but it was still good for her to make the effort.

'Come on, Mam, how about a cup of tea?' I'd say.

'You'll have to get your own.'

'Bloody hell, Mam, that's the trouble with you packing up work, you're all self. What about the rest of us?'

She laughed and told me not to swear.

Albert, David and me visited her every Sunday, but our Ronny did the lion's share of looking after her. Sometimes he'd be around at the bungalow four times a day. He picked up her pension, shopped for groceries and even did the laundry and cleaning.

Before he went home he'd make her a bit of supper – a sandwich and a cup of tea – and put them on a tray next to her. The next day, he'd ask, 'Did you eat them sandwiches, Mam?'

'They were lovely, them,' she'd say.

A few days later he'd be tidying up and find the sandwiches in the drawer next to her chair. He wouldn't say anything. He'd simply throw them away and keep fussing over her.

Ronny kept a lot of the worst from us. He took on all the responsibility himself. He even kept it secret that she was incontinent. Meanwhile, he put pads on the chairs and cleaned up the accidents.

He told us the story of the radiator leaking in the bathroom and how he'd found this puddle on the floor.

'Before you start, I never done that,' she announced.

God we laughed.

Her mind had always been sharp, but towards the end it started playing tricks on her. She phoned Albert after midnight one time.

'Are you on your way to get me?'

'Why?'

'I'm supposed to be at the hospital.'

Albert looked at the clock. 'It's one o'clock in the morning, Mam. Your appointment is this afternoon.'

'Oh, blimey. I'm sorry. Day and night have become one.'

Not long after that I went to pick her up for her Friday blood test. Ronny was at the bungalow cleaning the windows. As I came in the front door, she pointed upwards and said, 'Shhh, you'll wake your Dad. He's been on nights.'

The bungalow didn't have an upstairs and Dad had been dead for thirty-four years.

Hobo Rick and the Hi-Fi Three played in some pretty rough pubs – places where fellas would tap you on the shoulder with a bar stool if you looked twice at them.

The line-up of the band had become fairly flexible. If one of the lads had work commitments, we recruited from the

pool of musicians who had become mates over the years.
This included fellas like John Cordwell, an ex-guardsman
and a wonderful banjo player, who is one of the best-read
men I've ever met.

Once a week we had a gig at the Bow and Arrow in
Huyton. Jossie Peters, a local scrap dealer, brought along his
family and sat right up front. He was a huge man, with a hard
reputation, but I didn't think twice about taking the piss out
of him because he knew I meant no offence.

The show was going well one day and I started telling a
joke about the Pope. Suddenly, there was a shout from the
back of the bar. I didn't hear what was said, so I carried on.

Next thing I noticed that the place had gone quiet. The
audience was no longer looking at me. Everyone had focused
on Christie McMullen, a hard case from a well-known
Catholic family, who was on his feet.

I carried on telling the joke, but Christie had heard
enough. He began shouting at me, red-faced and ranting. I
killed him with the ad-libs and had everyone laughing, which
only made things worse.

Christie turned to his wife. 'Give us your bag.'

He pulled out a revolver and aimed it directly at me. The
hole in that barrel looked about twelve inches wide. Scoggo
and John Cordwell were behind me, still holding their
instruments.

'Pack your gear,' I said. 'I don't mind getting heckled but
I'm not getting shot.'

We walked out. I heard later, but I can't vouch for it, that
there was mayhem at the pub. Jossie Peters wanted a piece
of Christie McMullen for having stopped the show. The
police were never called. That's not how things were done.

Apart from gigs with the band, I also did stuff on my own,
normally as master of ceremonies for particular functions or

concert nights. I did a show out Runcorn way for the local constabulary, who were entertaining a visiting dignitary – a high-ranking Malaysian policeman.

A number of acts had been lined up including a stripper and Blaster Bates, a wonderful comic, who worked as a demolition guy during the day, using dynamite to blow up chimneys and cesspools.

The stripper was a stunning Jewish girl and she told me backstage that she was saving up to open a tropical fish shop. That's the sort of detail you remember because it is so unusual.

The organiser of the show, a senior policeman, pulled me aside beforehand.

'Look, Hobo, as you know we got this visiting bigwig. Nothing too blue, OK. And can you tell the stripper to make sure she keeps her tassels and her G-string on. We don't want to upset this guy. He's probably a Muslim.'

We did the first half of the show and then took a break while the police made a few speeches about the spirit of cooperation between law enforcement bodies. While this went on the entertainers were told to help ourselves to drinks in the lounge. We all got stuck in, but the stripper had more than her share as the interval dragged on.

We started the second half with Blaster and then a few other acts. It was hot backstage and the stripper kept having to reapply body glue to hold her tassels on her nipples.

'Look, just do your best,' I told her. 'If you look like you're losing them, turn your back.'

I did five minutes of stand-up and then introduced her. I couldn't see her performance from backstage, but I assumed she was going down a treat from all the wolf whistles and cheers.

Next thing there was uproar. Some bloke had launched

himself on stage and people were trying to hold him back. Her tassels had fallen off and she'd turned her back. There were howls of protest. She ran off stage, almost in tears.

'What was that all about?' I asked the organiser.

'Stupid bastard tried to get his hands on the stripper.'

'Why didn't you throw him out?'

'I couldn't. He's the Malaysian bloody policeman!'

Because of the licensing laws, all sorts of drinking and social clubs flourished in Liverpool. People wanted somewhere to go when the pubs shut. Some of the clubs got around the licensing laws by serving food, while others seemed to always know when police raids were planned.

The Colombo Club in Seel Street (formerly known as the Rum Runner and then Maggie May's) was one of the most notorious. The owner, Tony Gallagher, was a little guy who used to be a boxer. He asked us to do a few gigs of a Sunday, which we had to squeeze in between our existing commitments at the Mediterranean.

The Colombo was always full of gangsters, conmen, hustlers, crooked lawyers, ex-boxers and hard cases. The only girls I saw there were mistresses or prostitutes who worked the ships. Liverpool had more hookers per square mile than anywhere else in the country.

After getting to know the regulars I was soon telling jokes about them without causing offence. It didn't worry me that I might go too far. These guys loved having their names mentioned and craved the limelight. That's why so much Mafia money is tied up in Hollywood and you see gangsters running nightclubs.

Families like the McMullens and the Fitzies were notorious, but they weren't bullies or tyrants. They wouldn't pick on your ordinary punter in the street because that wouldn't be fair.

Instead they targeted other gangs or families with similar reputations.

Eddie Palmer, a former heavyweight boxer, worked on the door. A good bouncer is worth his weight in gold because he can sort out trouble quickly or stop it before it happens. Eddie was basically a knockout merchant and a psychopath.

I was in the club one night when a foreign sailor tried to get in. The lad was a bit of a nuisance, but harmless enough. He just didn't know the score. In the end Eddie hit him and knocked him out.

That should have been the end of it, but Eddie went inside the club, where he kept a metal railing behind the bar with a lump of concrete on the end of it. He was going back out to hit this guy, even though he was already unconscious. We had to wrestle the railing off him.

Eddie had spent time in jail and was meaner than a junkyard dog. Sometimes he'd go into clothing shops, choose an outfit and walk out without paying. Most of the time people were too frightened to challenge him.

It didn't come as any surprise when Eddie turned up dead. Someone near took his head off with a knife. When the local police found his body they sent out for a crate of champagne to celebrate. I can understand why. You live by the sword, you die by the sword.

The Colombo was surprisingly free of trouble, maybe because of the clientele. Nobody was game to start a fight because it could have escalated so quickly.

Someone let off a double barrel shotgun during the show one Sunday afternoon. Both barrels. Bang! Bang! Everybody hit the floor. Tony Scoggo and Tommy Scully were lying on the stage. I was hiding under a beer mat.

The smoke slowly rose and gangsters were peering over the tops of tables. At the far end of the room, Tony Gallagher vaulted the bar, ran through all the tables and jumped on the stage. He grabbed the microphone.

'That's it! That's it! I've had enough. Shotguns in my club, is it? Well from now on nobody gets in without a bloody tie!'

The Colombo was full again the next weekend. The gunman was never identified and things went back to normal.

One of the most popular parts of the show every Sunday was the worst singing competition. The winner would get a teapot without a handle or maybe an old boot.

During one particular show, I had a fella down the front who kept trying to get my attention. I told him to wait, but he wouldn't give up.

'All right, come on then, ya pillock,' I said, giving him a clip around the back of the head as he climbed on stage. 'Give us a bit of order for this dopey twat. He's gonna give us a song.'

I handed him the microphone and he cleared his throat. In a big loud voice he announced, 'My name is Detective Inspector Coffee and this is a raid.'

Six policemen with clipboards under their arms came marching through the main door and down between the tables. There was a little fire escape at the side of the club, up about four stairs. It was only about two foot square. A hundred people went through that door in about seven seconds. A young policeman outside raised his arms and managed to say, 'Stop! Police!' before disappearing under the stampede.

They never got a single name, unless you count mine and Scoggo's. In the end they tossed the clipboards on the bar and had a drink.

A few years later a couple of us decided to open a banjo parlour in Liverpool. John Cordwell had played in one in America, which gave us the idea. Scoggo, Cordwell, myself and a fella called John Carberry began making plans. We found a near-empty building (Liverpool was full of them in those days) and negotiated a lease. It was seven storeys high and the only other tenant was King Conner, a local bookmaker, on the ground floor.

Gripped by the entrepreneurial spirit, we had plans to turn the cellar into a dockside café that Mam would run. One of the upper floors was completely open, which made it perfect for a five-a-side football pitch.

Getting stuck in, we cleaned the rubbish, skimmed the walls and began the painting. In the meantime, Cordwell, Scoggo and me would take the van to collect old-fashioned bits of furniture to make the bar look like 1920s Chicago.

I had the task of getting the liquor licence, which meant getting permission from the local police. At the station I was directed to an office upstairs where I knocked on the door and entered. The officer had his back to me.

'I've come about this application for a licence.'

He turned. It was Detective Inspector Coffee. My heart sank.

With nothing to lose I pressed ahead and told him about the banjo parlour.

'Oh, yeah, I can't see a problem with that,' he said, signing the form.

I couldn't resist asking him about the raid on the Colombo. Why had it taken the police so long to act?

'We watched that club for years,' he said, shaking his head sadly. 'We didn't close it down because it served a purpose. We knew where all the gangsters were.'

'So what changed?'

'It got too bloody popular. All the local publicans were complaining that an illegal drinking club was taking away their trade.'

Ironically, it was the same sort of opposition that killed off the banjo parlour. When the council came to rule on planning permission, the Catholic social club across the road, Our Ladies of Burlington Street, raised objections.

This was due to a misunderstanding. The club had heard rumours of gangsters being involved in the banjo parlour. By the time they discovered the truth the objection had already been lodged and it was too late to change anything.

The council made some excuse about insufficient parking for patrons and turned down our application. We could have appealed, but it would have taken eighteen months. Instead we called it a day, writing off the money that had already been spent.

Although in my late twenties, I was still politically naive. I had a mixture of left- and right-wing views, having been a shop steward and at the same time coming from a very patriotic family.

I found most left-wing literature beyond my caring and newspapers like the *Daily Worker* or the *Morning Star* were often full of diatribes that you needed a dictionary to understand.

On one building site a little guy called Wally would come around selling a broadsheet paper. I can't remember what it was called, but it was a mouthpiece for the National Front.

I am not the brightest guy in the world, but sitting on an upturned bucket on a building site, eating a cold cheese sarnie and worrying about where my next job would come from, some of the right-wing arguments seemed dead easy to understand.

Wally argued that immigration was the reason that none of us had enough work.

'It's totally out of control,' he said. 'We're getting swamped and nobody wants to do anything about it. We need to let the politicians know. We need to change their policies.'

'What can the likes of us do?' I asked.

'You can join the National Front.'

I thought about this for a while. It seemed so simple. First identify the problem – immigration – and then solve it – less immigration. All the ills of the country – the overcrowding and the lack of jobs – had been caused by too many people coming in. If we could stop the flood there would be plenty of jobs and houses to go round.

Then came the 'Rivers of Blood' speech by Enoch Powell in April 1968. Speaking to a Conservative meeting in Birmingham he painted a picture of a nation swamped by immigrants, resulting in a host of social and cultural problems. He advocated a virtual end to black and Commonwealth immigration along with a policy of assisted repatriation. Unless this happened, he argued, 'As I look ahead I am filled with foreboding; like the Roman, I seem to see "the River Tiber foaming with much blood".'

The Tory leader Ted Heath sacked him from the shadow cabinet. It was a decision that angered a lot of people, including the *Daily Telegraph* which argued, 'Whatever the deficiencies of his [Powell's] statistics and the exaggerations of his language ... he was expressing anxieties felt by millions of people ...'

I was one of them. I fell hook, line and sinker for the anti-immigration arguments. I thought our culture was under threat and working-class jobs were being taken.

When I heard people arguing that Britain owed a duty to people from Africa and India and the West Indies who had been exploited in building the Empire, I responded, 'Well, it wasn't me.'

The people who exploited them were the upper classes –

the same aristocrats and business leaders who had been exploiting the working classes for a lot longer than they exploited the Africans and Indians.

It seemed to me that I was supposed to take the blame for what my forefathers did. I had done nothing to hurt these people. Why should I pay for something Winston Churchill's grandfather did or that the Royal Family did?

At the same time I tried to think back to a great time in Britain, when everybody was doing well. I couldn't find one. People talk about booms and busts, but it only ever 'booms' among the money men, the stockbrokers and the employers. The working classes never experience boom and bust. They have bust, bust and more bust. Take my word for it.

In 1968 I filled out an application form to join the National Front and didn't hear anything more for a few weeks. I was performing one night with the Hi-Fi Three when two blokes came to me after the show. They introduced themselves as being from the National Front. I don't know how they found me, but I was getting pretty well known by then. I was invited to a meeting at a nice semi-detached house up by Alder Hey Children's Hospital. The owner of the house, John, was in a wheelchair.

There were six or seven fellas, sitting in the front room. One was a taxi driver and another a school caretaker. They were all dressed in collar and tie or smart casual.

I can still remember some of the others. Henry Bimpson was a member of the British Israelite Association and firmly believed that Jesus Christ had come to Britain during three missing years of his life. We were all descended from one of the tribes of Israel, he said, which made us almost direct descendants of Jesus.

Davey Jones was a good-looking lad, with lovely manners. He was quietly ambitious and wanted to take charge. Bill

Clarkson, a total convert, would get fired up at meetings and become a different person. These were fellas with ordinary jobs and ordinary lives, but the one thing they all shared was a concern for the future and their children. They were saying things like, 'How can we get rid of unemployment when there are tens of thousands of immigrants flooding in each year? How can we make sure that our kids get houses when they grow up?'

This might sound naive, but it was never an issue of race. I didn't regard whites as being superior to other people or want to discriminate against anyone. My Grandad was as good as black and colour had never been an issue when I was growing up or when I started performing. At the Blue House every week, I swapped gags and took the piss out of a black entertainer called Jimmy Gabriel, a lovely man and a great mate.

The immigrants who had come to Britain were welcome. Most were doing the nation proud. I just wanted to draw the line under how many we could take because there didn't seem to be enough jobs to go round. Colour wasn't the issue. I didn't want Australians or Canadians coming in either.

We had meetings about once a month and, although there was a chair and someone taking notes, it was really just an excuse to talk and bounce around ideas. The arguments being put forward are as relevant today as they were then. People are still concerned about employment, welfare, housing and cultural identity.

My mates in the band couldn't understand me. Scoggo and Cordwell were both left-wingers and so was our new guitarist Billy Witty. It didn't interfere with our friendship. Instead we had great debates and discussions. Eventually we agreed to disagree. Politics was never going to test the bonds of our friendships. We were too close for that.

A few months later I went to a regional meeting of the

National Front in York. Martin Webster, a senior figure in the organisation, whipped up the crowd with a stirring speech. People had come from all over the country, yet I didn't get a sense of a strong national organisation. The party played on this underdog status.

'Do you realise how small we are?' he said. 'Do you realise how much work we have to do? Are you up to the challenge?'

Half a dozen of us went to London for a National Front demonstration in June 1968. A few hundred people gathered and marched, including old men with the Union Jack around their shoulders and mothers pushing prams. The left wing organised a counter-protest that drew far greater numbers. We had the shite kicked out of us, but scenes like that on TV always increased the membership of the National Front.

Back in Liverpool at our monthly meetings we hatched a plan to seize control of City Hall. Not quite! The local elections were coming up and we decided to field candidates in every borough. Since there were only ten of us, we had to eventually lower our sights and we registered a handful of candidates, including myself.

We had no money for campaigning, so I offered to put on a fundraiser at Ozzie Wade's. I managed to raise twenty-five pounds, but it didn't go very far once we had paid our nomination fees and printed a few leaflets.

Whitewash and a brush were far cheaper. We spent six hours one night painting 'VOTE NF' slogans on a huge wall out by Thomas Lane. Next morning I rode past it on my motorbike. The wall had been demolished as part of the reconstruction work. We couldn't have organised a piss up in a brewery.

On polling day I seem to remember getting about fifty-five votes and finishing last. I felt as though I had made a point and stood up for my beliefs, which most politicians seem to say when they lose.

By then I was already beginning to lose interest in the National Front. This had nothing to do with the darker motives and policies espoused by the leadership and far-right figures like Martin Webster and Colin Jordan; I was still ignorant of such things. My dissatisfaction stemmed more from a sense of disquiet.

When I went to York and met with the hierarchy of the party, I came away with the impression they were a little too aloof and self-important. These were upper-middle-class guys who seemed to be embracing power a bit too eagerly.

My involvement with the National Front fizzled out, but I still held the same beliefs. It took another four years before I realised that by attacking immigration I was looking for a scapegoat for this country's ills. When you're at the bottom of the greasy pole, mired in shit, you're always looking for someone else to blame.

I don't know what happened to a lot of the other guys. The last time I saw Davey Jones he was in a pub in the South End sitting next to a pretty black woman.

'By the way, Rick, this is me partner,' he said, introducing us. 'She nursed me Mam when she was ill.'

I bought them both a drink and marvelled at how Davey had gone the full circle. Good for him.

My previous political affiliations have generated some harsh criticism, particularly from right-wing columnists and commentators in the media. I can't quite work out if they're angry with me for joining the NF or abandoning the right. I can't change my history and I'm not about to run away from it. I believed certain things in 1968 and I don't believe them any more. I was wrong. I was politically naive and poorly educated.

Nothing is ever as simple as the National Front makes out –

the problem or the solution. Enoch Powell had been trying to defend the idea of 'Britishness' and to sound a warning, but he overreacted in his speech. He made outrageous claims that haven't come true. At the same time it would be ridiculous to suggest that racial harmony exists in the inner cities and on housing estates.

I still feel anxious when I see illegal immigrants or asylum seekers torching a thirty-million-pound refugee centre. Nobody has the right to do that, whether born and bred here or seeking refuge.

And when I see images of race riots in Birmingham or the nightly stampede of refugees trying to get through the Channel Tunnel from France, I can understand how people get frightened. That's why politicians and community leaders have to tell people there isn't any need to panic. Talk to them. Reassure them. Educate them. Now is the time for tolerance and calm heads.

The doorman at the Adelphi Hotel in Liverpool in 1969 was a fella called Harry Haycock, who was almost as well known as the hotel itself. He wore a uniform and acted as though he owned the place, guarding the entrance and keeping out the riffraff.

I met Harry when he advertised a boat for sale in the *Liverpool Echo*. On a complete whim, a few of us had decided that we wanted to buy an old boat and fix it up for the summer. We had visions of cruising along the Leeds–Liverpool canal, stopping at pubs and lazing in the sun.

The syndicate seemed to grow by the day, but in the beginning it included Albert, Billy Wishman, Colin Walker and three footballers from Everton, Davey Johnstone, Stevie Sargent and Terry Darricott.

Billy was often called 'the fifth Tomo' because he spent so

much time with us and was like part of the family. A real jovial sort, he'd done a bit of boxing in the Army and had a broken nose that had never been fixed. Although very quiet compared to the rest of us, when it came his turn to sing he was right in there, belting out his favourite song, 'Far Away Places'.

He lived in Elmore Street, next to the blocks that had been bombed during the war. His wife, Cissy, is a real gem. Sometimes we'd have all-night card games at his place and Cissy would make us sandwiches and cups of tea. We used to tease her rotten and she never once complained, not even when we tied her to a dining chair and left her in the middle of the bombsite.

'I haven't got two kids, I've got seven,' she laughed.

Colin Walker was a great mate of Albert's and used to drink at the Brittania. A big man with round shoulders and a wicked sense of humour, he never married, but always found attractive women to look after him.

Our new project was a 28-foot flat-bottomed Army pontoon. It was out of the water at a boat yard in Bootle, surrounded by a host of other vessels, big and small, smart and rough. She could have been the *Marie Celeste* for all I knew about boats, but she had what estate agents refer to as 'great potential'.

Harry Haycock's house was right by the boat yard. As soon as he arrived home he would take off his Adelphi uniform and put on a blazer and a naval cap. From then on if you called him Mr Haycock, he wouldn't answer. He had to be addressed as 'Commodore'.

We paid two hundred pounds for the pontoon and he offered to provide advice on refitting the boat and getting it back in the water. The first task was fixing up the timbers and plugging leaks. Then we stripped the diesel engine and soon had it working, with two speeds forward and one back. We built four bunks inside and installed a chemical toilet, while Marlene and the other wives sewed curtains for the windows.

A mate of mine, Harry Jones, put a safety rail round the deck. Harry looked a bit like Tom Selleck, with his fine head of hair and heavy moustache. We'd grown up in the same area and drank in the same pubs. He was a real Mr Fix-it, who very rarely does. After building the safety rail, he casually leaned against it and disappeared over the side, nearly breaking his neck.

Whenever it rained we took shelter inside, lighting candles and breaking out the cards. I even took my banjo along and we had sing-songs. It was so much fun that I didn't care if we never finished the boat. We were like a gang of kids living a dream and nobody would have guessed that we were all married.

Names for the boat had been bandied about and some, like the *Gypsy Moth* and the *Mayflower*, had already been discounted. Eventually we settled on the *British Heart* because we were all raving Land-of-Hope-and-Glory types. She'd be painted red, white and blue and would be manned by pure Englishmen, with hearts of oak.

The cocky watchman at the boat yard was an old guy with a wooden leg, a withered arm and a watery eye. Every night he came round and said the same thing, 'How's it going, boys?'

'Can't grumble,' Albert replied. He always slipped the watchman a couple of bob and the old guy headed straight to the nearest pub.

At the last minute we decided to change the name of the boat to *Can't Grumble*. This was a tribute to Albert, who had done most of the work, and also the old cocky watchman who had given us so many laughs.

After twelve months of work we were almost ready. All that remained to be done was the painting. Billy Wishman had a day off and offered to do the honours. I gave him the money and told him how much paint we needed.

I didn't think Billy would do it all in a day, but he proved me wrong. We arrived that afternoon and just stood and stared. The boat was magnificent, done out in red, white and blue. Billy stood there, with a roller in his hand, beaming with pride.

Then I looked at one of the paint cans and my heart sank. Billy had used water-based emulsion paint, which would have polluted the canal if the boat had gone in the water. He looked crestfallen. The hull had to be resealed and painted again.

We planned to launch the pontoon on Saturday morning and I turned up with Colin Walker and Billy, who had brought Cissy and the kids along. They were planning to take the boat for a weekend away and Cissy had already stocked the galley with food and made up the bunks.

Harry Haycock had promised to be there to oversee the launch, but the Commodore failed to show. We figured that we could probably do it without him.

The boat sat in a large wooden cradle, with the stern facing the canal. We planned to ease it into the water back-first, using ropes and a main winch. I controlled the winch, while Billy had a rope on one side and Colin had a rope on the other. They each hammered a peg into the ground and wrapped the rope around it to stop their hands getting burned.

We manoeuvred the boat into position and I released the winch, letting it down in one smooth motion. I knew the stern would go under briefly and take a little water, before bobbing up again.

Suddenly, the rope jammed on Colin's side.

'Winch it in! Winch it in!' he yelled.

It wouldn't budge.

The stern was sitting beneath the surface taking in water.

'Let it go! Let it go!'

'It's jammed.'

He looked everywhere for something to cut the rope – a broken bottle, a rusty can, anything. Meanwhile the boat was quickly taking in water and becoming heavier. The weight was too much for the winch, which spun out of my hands. The pegs were dragged out of the ground by the ropes and the boat went under. It took only a matter of seconds.

The 28-foot pontoon had sunk crossways in a 30-foot-wide canal. It barely seemed possible.

Billy started crying and ran one way, while Colin started crying and ran the other. I stood there, transfixed, with my mouth open, watching teabags and upholstered seats float to the surface.

The worst bit was having to tell our Albert. I knocked on his door and he knew something was up from the moment he saw my face.

'What's the matter?'

'The boat sunk.'

'Who was in charge?'

'I was.'

'Well, why didn't you go down with it?'

The next day all the lads met at the boat yard. We stared at the water and scratched our heads. A fella called Peter Caddick from the Bootle Barge Company came to have a look and roared with laughter.

'Yeah, I'll get it up for you,' he said. 'It'll cost you a tenner.'

'OK.'

He hired a pump with a six-inch-diameter pipe then began

directing the salvage operation. We filled sandbags and then most of the lads put on swimming trunks or stripped down to their underpants.

Our Ronny was one of the first into the black water, disappearing beneath the surface to sandbag the entrances to the boat. He was underwater for what seemed like ages and I began to panic. The canal was full of abandoned prams, bikes and sprung mattresses and I was petrified of him being caught up.

Colin went in next, followed by Billy, Harry Jones and others who had come to lend a hand. I couldn't go in because I couldn't swim.

Once the hull was sealed, the lads from Sykes Pump Hire put a hose into the boat, with the outflow pipe along the edge of the canal. They started the generator and the pump began sucking water out of the hull quicker than it could leak back inside. The outflow pipe looked like Niagara Falls.

Within seconds the sandbags appeared on the waterline and *Can't Grumble* broke the surface. We dragged her to the side of the canal and tied her up.

If Harry Haycock had been about I would have made him walk the plank, making sure I filled his pockets with lead first.

We could have fixed *Can't Grumble* up again, but our hearts had gone out of the project. It had filled a glorious year, from summer to summer, and had given us some wonderful memories, which was satisfaction enough. In the end we let the lads from the boat yard scavenge bits and pieces until there was nothing left of the boat.

Even now, after all these years, we all still talk about *Can't Grumble*, or the *British Heart*. The story has been told so many times over countless pints of beer that the tales have grown taller and taller. Instead of it being a nice calm day when we launched the boat, it was a howling tempest, with thunder and lightning. Sparks flew from the winch and ropes snapped. Guys held their breath for ten minutes at a time when they went under to do the sandbagging.

We had to call a halt to the telling of these stories when Harry Jones, now a local councillor, described in a trembling voice how he dived into the murky water with a sandbag and came face to face with a shark.

7

Playing away from Home

The clouds have grown darker. People are carrying umbrellas and they glance skywards as they leave the church. I know it's not going to rain. Not today.

As all four sons carry the coffin out of the church a newspaper photographer starts snapping photographs. I'm obviously distressed and Tony Parr, a mate of mine, bails up the photographer and has a quiet word about respecting people's grief.

A woman comes over and gives me a little kiss on the cheek. It's Bessie Highfield, the girl whose suitcase I found in the bombdie when she was planning to elope with her boyfriend.

Lots of hands shake mine or squeeze my arm. I manage to hold myself together and climb into the car. We follow the hearse through the front gate and quickly turn down Mere Lane. There's a pub on the corner where Peter Miller used to drink. Further down the lane we pass the Derry Social Club, which is looking a bit worse for wear. It used to be an Orange Lodge club, but nowadays they can't afford to be so fussy.

As we pass Anfield Football Ground, the cars all stop in the shadows of the Shankly Gates for a minute's silence because Mam had been so fond of the famous manager.

Alongside the gates there are fresh flowers propped against the Hillsborough Memorial and red-and-white scarves are tied to the railings. The names of the ninety-six fans who died on 15 April 1989 are etched into the marble.

Football ceased to be a game for a lot of people after that. It had already started to change. Once it had been a working-class game and you could get in for a few shillings. Nowadays a season ticket sets you back thousands of pounds and they change strips more often than underwear to squeeze more money out of the kids. Clubs care more about corporate boxes than die-hard fans. It's a bloody shame.

The crematorium is less than half a mile away from Anfield across Stanley Park. This used to be one of my playgrounds as a kid; catching the No. 19 tram for a penny return, carrying a sandwich that Mam had made and a bottle of water mixed with a touch of orange cordial.

At school we played our football matches at Stanley Park. There were permanent goal posts on the pitches, with the penalty spots worn bare by the traffic. There was even an outdoor swimming pool, but it was always too cold for anyone to use and thick with leaves that gathered on the bottom and turned to sludge.

I could spend all day in Stanley Park, playing on the swings and climbing frames or fishing in the lake with cotton line and a matchstick float. I only ever caught tiddlers, but I've been in love with fishing ever since. Not the 'catching' but the quietness.

I used to arrive home exhausted and filthy dirty. Mam would scrub me until my skin turned pink and scold me for sins she imagined I committed or even just contemplated.

Stanley Park is very different today. The swimming pool has gone and the Palm House is derelict. Like so many other parks it has been taken over by drug addicts and the destitute, particularly at night.

Liverpool Football Club wants a huge slice of this public land to build a brand new sixty-thousand-seat stadium and car park. People are fighting against it because the park belongs to everyone – not just rich football fans who fly in for the games and leave again afterwards.

Marlene will tell you that I wasn't a perfect husband. I made mistakes and took her for granted. And there were nights that I didn't go home and I lied about where I was. Yet I never stopped loving her. That's the truth.

Working the pubs and clubs, getting laughs and applause, there was always a real buzz at the end of the evening and lots of women around, some married, some single and others not advertising either.

Mandy Simmons was a lovely girl with a beautiful face who I met at Ozzie Wade's one night. I poured her a drink, pulled out her chair and pretty soon had her laughing. From then on I began dropping by her place and doing the honours, while her husband Frank was working nightshift down the mines four days a week. Mandy would even phone me at the club.

'Are you comin' round tonight, Rick?'

'I think I better go home, love.'

'But I've made a little bit of supper.'

'You shouldn't have done that. OK, I'll see if I can drop by.'

Of course once I arrived the inevitable happened and we finished up in bed.

This went on for a few months until I had a gig one Saturday at the Cumberland Arms. Albert and a few other mates had come along to watch. In the parlour during my break, I glanced up as the door opened across the bar and Mandy walked in. She looked a million dollars. I nodded but she didn't respond. Who comes in behind her, but her Frank wearing a face like thunder. Me heart stopped. He knew!

I quickly picked up the banjo and motioned to Brian Kurs, the singer for the gig. We started playing and I tried not to look at Frank or Mandy. All the while I'm talking to myself, 'What am I gonna do here? He's gonna kill me.'

As soon as the set finished, I put down the banjo and went to the toilet. Frank put down his drink and followed me. There were three urinals and Eddie Walker had already taken the middle one. He and his brother had a coal round, delivering hundredweight sacks on an open wagon. They were both over six feet tall, with huge hands, and they handled these sacks as though they were shopping bags.

I stood on one side of Eddie and Frank on the other. I was so nervous I couldn't piss.

'What's your fucking game going down to see Mandy?' he said.

'What are you talking about?'

'You know what I'm talking about. You've been going down annoying her.'

'No. You've got this all wrong, Frank.'

'Have I? Have I now? She bloody told me.'

The next minute Eddie Walker put his oar in. 'What's all this about, Tomo?'

I shrugged.

'You stay out of it,' said Frank.

'Hold your horses. I'm just trying to sort things out.'

'It's none of your fucking business.'

The two of them started arguing and I thought, right, I'll get out of here. Frank followed me and Eddie followed him. The three of us couldn't fit through the door together, so I went first. They were still arguing. On the far side of the bar, in the parlour, people could see the commotion but they couldn't hear what was being said.

Eddie suddenly had enough and head-butted Frank in the face. His nose blossomed red and he fell forward on to me, spraying blood all over my shirt. Mandy looked up as Frank slid to the floor. She screamed, 'Don't hit him! Don't hit him! I love him.'

She ran around the bar and I figured she was going to protect Frank, but instead she threw her arms around my neck and kissed me. I could have died of embarrassment.

Afterwards, when Frank had been carried out and Eddie had been thrown out, I had to carry on with the show. Everybody realised that I must have been screwing Mandy. Poor Frank had done nothing wrong and finished up with a busted nose.

I didn't see Mandy again and it was another thirty-odd years before I ran into Frank at a little social club in Liverpool. Ironically, I found myself standing next to him at the piss stalls. Talk about *déjà vu*!

'Hi ya, Frank,' I said.

He blanked me and left without saying a word. I felt about an inch tall.

By 1969 Marlene and I had been married for seven years and there were still no children. This caused an unspoken tension and a silent regret that was obvious when you saw her looking at other children and jumping at the chance to babysit.

She looked after Tommy Scully's little girl, Alison, one weekend. When the time came for her to go home, Marlene didn't want her to go. Although she was a rational woman, I had to sit down and explain to her that we couldn't keep someone else's child.

The disappointment was exacerbated when a letter arrived from the local council, notifying us of a compulsory purchase. They were buying all the houses in Salop Street and knocking them down.

They offered to rehouse us in Skelmersdale, which is the back of beyond. It had been created as an overspill town, with lovely new houses and bungalows, but no infrastructure or amenities like corner shops, pubs, libraries or playgrounds.

It's also probably the easiest place in the country to get lost because of all the roundabouts.

The council wasn't offering any compensation. It was to be a direct swap – our house for any one they chose to give us. I lodged an objection and a council inspector turned up on the doorstep. He claimed our house was unfit to live in and tried to point out gaps under the doors and cracks in the walls.

'You're joking,' I said. 'I'm a City and Guilds plasterer and I've done up this house myself. I can get a dozen builders who'll give evidence that this house is sound. And if that's not enough, I'll get a dozen more.'

The inspector started backtracking. I wouldn't listen to his excuses.

'I'm going to see a solicitor and after that I'm going to the newspapers,' I told him.

Almost by the return of post we received a cheque for £1,100.

We used the money for a deposit on a new semi-detached house in Golborne, Lancashire, about twenty miles from Salop Street. It cost £3,300, and had three bedrooms, an internal bathroom and gardens at the front, back and down one side.

Our neighbours were moving to Golborne so I figured that Marlene would have friends nearby and it was much more accessible than Skelmersdale. Unfortunately, it was also further away from Wrexham, which made it more difficult for Marlene to get home.

In hindsight, we should have gone and lived in Wrexham, closer to her Mum, but she had never asked to move back to Wales. And if she had I would have made excuses about there being no jobs. What would we do for money?

Living in Golborne meant more travelling for me, but if I

finished late I could stay in Liverpool at Mam's rather than drive home. The van broke down one Sunday when I was due at the Blue House. I spent half an hour trying to thumb a ride, carrying a suitcase full of props. Eventually, I opened the case and took out a clerical collar and snapped it on. The first car stopped.

'Where can I take you, Father?' said the driver, thinking I was late for a service.

I directed him to the Blue House and I could see his eyes widen when he saw the pub and the queue outside.

'Sometimes I have to seek out sinners,' I explained, giving him a blessing.

That afternoon I met Mary Jackson. She and her sister Sandra came into the pub to watch the show. We were dragging people out of the audience to sing and Mary and Sandra got up. You should have heard them. They were brilliant.

The Jackson Sisters were a semi-pro act and had come down from Glasgow. They were real sisters, from mixed-race parents. Mary was only five foot one, with blonde hair and a lovely pale complexion. She played the guitar and was even better on the piano. Sandra was taller, with black hair, beautifully smooth dark skin and an amazing voice.

Over the following weeks I began seeing more of Mary and Sandra. On weekends they usually had their gigs, but on Mondays they came to see us in the Blue House. Normally I dragged them up on stage to do a spot or Mary would play guitar, while others performed. She was a cracking-looking girl and all the lads fancied her. She was about my age, but out of my league.

One of my mates had started dating Sandra Jackson and came to me one night near the end of the show.

'Mary wants to know if you'll take her home.'

'Are you sure?'

'Positive.'

The sisters were sharing a flat in Saint Domingo Road. I took Mary home, feeling a mixture of excitement and apprehension. We had a cup of tea, a laugh and a cuddle. She was beautiful and far more talented than me. She had travelled all over the place, including overseas, as a professional musician. I was an amateur by comparison.

Mary and I started an affair. She knew I was married. I didn't try to hide the fact, but she didn't say anything. Some nights I stayed in her flat and told Marlene I'd bunked down at Mam's or at a mate's place. I'm not proud of having lied, but there's not much I can do about it now.

Mary Jackson infatuated me. She was bright, beautiful and enormous fun to be with. We gave each other silly names and we wrote little nonsense letters to each other, with the wrong spelling and mixed-up words.

At the same time, I had never stopped loving Marlene. We weren't in the same place any more. We had different interests and ambitions. She was spending most weekends in Wrexham, leaving on Friday morning and not coming back until Monday afternoon. This didn't bother me; if anything it probably helped ease my guilty conscience about falling in love with somebody else.

People are going to say I was a greedy bastard – I wanted my cake and I wanted to eat it too. I reckon I was lucky that two such amazing women loved me. I didn't deserve either of them.

Having Mary in Liverpool and Marlene in Golborne was like having two wives. Sometimes Mary would turn up at the pub with a cooked dinner for me complete with a little napkin and salt and pepper. Nothing was too much trouble for her.

When I stayed overnight she woke me in the morning with a cup of tea and then went off to work. She had a daytime job as a secretary at a timber business. At midday she caught a taxi home so we could have lunch together. It was lovely.

Her father came down from Glasgow one weekend to visit. Mary and Sandra's flat only had two bedrooms so they bunked in together and gave their Dad the other bedroom. Mary sneaked me into the flat after a gig that night and I slept between her and Sandra. Next morning Mr Jackson knocked on the bedroom door.

The girls were motioning frantically for me to get under the bed, which I did without complaint. Not many fathers look favourably on fellas who spend the night with *both* their daughters.

'I'm just making breakfast,' said Mr Jackson. 'What do you fancy?'

He came into the room and I could just see his shoes from my hiding place.

'I'll just have a cup of tea, thanks, Dad.'

'What about you, Sandra?'

'Tea and toast will be fine.'

He was just about to leave when he turned at the door. 'And what do you want, Rick?'

I wanted to shrivel up and slide between the floorboards. He had known all along. I crawled out from under the bed and went down for breakfast. What else could I do?

Mr Jackson turned out to be a really nice fella. He came to see a show at the Blue House and another at the Colombo Club. He didn't mind the blue jokes and banter. And he seemed pleased that Mary had found someone who made her happy.

Mary moved to a flat just by Sleeper's Hill, near Anfield.

I used to drive right by her window when I came into town to Ozzie Wade's. We had a row about something one day. I can't remember the reason. I stormed out the door and told her I wasn't coming to see her any more.

For three days I stayed in Golborne doing work around the house. When I finally drove into town, I passed her place and saw her sitting in the window. She waved. I parked the van and walked up the path.

She looked exhausted from lack of sleep. 'What's the matter?'

'I've been waiting for you.'

'How long have you been waiting?'

'Three days.'

I believed her. For all that time she had sat at the window waiting for me to drive by.

My affair with Mary could only end in tears, but I was in absolute denial. I didn't think any further ahead than our next meeting.

Frank Wormsley, a piano player, did the dirty on me. He told his wife, who told a friend, Sheila, who lived two doors away from us in Golborne. Out of loyalty to Marlene she revealed the secret.

I came home that night and found Marlene sitting up in bed. She had obviously been crying.

'You're carrying on,' she said.

'No, I'm not.'

'I know you are. There's no use lying about it.'

'It's not true, pet. It's a load of codswallop.'

I denied and denied, but Marlene didn't believe me. I was playing a dangerous game.

Next morning she dragged me along to Sheila's house and I was nailed bang to rights. Sheila told me the source of her information and even knew Mary's name. There was no point in denying it any longer. I held up my hands and apologised to Marlene. Then I went down on my knees and promised I wouldn't do it again. I told her that I'd been lonely. I might have been the busiest man in town – working on building sites all day and doing the clubs at night, but I was still lonely.

Marlene didn't cry. She calmly walked back to the house, went upstairs and closed the bedroom door. I had to go to work. When I arrived home that afternoon she was gone. The house was empty except for a chair, a table, the bed and my clothes.

I lay in bed that night, replaying events and trying to fathom how I could have messed things up so completely. I loved Marlene. I also loved Mary. I was torn. Nobody in my family had ever divorced. What would my Mam say?

I don't know what went through Marlene's mind. Maybe she was looking for a reason to leave me and go home. I had certainly given her one.

For the next few weeks I wandered about in a daze, not knowing what to do or to say. I was too frightened to contact Marlene in case she asked for a divorce. I had never been in this position before. Maybe it would resolve itself.

A fortnight after she walked out, I received a letter. She had never been a confident writer and I knew it must have taken her a while.

'Dear Rick,' she wrote.

'I thought you should know I have been to see Dr Wallace [her old family doctor] and I am three months pregnant. I don't want you getting the wrong idea about who the father is. You're the only one I've been with. I'm just telling you this because I think you should know the score.'

Suddenly, everything had changed again. I knew exactly what I had to do. I went to see Mary and had one of the hardest conversations of my life.

'I'm going to Wales,' I told her. 'I have to try to win Marlene back. She's having our baby.'

Mary looked devastated. 'If you stay with me I'll give you six babies,' she said. I knew she meant it.

Morally and emotionally I had made a commitment to Marlene when I married her. Now she was pregnant and alone. Maybe she wouldn't have me back, but at least I had to try.

Saying sorry was never going to be enough. I had to win her back slowly with letters and phone calls. I had to prove I still loved her and wanted to be with her.

Marlene made me wait, as the baby grew bigger inside her. Nothing was certain except for one thing – if she accepted me back it meant leaving Liverpool.

I saw Mary only once more. It was in 1971 when I went to Wembley to watch Liverpool play Arsenal in the Cup Final. They lost 2–1, with Charlie George scoring the winner.

She had moved to Southend-on-Sea and someone had her phone number. I can still remember the phone number thirty years later despite only calling it once.

A bunch of us were staying at a little hotel in north London. I phoned Mary and asked if I could see her.

'I don't think that's a good idea.'

'I have something for you. Can we just meet for a few minutes? Please.'

We agreed a time and a place on Sunday morning.

Just by chance a few weeks earlier I had made a tidy bit of cash in one of those business deals that only seem to take place in pubs. I wanted Mary to have something so I took some cash and sealed it in an envelope. I know it sounds as though I was trying to buy her off or somehow lessen my own guilt, but I hope that's not what she thought. I wanted to say,

'I'm sorry. These things happen. It wasn't your fault. I know I can't make it up to you, but I want to give you this.'

I waited on the platform for her train to come in. Only a few people got off. She looked magnificent in a long, calf-length coat, black boots and a wide-brimmed hat and seemed to glide along the platform towards me.

I gave her a kiss and we went out of the station and crossed the road to a café. I ordered tea and she had a piece of cake.

'How are things?'

'OK.'

She chatted about Southend and how she had found a job and was still playing the guitar and piano. A couple of times she came close to tears, but managed to hold herself together.

Much too soon our time was up and I walked her back to the station. I gave her one last kiss and handed her the envelope. I felt choked. A part of me didn't want to let her go.

The train pulled away and took her out of my life. I don't know what happened to her, but I think about her often. Did she get married and have children and grandchildren? I hope so.

8

Fatherhood and
the Flying Pickets

The last time I was at the crematorium was for Peter Kerrigan's funeral. His family asked me to say a few words and I remembered him as a wonderful actor and a real gentleman. I don't want to say anything this time. I'm trying to hold everything inside.

After a nice little service the music plays and the coffin slides away. This is the end, the last act in the human drama. As the curtains slowly closed I glanced across at Albert and noticed him wipe away a tear.

We lead the congregation out into the open air and the smokers among them light up. People mill around and catch up with old mates, neighbours and relations. The only time I meet my relations now is at funerals. Some of them I haven't seen in forty-odd years.

'Does everyone know where we're going?' I ask, organising lifts to Our Lady of Sorrows, a social club off the East Lancashire Road. The concert room is lovely and clean, with polished tables and good bar staff. People help themselves to the buffet and the free bar. Nobody abuses the privilege.

I drift among the tables, hearing loads of stories. My aunties talk about when Mam and Dad were courting. He used to wear two-tone patent leather shoes and they called him a 'jazzer' rather than a dancer.

Jimmy Hackett reminds me of the Christmas a few years back when I was living on the bones of my arse. I owed money to everyone and had the bailiffs chasing me. Scraping together a few bob, I bought Mam a Christmas card, but I couldn't take it round to her. I was too ashamed. Jimmy delivered the card for me.

'How is he, son?' Mam asked.

'He's OK. He'll bounce back.'

'Tell him to come and see me.'

'I will.'

People start to laugh and relax, remembering the good things. I feel warm inside and proud to be part of this family. All my kids are here, Clifton, Gareth and Kate, as well as my granddaughter Paige.

Mam always had a real soft spot for Gareth and never tried to hide the fact that he was her favourite. He used to phone her every day, which not many grandkids do for their Nanna. Mam would say to him, 'Are you being yourself, Gags? Your Dad's very proud of you.'

People stay for hours and I hear lots of nice stories about 'Peggy' and comments about the wonderful funeral. Ronny has surpassed himself, but we expected nothing less. He would never have let Mam down.

Despite all the magnificent food, I can't eat a thing. I feel empty inside. None of this has really sunk in yet, but I know it will.

Marlene forgave me, which is more than I deserved. We started a new life in Wrexham, living in a council flat and later in a two-bedroom council house in the same road with a tiny garden at the front and a larger one out back.

There were fewer work opportunities, but plastering had never been very good for my health. The dust played havoc with my asthma and I spent a lot of my time soaking wet from damping down the walls.

I managed to get work on the Wrexham bypass, a road

construction project employing hundreds of men. Basically, I was digging holes and erecting 'McAlpine' signs, just in case anybody forgot who paid our wages.

My music and the band had to go because I lived too far away. Instead I made do with one-off gigs and bits and pieces of compering of a weekend. I did Sunday afternoons at the Cantril Farm British Legion in Liverpool, where Tommy Scully and the boys were performing.

Marlene went into labour on 7 December 1970 and I took her to the Wrexham Maelor General Hospital. She was a long time having the baby and I couldn't stay because I had to be at work. That afternoon I arrived at the hospital and walked down the passageway. A nurse said to me, 'You have a lovely son.'

I jumped and punched the air like I'd just scored the winning goal in the Cup Final. I had always dreamed of having a son. I think every father secretly does.

My Dad had been called Albert Edward Tomlinson, after the old King, and Marlene's father was Charlie Clifton. So we came up with Clifton Charles Albert Edward Tomlinson. If he had nothing else in life, he would have an imposing name.

Having a child made an enormous difference to our marriage. Our lives were bound together and we grew closer than ever before. Marlene doted on Clifton and became the mother she always wanted to be. If we were out somewhere and it was time for Clifton's feed, she would run all the way home pushing the pram. Nothing stood in her way.

Mam came to see us just after the birth. As she cradled Clifton in her arms, Marlene kept giving her advice about supporting his head and watching his back. Mam had raised four children and had three grandchildren by then so she knew one or two things about babies. As she was leaving she whispered to me, 'Your best bet, Rick, would be to put him in a home until he's twenty-one.'

As so often happens when you wait so long for a child, Marlene fell pregnant again very quickly. Eighteen months later, with a tug of the forceps, Gareth David Ronald William Tomlinson arrived in our lives. Albert had been honoured when we named Clifton, so this time I looked after my other brothers, along with Billy Wishman, the 'fifth Tomo'.

I loved being a Dad. I couldn't wait to get home of an evening to see the boys before they went to bed. They were each completely different. Clifton had some of my Grandad in him, with dark eyes and dark hair. He could ride a bike when he was two years old and had wonderful hand-eye skills which later set him apart as a sportsman.

Gareth had blond hair and blue-green eyes. He was always getting into mischief, investigating things and taking them apart. He loved hammering nails into wood and going fishing, coming home with fantastic stories about the big one that had got away.

Money was often tight in the early years but Marlene found ways of making the pennies stretch. She washed our clothes overnight and backed up the fire so they'd be dry in the morning. And she knitted pullovers and cardigans to keep us warm.

Working on the Wrexham bypass was a real eye-opener because I expected conditions to be a lot better. There were hundreds of men on the site and only a couple of toilets, which were always blocked up and stinking. Fellas would have to get cement bags and go behind the bushes or in the middle of fields.

Some of the incidents were terrifying. One lad cut his head open working down a ditch, but wouldn't go and get it seen to until his lunch break because he was frightened of losing his job.

I had always believed in trade unions, even as an

apprentice plasterer, and had never missed paying my subs or attending meetings. Just as on the Carrington site, nobody else had stepped forward so I found myself becoming the site convener. Every morning I drove around the site, checking that lads had the proper safety equipment and knew their rights. At the same time I signed up new members for the union and collected the weekly subs.

During regular talks with management, I discussed terms, conditions and site bonuses. Occasionally there were sticking points and threats of industrial action but we usually found a satisfactory compromise.

I learned an important lesson one day when I took the lads out over something that didn't really justify the action. I phoned up Alan Abrahams, who I'd known since my days on the Carrington job. Alan had since become a full-time union official.

'Get them back to work,' he told me.

'How do you mean?'

'Gain something and get them back to work. These men have families to feed.'

He was right. I had overreacted and now they were likely to suffer lost wages for no reason. The idea that workers enjoy going out on strike is rubbish. They often lose far more than they ever gain.

Although I respected Alan enormously, some of the other union officials were lazy and corrupt. One in particular would never return my calls or come to the phone. One day I rang and said I was calling from McAlpine's. He came to the phone straight away, sounding like a grovelling toad. I don't know if he was in cahoots with the bosses, or just after a quiet life, but he didn't deserve the support of the workers.

There were dozens of different specialists and trades working on the bypass including steel fixers, concreters, mechanics, fitters, ground workers who dug the trenches and did the backfilling, safety lads who hung the lanterns and bunting and the 'black gang' who drove the bulldozers, cranes and pile-driving machines.

On top of this were ancillary workers like old Len the 'can lad' who brewed up tea for the 'black gang'. We all chipped in 'can money' every week and Len would buy the milk, sugar and tea. He worked hard, washing cups and keeping the kettle boiling, but the bosses paid him buttons.

Len loved his work. He had a little hut with a table and benches, which he kept spotless, using the pages of the *Evening Leader* as the tablecloths.

A former miner, he was barely five foot tall and wore a boiler suit tucked into Wellingtons and a trilby hat. He had this scar across the bridge of his nose, which looked like a tattooed blue line where coal dust had become ingrained into his skin.

At one point I negotiated a bonus for the workers of half a crown an hour for a forty-hour week. It included everyone, even old Len. He was made up. Usually people forget about workers like him. Next morning he brought me a present: a bird in a cage.

'It's called a German Roller Bird,' he said. 'Just give it a bit of seed and some water.'

I took it home for the boys and every time it sang I thought of old Len.

The building industry was rife with problems. With so many different trades and building sites spread across the country, it was very difficult to unionise and get uniform conditions and safety standards. On average a building worker was dying every day in the UK because safety equipment either wasn't provided or policed.

The biggest stumbling block was known as 'the lump'. This

was the colloquial name for self-employed contractors and sub-contractors, many who employed unqualified labourers and were notorious for cutting corners, doing shoddy work and ignoring safety.

These weren't licensed builders or card-carrying members of the union. They were cowboys, who disappeared as soon as a job was done, didn't pay taxes and didn't train apprentices. At the same time, they were undercutting proper tradesmen and forcing down wages to below poverty levels.

In 1972 the two biggest building unions – the TGWU and the Union of Construction Allied Trades and Technicians (UCATT) – called Britain's first national building strike. The aim was to secure a minimum wage within the industry of thirty pounds for a thirty-five-hour week, as well as rigid enforcement of safety regulations and the outlawing of 'the lump'.

After negotiations broke down the strike action escalated in early August. One morning on the Wrexham bypass we were visited by pickets. A brickie called Barry Scragg addressed the workers. He explained what the dispute was about and we voted to join the strike. I became a member of the Wrexham Strike Action Committee.

There were various local committees in the North Wales area. We met regularly at a pub in Chester, the Bull and Stirrup, where we hired a room upstairs. Each group gave a progress report about who had joined the strike and we heard what the bosses were offering. Trade union membership was only about 10 per cent in North Wales because most of the building sites were small and scattered.

Very few of us had much experience with the mechanics of picketing. And right from the beginning it was pretty obvious that conventional methods wouldn't work. There were no factory gates to picket. Building sites were often large open areas with nowhere to focus the action. Either that or they were small sites, with only a handful of workers, dotted all over the countryside.

Many employers were telling workers that the strike was unofficial and poorly supported. In some places they even organised anti-strike gangs, who attacked and injured pickets.

The other problem was convincing people to strike for thirty pounds for a thirty-five-hour week, when some of the 'lumpers' were getting more than that. Where was the financial incentive? Greed drove people to think of themselves rather than for the good of the whole industry.

To overcome these problems it was important to get as many people on the picket lines as possible to convince other workers they weren't alone and give them the courage to lay down their tools.

Stopping the big sites was relatively easy, because the workforce tended to be more organised. It was far harder to close down the smaller sites – the one-man bands and small family firms – but this had to be done if we were to win.

Flying pickets became our most effective tactic. We could spread the message by hitting as many sites as possible, talking to workers and trying to convince them to join us.

I became very passionate about the dispute, but some people were very suspicious of me because of my past links with the National Front. I could understand that. At one of our regular meetings Barry Scragg suggested I was a traitor.

'There is someone here who I don't think should be here,' he said.

Alan Abrahams, Dezzie Warren and Billy Jones leapt to my defence. Dezzie and Alan were members of the Communist Party and they knew I believed in solidarity and workers' rights.

We were all on the same side, but didn't always agree on tactics. Alan argued at one point that if a particular employer accepted our terms then workers at that site should be allowed to go back. I disagreed totally.

'It's a splitting tactic by the bosses. How can we let some lads work while others are on strike? It will undermine the whole dispute. It has to be one out all out.'

From the outset I knew it was going to be hard. We had no savings and Marlene wasn't working. As the strike dragged on we borrowed money and relied on the charity of friends and family.

The Government stopped us getting the dole, claiming we were getting strike funds, which was a load of crap. We were getting petrol money and little more.

As the weeks turned into months, some of the lads fell away; a few I would never have suspected. A lot came under pressure from their wives who wanted them back to work. Some became quite antagonistic towards me, but it went both ways. A lot of friendships were destroyed.

It was sometimes very difficult being in charge and having the responsibility. At one point I discovered my brother-in-law, Dennis Clifton, a master bricklayer, was employing a few lads on a job in Wrexham. I had to go down and tell him to withdraw his labour. Dennis did the right thing.

For the most part, the picketing had been peaceful and good-natured. I even took Clifton with me sometimes. At nearly two years old, he sat on my shoulders and ate the sandwiches that Marlene packed for us.

At the regular meetings of the strike committee I became friendly with lads like Dezzie Warren, Ken O'Shea, John Carpenter, John McKinsie-Jones, the treasurer, and John Llywarch, a slim, shy Welshman who had worked with me on the Wrexham bypass. Dezzie, in particular, was a forceful

Welcome to the neighbourhood. This is the bottom of Lance Street, Liverpool, where I grew up. The bombdie (bombed-out house) where we used to play was right next to the Horlicks sign.

The likely lads – out for the night with some mates, aged about seventeen. (Left to right: Lenny Johnson, me, Derek Chapman, Richie O'Neil.)

My granddad 'Black Dick' and my Aunt Fan.

Dad and my youngest brother Ronny, with Marlene soon after we married.

Mam and her four lads (left to right) David, me, Albert and Ronny.

Our wedding day – 22 March 1962. Marlene looks overawed and Albert is more like a clothes' horse than a best man.

Growing woollier by the day – with Marlene and the boys Clifton (right) and Gareth.

The Hi-Fi Three (left to right: Tommy Bowness, Tommy Scully and Tony Scoggo). I was the scruffy member of the band. We became known all round Liverpool as Hobo Rick and the Hi-Fi Three.

Above and right: one of our improvised sketches at the Blue House. Donny the Walton Road Gooser is the one in the frock and sombrero. Don't I look fetching in blond pigtails?

The day that changed my life forever. 6 September 1972 – picketing building sites in Shrewsbury. I'm in the middle with my head down, listening to Dezzie Warren give a speech. John McKinsie Jones is next to Dezzie and Barry Scragg is just below to his left, looking out at the camera.

Talking with a senior policeman. John McKinsie Jones is on my right. We were congratulated for running a peaceful picket.

Arrested, charged and put on trial. Police are lined up around Shrewsbury Crown Court on 3 October 1973.

A Christmas card sent out by the Shrewsbury Independence Fund, which campaigned for our release from prison.

**HAPPY CHRISTMAS – AT HOME OR IN GAOL?
REMEMBER THE SHREWSBURY PICKETS
DENNIS WARREN AND ERIC TOMLINSON**

Reporters and cameramen crowd around me outside the prison gates.

Free at last! Clutching Marlene's hand as I walk from Leicester prison on 25 July 1975, flanked by Jim Nicol and Peter Carter.

Fighting for justice at the TUC conference in September 1975. The union bosses had abandoned the Shrewsbury pickets.

Another demo in 1975. Everyone has the right to work, but I had been blackballed since leaving prison.

orator who always led from the front. I like to think that I did the same.

Unfortunately, one among us was a police informer. We should have realised sooner because every time we turned up to picket a site, the police were already there. Sometimes we sent only a token picket of half a dozen guys and at other times we organised a real show of force, but the police contingent always matched us, like for like.

At one of our regular meetings at the Bull and Stirrup on 31 August 1972, we discussed picketing in the Shrewsbury area, where many of the big sites had still not come out.

We voted to organise a big picket for the following week, with coaches bringing building workers from the surrounding districts. On the morning of 6 September, I boarded the coach from Wrexham and we drove to the meeting point, the Oswestry Labour Club. We all looked like extras from *Auf Wiedersehen Pet*, dressed in donkey jackets and duffel coats, with sandwiches in our pockets and flasks of tea.

The atmosphere on the coach was almost like a day out, with lots of banter and jokes about scabs. At the same time, we all knew we had a job to do.

Coaches also arrived from Chester, Flint and Prestatyn – about two hundred pickets in all. Dezzie Warren made a short speech thanking the lads for turning up and I also spoke, reminding them of what the strike was all about.

Alan Abrahams couldn't be there, so there was nobody in overall charge. Each of us took responsibility for the various coaches as we made our way to the first building site.

In the days, weeks and months that followed there were many accounts of what happened that day, but I can only tell you what I remember. Building sites are the same the world over – covered in holes, open drains, half-built walls, scaffolding and machinery. We visited seven such places during the day. The coaches pulled up and we marched to the site office.

If we could find the site manager or an employer repres-entative, we asked for permission to address the workers. If there was nobody about, we talked to individuals or groups of workmen.

The reaction at each place was different. Some fellas simply put their tools down, let us approach and listened to what we had to say about the strike. They knew they were blacklegs (scabs), working the lump, with no guarantees or safety conditions.

'What about handrails on the scaffolds?' I asked them. 'If one of you gets hurt, who's going to look after your families? And look at these makeshift shitty holes they call toilets. I wouldn't let a dog crap in one of them. I see bosses have proper toilets and sinks . . .'

A lot of the lumpers were totally clueless about what had been going on and had believed their foremen who had told them the strike was a non-event.

However, not all of them wanted to listen. At some sites they flung down their tools and ran like hares as soon as the coaches pulled up. I guess they figured if they could get away, they could come back tomorrow and claim to have no knowledge of the strike.

This caused frustration and tempers boiled over. A few doorframes were damaged and windows smashed. A partially finished brick wall was knocked over, drainage pipes were kicked into a trench and two workers were injured in scuffles.

The most serious incident was directed against the pickets. A worker on the Kingswood Estate pulled a shotgun out of his car and waved it at the lads on the coaches. The gun was snatched from his hand, broken and handed over to the police.

Nobody from the Wrexham coach was involved in any trouble. Barry Scragg talked to the lads on the Flint coaches and told them to 'cool it'. He said if they stepped out of line again he would turn the coaches back.

Although it may have looked disorganised to an outsider, the picketing was good-natured and effective. Flying pickets were lawful and we were escorted by police to all but one of the sites. Afterwards, a senior policeman, Chief Superintendent Meredith, shook hands with Dezzie and me, congratulating us on a peaceful picket.

The national strike officially ended after thirteen weeks, but there was no celebration. Most of us were just relieved to get back to work after eleven weeks without a wage. It had been a great victory and we won most of our demands.

North Wales had been just a tiny part of a national campaign which had involved tens of thousands of workers. Maybe the next generation would appreciate our sacrifices, but for the moment I just wanted to put some money in my pocket.

I went back to work on the Wrexham bypass, attached to the safety officer. A few weeks later, I had a message to go to the foreman's office and he asked if I wanted a job as a work's manager on a road project.

'There's a job going in Portugal. The company will cover all the travel costs.'

'I'm a City and Guilds plasterer,' I said. 'I can't even read a theodolite.' (A theodolite is the instrument used on construction sites for reading horizontal and vertical angles.)

'That doesn't matter.'

'No, thanks, just the same. I'll stay where I am.'

I knew exactly what was happening. They wanted me off the site and hundreds of miles away, but they couldn't risk sacking me so this was the next best thing.

The building strike and, in particular, the use of flying pickets had caused a lot of anger. This was obvious from the publicity emanating from the right-wing press. I can't remember seeing a single article supporting the strike. Instead, there was a barrage of scare stories and daily accounts of how people wouldn't be able to get into their new homes for Christmas because of the dispute. Not a word appeared about workers building houses they could never afford to live in, even if they worked for a hundred years.

Once the strike had ended I assumed that this bad feeling would evaporate. We had won our thirty pounds for a thirty-five-hour week, which still put us right at the bottom of the wage pile, but that was OK.

What I didn't bank on was the anger of major employers who were hell-bent on revenge and Tory MPs who were under pressure to outlaw flying pickets and punish the organisers of such tactics.

The Home Secretary Robert Carr made this perfectly clear:

'Following disturbing evidence of intimidation from many areas during the national building strike, I intend once again to draw the attention of Chief Constables to the provisions of the law and discuss with them what further action they might take to defeat such violence and intimidation in industrial disputes.'

Three months after the strike ended two detectives arrived at the bypass and asked to speak to me. I had no idea what they wanted. I had never had any problems with the police.

They started asking me questions about the day we picketed the sites around Shrewsbury and Telford. We chatted politely and I answered general questions about numbers of pickets and having hired the Wrexham coach.

'What's all this about?' I asked.

'Well, there may be prosecutions pending.'

'What for?'

'Well, we have reason to believe that certain things were done which were untoward and we'd like you to help us get those responsible.'

'How can I help you?'

'We'd like you to be a prosecution witness.'

'How can I be a prosecution witness? I was there. I was one of them. I was one of the strike committee.'

'We know.' The detectives glanced at each other and then suggested that because of my political background they thought I might be interested in helping them.

'What about my background?'

'The National Front has no time for commies.'

'Is that what you think this is about?' I laughed. 'We're just building workers. Politics have nothing to do with it.'

'That's unfortunate.'

The whole conversation had been so surreal I wanted to laugh. In a three-month national strike, why were they concerned about one day of picketing in a distant corner of Wales? We had done nothing wrong. The police had been with us all day. I had seen more hostility at a kiddies' Christmas party.

A few weeks later, at home in the council house, I had a visit from the same two detectives just after tea. The boys were both asleep upstairs. Marlene had hold of my arm.

'What's wrong, Rick? Why are they here?'

At that same moment they were reading me my rights. I put my coat on and they escorted me to a Black Maria.

Similar vans were going round the other houses, picking up members of the strike committee. We were taken to police stations, photographed, fingerprinted and questioned for hours about 6 September.

The following morning we were taken to court to be officially charged. The police van was flanked by motorcycles and Alsatian dogs stood on guard as we were marched into court. There were 210 charges brought against twenty-four men, including affray, unlawful assembly and damage to property.

The most damaging charge came under the obscure 1875 Conspiracy and Protection of Property Act. For ninety-eight years no Government had ever used the conspiracy law. Unlike the other charges, which carried a maximum sentence of about three to six months, a conviction of conspiracy could see us jailed for life.

It was ludicrous. If the offences were so serious why didn't the police take action at the time? Why did they wait five months to charge us? We weren't militants. We were ordinary hairy-arsed building workers.

Having been formally charged, I was granted bail and advised that the trial was eight months away, but I should think about getting a lawyer.

I went home to Marlene and the boys, unable to understand or explain what had happened. I kept thinking it had to be a mistake. At any moment someone was going to realise and apologise to us.

Organisers like Alan Abrahams and Barry Scragg had a much clearer sense of what we were up against. They immediately began organising funds for our defence and contacting solicitors to represent us.

A Manchester firm, Casson & Company, took on the case and our solicitors Campbell Malone and Tony Casson spent a long while going over our statements and explaining what lay ahead.

The prosecution was to argue that the picketing at Shrewsbury had been violent and calculated to intimidate building workers. More so, it had been planned and orchestrated in a conspiracy hatched in the upstairs room of the Bull and Stirrup pub.

Six of us were to face trial first – myself, John Carpenter, Ken O'Shea, John Llywarch, Dezzie Warren and Mackie (John McKinsie-Jones). All of us had been at the 31 August meeting, except for Mackie. He had been handed a large sum of money in the downstairs bar for the strike fund and thought it best to take it straight home. How can you be part of an alleged conspiracy if you're not even there?

The press had a field day when the charges became public knowledge. We were labelled as thugs and criminals. The *Sunday People* wrote that Dezzie was getting so much on the dole that he drove a Jaguar and had a colour TV.

'I'm not having this,' I told myself. 'If the story's right, there'll be fucking murder.'

I drove up to see Dezzie. He had a battered old Jaguar in his front yard that hadn't moved in two years. Several litters of kittens had been born on the back seat. His so-called 'colour TV' was a black and white set with a coloured filter over the front which turned everything green.

I felt guilty about doubting him. We had been through a lot together and, despite coming from opposite ends of the political spectrum, we had found common ground on the picket line.

Ordinary rank and file trade unionists were shocked and angered by the charges. Most of them realised how easily it could have been them. Strangely, the leaders of UCATT and the TGWU didn't seem to share this sense of outrage. They should have been screaming bloody murder. Ordinary workers had been dragged from their homes, fingerprinted and charged; our wives and families had been interrogated; we had lost our jobs or been forced to quit. There should have been mass demonstrations and threats of strike action.

Instead the union executives decided to cut us loose because of fears that a long trial would bankrupt them. We were expendable. As a result, the only union leaders who came to give evidence on our behalf had to be subpoenaed. Once again it was a case of the leadership being out of step with the rank and file.

From the outset it was obvious this wasn't going to be an ordinary trial. West Mercia Police had spent three months investigating a normal day of picketing and interviewed over eight hundred people. And mystery surrounds a report submitted to the Director of Public Prosecutions by the investigation, which casts doubts on whether the conspiracy charges could be justified. Although never made public, strong rumours circulated during the trial about the content of the report. It apparently claimed that any violence during the picketing had been spontaneous and had been instigated by men whom the police had been unable to identify.

Rumours such as these simply confirmed my belief that the decision to prosecute had been a political one. The Government wanted to make an example of the building workers pickets. We were like lambs to the slaughter.

A few weeks before the trial started, I went to London to meet my QC, Keith McHale. He asked me how I was going to plead.

'Not guilty.'

'You realise that you stand to get two years in prison?'

'But I'm innocent.'

He smiled dryly. He knew something that I didn't.

9

Rough Justice

Ronny wants us all to come and choose a few keepsakes from Mam's bungalow. He's cleaning up the place and packing her things before handing the keys over to the council.

Her cupboards and wardrobes are crammed with shawls, cardigans, scarves and coats, a lot of them still in the wrappers and with labels attached. Mam could never stop counting pennies. That's the truth of it.

I used to ask her what she wanted for birthdays or Christmas.

'What do I want at my age?' she'd say.

'You must need something.'

'Maybe a cardie or a shawl.'

So what does she do? Puts them away and wears the same old cardigan until it falls apart. It was the same with food. I couldn't buy her a nice food hamper because she wouldn't open the fancy jams. And everything had to be in small quantities because she worried that she wouldn't be able to finish a large jar or can.

She hated waste and drummed this message into us right through my childhood. That's why I'm the size I am – I can't leave anything on my plate.

My two aunties, Liza and Elsie, come round and take coats, cardigans and stuff like that. Albert chooses a nice bedroom suite for his granddaughter and David takes a little freezer, fridge and washing machine for a house that accommodates troubled teenagers.

Mam had an old Asian-style vase, which had been left to her by her mother and was obviously very old. There were also two long fluted vases, which were kept in the front room near the window when we were growing up. I remember her saying that a fella once knocked on the door when we lived in Lance Street and offered her five quid for these vases. He must have seen them through the window.

Mam turned him down, but he called back the next night and offered her twenty-five quid. That was about a month's wages in them days, but again she said no. The vases had been a present from her mother.

Ronny is going to take those, which I'm pleased about. I think he should have everything, but he insists we all choose something. There's nothing I really need or want, but I don't want to see Mam's stuff thrown away.

In the end I take most of the ornaments, clocks, pictures and furniture, which I'm going to store in a house I'm renovating. I don't know what I'll do in the end, but all of her grandkids will get something and I'll find a home for every piece.

Hundreds of police were lined up outside Shrewsbury Crown Court holding batons and shields. Barricades and surveillance cameras had been set up on the street and police dog handlers patrolled the footpaths. It looked like the start of a mass murder trial or one for IRA bombers.

In the interview rooms beneath the new courthouse, I sat and stared at my polished shoes. Dezzie Warren paced up and down like a caged lion.

My barrister, Keith McHale, came downstairs. He wore a black robe and carried his horse-hair wig on a bundle of files.

'The prosecution is offering a deal,' he said. 'If you agree to plead guilty, you'll each be fined fifty pounds. The unions will pay it for you. This could all be over today. You can walk out of here and get on with your lives.'

'With criminal records,' I said.

'Yes.'

He gave us each time to think about it, but I already knew my answer. We took a vote. Four of the lads were in favour of taking the deal. Dezzie and I were opposed.

'I've never been arrested for anything in me life,' I told them. 'I've done nothing wrong. I'm not going to let them do this to me.' At the same time I told them to take the deal if they wanted. We all had families to think about.

Mackie said, 'OK, if you're not then I'm not.'

Ken O'Shea and John Llywarch nodded in agreement. We all looked at John Carpenter. I could see he was torn.

'Fuck 'em,' he said. 'Let's fight.'

The prosecution offer galvanised our resolve. Clearly they wanted this case to go away. Messages of support had arrived from all over the country and abroad as rank and file trade unionists began to realise this was a show trial.

It took a long while to choose a jury. Some of the prospective jurors had been lumpers on the building sites and, to be fair to them, they asked to be excused.

Finally we were ushered into court and I glanced up at the huge coat of arms on the front wall. I had always had enormous admiration for the police and judiciary. I had been taught by my father to respect the law and that the British judicial system was the finest in the world.

Maurice Drake, QC, made his opening address on Wednesday 3 October 1973. Using emotive language he painted a picture of a rampaging mob, tearing things apart, knocking down walls, terrifying workers. We were 'like an Apache horde', he said, hell-bent on destruction.

He argued that the strike action committee was a wild,

unofficial body, acting without the authority of the unions; and the six of us in the dock had conspired to intimidate other workers and cause criminal damage.

'These charges are in no way an attack or challenge on lawful trade union activity,' he argued, 'but what happened at the building sites in Shropshire is something which no trade union would ever seek to excuse.'

What took place next will stay with me forever. Witness after witness swore an oath and then described how terrified they had been by this rampaging mob, armed with sticks, using obscene and hostile language.

Under cross-examination, it emerged that the original statements had been lost and witnesses had been asked to make new ones only weeks before the trial. They were also shown photographs of Dezzie and me before they entered the witness box so they could point us out in the courtroom.

Terence Callaghan, one of the site managers, claimed we had stormed off the coaches shouting 'Kill! Kill! Kill!' He pointed to John Llywarch and claimed that John had told him, 'We have just left Cubitts and the contracts manager, the agent and the general foreman are in hospital so let's start talking, you bastards.'

Dezzie apparently boasted, 'This is not a strike, this is a revolution.'

Under cross-examination, it emerged that John Llywarch hadn't even arrived at this site until late. He had been at the local police station handing over the shotgun that was pointed at pickets.

In a classic example of how words were twisted, another witness claimed that Dezzie had threatened to burn down the canteen when addressing the workers. Later it emerged that Dezzie had actually said, 'Look at this lousy place. It's filthy. It's only fit to have a match put to it.'

Another time I was alleged to have said, 'Come on, lads, smash it up.'

The same witness admitted under cross-examination that I may have said, 'Come on, lads, break it up.'

Sometimes I didn't know whether to laugh or despair as I listened to the prosecution witnesses describing their 'terror' and 'fear'. Some of these lads shared cups of tea with us. Others had taken off like hares as the coaches pulled up. They weren't frightened of violence. They were scared of being identified as scabs. I firmly believe that. We were all in the one industry – working for shit conditions and shit money. And when the strike ended, these same men were happy to accept all the benefits that we had won for them. A free ride is what you call it.

At the Brookfields site, a hod carrier called Cliff Growcotte was working on scaffolding when he claimed he was threatened by twenty to thirty pickets. He described some argie-bargie and said he was hit on the back of the leg with a brick and dragged off the scaffolding by his ankles.

During the trial he couldn't identify anyone from the photographs, although nearly thirty years later, when approached by a tabloid newspaper, his memory suddenly came back to him and he claimed that I was one of the ringleaders, urging them on.

Another witness told of pickets standing over a plumber and holding four-inch nails like daggers. Strangely, he hadn't mentioned this in his first statement to the police nor in his second statement six months later.

'Why do you remember it now?' asked a defence barrister.

'Oh, it changes every time I think about it,' he replied, to roars of laughter.

At one of the sites someone had smashed up a workman's hut, breaking crockery, windows and furniture with a shovel.

This person was never identified, named or charged. Later, in court, he was described as having a distinguishing birthmark on one side of his face and spoke with a Geordie accent and his breath smelled of meths. This sounded more like the local drunk than one of the pickets.

Our lawyers were brilliant. We had a star-studded line-up of silks, including Keith McHale, David Turner Samuels, John Platts Mills, Marist Young and Philip Phillips. Thanks to their cross-examinations, many of the prosecution witnesses were shown to be lying or exaggerating their claims.

At the same time, the defence struggled to get any special consideration from Mr Justice Mais, an ecclesiastical Judge, who had been chosen to preside over the trial. Justice Mais had been a Tory Government appointment to the High Court in 1971, having never taken silk, though he had been a County Court Judge. He seemed to take a particular dislike to Dezzie, who was being portrayed as the arch-villain.

I was also labelled a ringleader, who had apparently threatened scabs, encouraged violence and attacked a site door with a shovel. Witnesses referred to me as the 'bearded man' – as though I was the only one. At least six people on the Wrexham bus had beards and God knows how many others. I was also described as wearing a white shirt, jeans and having a Welsh accent. I wore a flowered shirt, light-coloured trousers and my Scouse accent is broader than the Mersey.

The police who followed us to the building sites suffered from a rare collective form of memory loss. One fella got in the witness box – enormous, he was – and described how he was petrified when he saw the pickets. Another claimed he was afraid to interfere and make arrests in case he was 'seriously assaulted'.

I'm sorry, but if that's true, why didn't the police call for back-up? Why didn't they turn the buses around and tell us to go home? Why did the most senior policeman on duty, Chief Inspector Meredith, thank us for a peaceful picket?

When asked this in the witness box, Chief Inspector Meredith admitted shaking Dezzie's hand. 'I didn't know he was a criminal then,' he explained.

When the court adjourned each day, most of the lads lived close enough to go home for the night, but Dezzie and me had found digs at a little boarding house, the Warwick Arms. The landlady really looked after us, cooking meals and washing our clothes.

On weekends I managed to get home and see Marlene and the boys. We had bought a run-down cottage in Coedpoeth, a small village about four miles from Wrexham. It needed a lot of work, but we had great plans to build extensions and do up various rooms.

I tried to get home before the boys went to bed so I could tell them a story or sing a song. Meanwhile, Marlene fixed me supper and when I sat down at the table she asked about the trial. I didn't want to talk. Instead I wanted to hear about things at home. Gareth had started walking and Clifton could already dribble a soccer ball around the garden.

Marlene didn't understand the issues and the politics behind the trial. She had always been non-political. Not in a head-in-the-sand sort of way, but because she had more important things to worry about like looking after the children. She supported me because that's what wives were supposed to do, in her view. Without her I couldn't have got through it.

The prosecution's opening statement had been widely reported and I know it upset Mam. I fobbed her off saying that it was a complete exaggeration.

'This is a storm in a teacup. What can they do? We haven't done anything wrong.'

Apart from the opening few days, the national papers didn't bother sending anyone to cover the proceedings. It was left to the *Morning Star* and the *Socialist Worker* to keep people informed.

For Mam's sake, I was relieved about the lack of publicity. I didn't want her reading all the lies that were being told about me.

She got upset one night after seeing a report on the evening news. Albert told her not to cry.

'Everyone will know it's our Rick,' she said.

'No, they won't. They called him Eric.'

'But they'll still know it's him.'

'How?'

'Because I've told them.'

The prosecution case lasted six weeks and featured over two hundred witnesses. Although appalled by the evidence, I had a sneaking admiration for Maurice Drake, the chief prosecutor, who had a very difficult task constructing a case out of lies and exaggerations. Drake was a good-looking man, with grey hair at his temples. He reminded me a little of Dad, who was slighter and not quite so tall.

In late November the defence case began and we finally had a chance to explain what really happened on that day in Shrewsbury. John Carpenter took the stand first, followed by John Llywarch. He described seeing a few smashed windows and bricks thrown at the building sites, but no other violence. He had calmed a few of the lads down, particularly after the shotgun had been waved in our faces.

Like me, he had first been approached and asked to be a prosecution witness, but when he refused to cooperate the police charged him.

Dezzie was brilliant under cross-examination. Maurice

Drake tried to portray him as a violent thug, but Dezzie countered him with humour. At one point Drake had rattled off a list of claims, each one prefaced with the phrase, 'Might I suggest, Mr Warren . . .'

Dezzie looked at him and said saucily, 'You're very suggestive, Mr Drake.'

The whole courtroom erupted and Drake's face turned pink.

I know some people were worried about me giving evidence. I was regarded as a hothead and they thought I might lose my cool. I have a big mouth. Always have. If I don't agree with something I say so. I get angry about hypocrisy and injustice. I'm passionate and emotional, which some people mistake for aggression.

I remember being nervous as I took the stand. Keith McHale, QC, took me through the events of that day and the meeting a week earlier at the Bull and Stirrup. The prosecution had tried to argue that the numbers were purely designed to intimidate. I explained that a big picket is much more effective than a small one. Lumpers and scabs can hardly go to their bosses and say they're refusing to cross a one-man picket line.

'We wanted to show them we were striking for the right reasons. We were sticking together.'

A small number of pickets had misbehaved, I said, and it was possible that a handful of workers may have felt threatened, but if we had gone to Shrewsbury intending to wreak violence the consequences would have been far worse.

I knew Maurice Drake was itching to cross-examine me, but he had to wait. The trial was adjourned and I was allowed to go home. I was put under house arrest and they stationed a police car outside the front gate. Even members of Marlene's family were refused entry. I couldn't see or talk to anyone.

Two days later I stepped back into the witness box. Drake did his smiling assassin act. Here was an educated man, who was going to try to make me look ignorant and foolish.

'And you were all shouting "Kill, kill, kill",' he said. 'You deliberately set out to intimidate these men. You were going to batter them into submission . . .'

'I used to take me lad Clifton on the pickets,' I responded. 'Do you really expect someone to take a toddler along if blokes are raging around shouting, "Kill, kill, kill"?

'A window got broke, a door frame got knocked over and a couple of walls were toppled. Some guy slipped off scaffolding and sprained an ankle. Another claimed a brick hit him. That was it! Nobody got carted off to hospital. There were no ambulances . . . no injuries . . . no arrests.'

I spent three days answering questions, but didn't waiver. Sometimes I had trouble remembering the sequence of events of fourteen months earlier, but this didn't alter the truth of what happened.

Maurice Drake tried to trip me up on whether I had 'asked' workers to join the strike or 'told' them to.

'It was both,' I said, 'but they weren't threatened with physical violence. They had to join because it was important for the building industry. It was a legal picket. Those who stayed and listened were asked to stop working and join the campaign. There were some harsh words and a few scuffles, but the hotheads were in a tiny minority and the police didn't intervene.'

In truth, I expected the cross-examination to be a lot tougher but Drake had to go by what the police had told him, which put him at a disadvantage because their statements were so conflicting. He also couldn't counter defence claims that if the picketing had been as violent as suggested, someone would have been arrested or charged or a policeman would have made some note in a notebook. None of this happened.

When it came time for closing arguments, Dezzie was portrayed as the chief rabble-rouser and the prosecution continued to insist that he had threatened to burn down a canteen.

John Carpenter's lawyer called the conspiracy charge baseless and 'a fantasy of the prosecution's imagination'.

John Platts Mills, QC, attacked the whole way the charges were framed. According to the wording, we had conspired to 'intimidate workers to abstain from their lawful occupation'. What lawful occupation? Most of the scabs were on 'the lump'. They didn't pay taxes or social security. The lump was a violation of the law.

Pointing to some of the prosecution's photographs, he said, 'Look at that scaffolding. Not a single bracing. Not a connection with the building. No guard rail. These breaches of the regulations not only endanger the public but the lives and safety of building workers.'

He also argued that the prosecution had failed to produce a single shred of evidence of any sinister agreement at our meeting at the Bull and Stirrup. Instead, the overwhelming evidence was that we had planned a peaceful picket.

'For ninety-eight years no Government has thought fit to bring a charge of this sort,' he said.

Justice Mais reacted furiously to this suggestion that the trial had been politically motivated. He thrust his finger at Platts Mills. 'This is an ordinary criminal trial.'

'And it was an ordinary trade union meeting, yet my client is now charged with conspiracy,' the QC responded.

Platts Mills stood his ground until he was ordered to withdraw the remark, which he did after throwing his wig on the bench in disgust.

In his summing up, he told the all-male jury: 'You are being asked to take part in history. You are being asked to turn the clock back to use the conspiracy act . . . a hideous weapon in the hands of the court . . .'

It had allowed the prosecution to rely on very dubious material such as hearsay and secondary evidence. And instead of having to prove who initiated the disturbances it could claim that by not calming other strikers down men were condoning what went on.

In his final statement to the jury, Judge Mais said that it didn't matter if the six of us had not been at the Chester meeting. We didn't even have to know each other. There could still be a conspiracy.

How he came to this conclusion is a complete mystery, but it made it extremely difficult to fight the charge. Similarly, he concurred with Maurice Drake's assertion that even being in the 'vicinity of trouble' was enough to prove the charges of affray.

The press benches, which had been deserted for most of the trial, suddenly filled up again as the verdicts grew nearer. Some of the reporters were running a book on the outcome. The betting was 'not guilty' to the conspiracy charge and even money on the affray and unlawful assembly.

The jury retired on Tuesday 18 December. I was quietly confident. In a separate trial, a week earlier, five Birmingham building workers who had occupied a site had been cleared on similar charges. The jury had been unanimous.

At the same time there was a nagging doubt at the back of my mind. Maurice Drake seemed almost too confident.

After deliberating all morning, the jury returned and the foreman announced they were still making up their minds on the conspiracy charges, but had reached a consensus on the other charges.

We were told to stand. I braced my hands against the polished wooden rail and stared straight ahead – convinced the prosecution hadn't done enough.

All six of us were found guilty of unlawful assembly. Dezzie, myself and Mackie were guilty of affray. John Carpenter and Ken O'Shea were cleared on the conspiracy charges.

I felt as though a fist had been driven into my stomach. My mouth had gone dry and blood pounded in my ears. How could they have convicted Mackie? His name had barely been mentioned during the trial. How could they have found me guilty of affray?

Mr Justice Mais asked the foreman if he felt that a unanimous verdict could be reached on the conspiracy charges. The foreman shook his head. The Judge then said he would accept a majority verdict and sent them back to the jury room.

I had already talked to my solicitor about what would happen if it all went wrong. He told me that I would have a chance to address the court before sentencing.

I started jotting down some thoughts and Dezzie did the same. The other lads didn't seem so interested. We were all in shock. None of us had really believed it would come to this.

For nine months I had clung to the belief that the British justice system would find us innocent. Now I realised the sad truth. The Government, business leaders and the Establishment had worked too hard for this. The trial had cost millions of pounds. You don't spend that sort of money for nothing.

These people from higher up – the giant construction firms – had decided to get the building workers. But they wouldn't take the big cities on, like London or Birmingham or Liverpool. So they came out into the sticks, into North

Wales, picked a bunch of ordinary building workers and put us on trial.

At five o'clock the jury came in again. They couldn't reach a majority verdict on the four remaining charges of conspiracy. Justice Mais sent them to a hotel, while the six of us were taken to jail for the night.

Nothing was said in the police van on the drive to Shrewsbury Prison. We sat in silence, lost in our own thoughts. Maybe some of the lads said a prayer.

It was dark by the time we arrived at the Victorian prison on high ground, overlooking the town and enclosed in a loop of the River Severn. We were processed and put in cells for remand prisoners, separate from the main prison population. Each cell had a bunk, a piss-pot, a chair and small table.

I had never spent a night behind bars. Every sound seemed magnified and the air had a coldness that wasn't just about the temperature. I sat down at the table and began writing an address to the jury, realising I might be going to jail.

I didn't sleep more than a few hours. Too many things were going through my head. In the morning the police were out in force again, surrounding the courthouse, fearing trouble from rank and file unionists.

The jury resumed its deliberations, but finally reached a decision at 1 p.m. The jury foreman, a schoolteacher, looked unhappy as he announced the verdicts. John Llywarch was not guilty of conspiracy, but myself, Dezzie and Mackie were guilty.

Later John Carpenter talked to the foreman and discovered the jury had been split eight–four for more than twenty-four hours. Eventually two of them were persuaded to change their minds by the argument that none of us would go to prison, but merely receive fines that the unions would pay. This finally broke the deadlock.

It was a wonderful piece of deception. Afterwards, as the foreman listened to the pleas of mitigation, he grew more and more upset as it became clear that prison sentences were to be imposed. He remonstrated with another member of the jury.

John Platts Mills and Keith McHale told the Judge that Dezzie and I wanted to make statements. I spoke first, feeling nervous and angry. I had kept silent for so long; now I could say what I thought.

The room was almost totally quiet, except for the occasional sob from the gallery. Marlene was among those crying.

'We have listened day after day as two hundred witnesses came into this court and systematically and automatically swore away our very character,' I said. 'It was said by Goebbels in the last war that if you repeat a lie often enough it becomes accepted as the truth. This I have observed put into practice in this court and now know it to be true . . .

'I can sympathise with the jury because they have been used in this charade in just the same way as myself and my colleagues. I have heard the Judge say this was not a political trial, but just an ordinary criminal case. I refute this with every fibre of my being. How can anyone say this was just an ordinary trial when a thousand police were on duty outside this very court because ordinary building workers were due to appear?

'. . . No sentence passed on me by this court, however lenient, however severe, can hurt me more than I have been hurt already. I have been almost totally unemployed since my arrest and this punishes my wife and two infant sons to a far greater extent than it does me.

'I know my children, when they are old enough, will

understand that the struggle we took part in was for their benefit and for the benefit and interests of all building workers and their families because we really do care . . .

'I have always considered myself to be a patriot and to love my country with a great passion. My politics may differ from that of some of my colleagues in the dock, but we shared a single common desire to help our fellow human beings . . .

'It is hoped the trade union movement and working classes of this country will act now to ensure that another charade like this trial will never take place again and the right to picket or strike will be defended even at the cost of great personal hardship or individual freedom.'

There was applause from the public gallery and calls of 'Hear! Hear!' Justice Mais hammered his gavel and threatened to clear the court if there was another outburst.

Dezzie spoke with power and passion. He told the court that there had indeed been a conspiracy, but not by the pickets.

'The conspiracy was one between the Home Secretary, the employers and the police. It was not done with a nod or a wink. It was conceived after pressure from Tory MPs who demanded changes in picketing laws . . . there is your conspiracy.'

As he spoke, I looked round the courtroom at the faces of my mates. Fellas were dropping their heads. Eyes misted over. It was as though the clocks had stopped.

'I am innocent of the charges and I will appeal,' said Dezzie. 'But there will be a more important appeal made to the entire trade union movement from this moment on. Nobody here must think they can walk away from this court and forget what has happened here. Villains or victims, we are all part of something much bigger than this trial. The working-class movement cannot allow this verdict to go unchallenged. It is yet one more step along the road to fascism.

'The greatest heroes in Nazi Germany were those who challenged the law when it was used as a political weapon by a government acting for a minority of greedy, evil men.'

Justice Mais was squirming. Right from the outset he had never been able to hide his contempt for Dezzie and now he was furious at being shown so little respect.

When Dezzie finished there was a long silence and then the noise started as a slow murmur. Justice Mais called for order and delivered the sentences.

He denied that we were martyrs and rejected completely any suggestion the trial had been politically motivated.

'You availed yourself of the freedom of the strike but you denied others an equal freedom *not* to strike,' he said. 'You succeeded in causing serious public disorder . . . Your conduct was totally unacceptable in this country and you knew full well what you were doing was wrong.'

John Carpenter, Ken O'Shea and John Llywarch were each given nine months' suspended sentences. Mackie was sentenced to nine months' jail and I was given two years.

There was an audible gasp from the court. I looked straight ahead. Suddenly, the foreman of the jury stood up in disgust and pushed his way out of the jury box.

'Disgraceful!' he muttered.

Another juror in the front row also rose to his feet and walked out. Justice Mais looked shocked. He mumbled something about dismissing the jury.

Both men had to be persuaded to come back because Dezzie still hadn't been sentenced. The foreman was close to tears as he listened to the Judge describe Dezzie as 'vicious and arrogant' before he sentenced him to three years' jail.

Within minutes we were bustled downstairs, surrounded

by police, and put into a van. Dezzie looked shell-shocked. Neither of us had expected sentences of this magnitude.

Friends and family gathered outside the courthouse, consoling each other. Already they talked of appeals and national campaigns to have us pardoned and freed.

I leaned against the wall of the van and thought of my two little boys . . . and of Mam. Then I remembered my meeting with Keith McHale, all those months earlier. He had told me then that I would get two years. How did he know?

10

A Prisoner of Her Majesty

The last time I saw my prison diary was about ten years ago in the cottage. I've moved a lot of times since then, living in different houses and sleeping on various sofas.

The diary ended up in an old garage owned by a mate of mine. That's where I found it, along with other bits and pieces, in a box full of old work records.

I used to spend hours writing it in prison. Mostly it helped pass the time, but somewhere in the back of my mind I thought about writing a book one day. I wanted to put everything down so that Gareth and Clifton would understand why I went away.

Mostly the diary is full of little stories about prison life; stuff fellas told me and things I witnessed. A bloke smuggled it out for me and I had it typed up, along with some of the poems I wrote.

Some of it is missing now but the memories they dredge up are just as strong. I ceased to be a human being when I entered jail. I became Prisoner 573143. I'll carry that number with me to my grave . . . just like Mary Jackson's telephone number in Southend.

There are dozens of letters and telegrams, many of them brittle with age and still folded in the original envelopes that carried them. There is one here from Southampton Students Union:

'Motion passed condemning your imprisonment. Seen as creation

of political prisoners in this country. We send our solidarity and will continue to support campaign for your release.'

Portsmouth Trade Council sent me season's greetings and pledged, 'fullest support to have the biggest miscarriage of justice changed and you be freed'.

I still have all my letters to Marlene and the ones she wrote back to me. She wasn't a great writer but she made a real effort to tell me all the news. I used to want to hear about the ordinary, everyday things – the routine of her life; what the boys were doing; how they were growing taller and learning new things. Mostly I wanted to be sure that nothing had changed . . . that I still had a home and a family waiting for me.

They shone a torch down my gob, made me strip naked, checked my hair for lice and handed me a prison uniform. Afterwards they said we could eat, but I had no stomach for food. Instead I had two dry rounds of bread and a cup of tea.

I spent that first night in a holding cell, shared with Dezzie and Mackie. It was only about twelve foot by ten foot. Mackie suffered from claustrophobia and fainted, but thankfully didn't hurt himself.

Right from the start Dezzie and me decided that we weren't going to soldier. Fuck 'em! We had done nothing wrong. Mackie just wanted to keep his nose clean, do his time and get out. I could understand that. With good behaviour he could be home in six months.

I wrote a letter to Marlene that night, before they turned off the lights and plunged us into a darkness that was deeper than any I had ever known.

My dear Mia,
    It seems almost a relief now that it's over. Now I

must get this sentence over with as quickly as possible. Having waited nine years for children I don't want to be away from them a day longer than necessary.

I hope you can come down to the prison, because I think they allow a visit. Please don't bring Clifton and Gareth with you. I don't have the courage to face them without showing some form of emotion. Everybody has an Achilles heel and, as is common knowledge, my weak spot is the kids.

Tell them I'm working away somewhere. I know you hate lying, but just this once. Later, when they're older, I'll explain everything to them.

It's strange being imprisoned for the first time. I'm not ashamed to meet people. It's not as though I stole something or hurt somebody. I'm a pawn in power politics and somebody had to be the whipping boy . . .

Well, my queen, I'll finish now. There's so much I want to say to you but these letters are censored and read by people in the prison. Maybe I'm a bit of a prude, but the feelings I have for you are not something I want read by other people.

Lots of love,

Rick.

The newspapers had a field day in the morning. The *Daily Mail* declared, 'LEADERS OF STRIKE TERROR GANG ARE JAILED'.

'Des Warren, the man who masterminded the flying pickets and brought a day of terror to building workers, was jailed for three years yesterday. Two other members of the 300-strong picket squad were also jailed for a total of two years and nine months at the end of the eleven-week trial at Shrewsbury Crown Court.'

The *Daily Mirror* included a photograph of Dezzie under the headline, 'GODFATHER BEHIND THE CAMPAIGN OF VIOLENCE'. Neither of these newspapers had bothered to cover the trial, only the outcome.

My first few days in jail were spent learning the routines of slopping out, meal times and lights out. I kept to myself, avoiding eye contact with other prisoners. Some of the cons didn't know how to treat us because they knew the background to the case.

On Christmas Eve we were taken to a Christmas carol service. Up until then I had always regarded carols a bit like hymns and didn't think it was possible to hear them sung badly. The prison choir was a shocker and one particular lad was so bloody awful I had to bite my arm to stop myself from laughing.

Christmas Day was spent thinking about Marlene and the boys. I could see the boys perfectly in my mind's eye – red cheeks, snug in their pyjamas, ripping open presents around the tree. I knew Marlene's family would take care of her. They didn't agree with my politics or some of my actions, but they loved the boys.

I began doing regular exercise, not just to keep fit and stay warm, but to make myself tired so that I wouldn't lie awake at night thinking about home. In the exercise yard, I made one friend, an Irish lad, who was doing a long stretch. He had read about our case in the papers and said he was sorry. Hardened crims were apologising to me. The world had come to this!

With broad, square shoulders and greying hair, Dezzie looked a bit like a present-day Richard Gere. He had grown up around Chester and had a similar education to mine. He and his wife Elsa had five kids and Dezzie always worked hard to look after them.

Early in January Mackie was transferred to an open prison, which was for the best. At the same time, Dezzie and I were transferred to Stafford Jail. Nobody bothered telling Marlene or Elsa. This set the standard for what followed – we were shunted between different jails, without warning, often in the dead of night.

Stafford was most memorable for actually making me miss Shrewsbury. It was ancient and falling apart; a real pighole. I had to strip off all over again in the reception centre and turn out my pockets. They let me keep two biro pens, a block of Palmolive soap, some newspaper cuttings about the case, and the telegrams and letters of support that had been arriving every day. Some were from ordinary people off the street while others came from shop stewards, trade councils, student unions, left-wing MPs and civil rights groups.

I was taken to a single cell – No. 37, ground floor, Crescent D. Wing. It was your classic prison wing – three floors built around a central square, with metal staircases running up to balconies. Nets were strung between the floors to stop shit being hurled from the top when the prisoners kicked off about something.

The only window, high up on the wall, had tiny glass squares with many of them missing or broken. The wind whistled through the gaps, making it too cold to sleep.

Finally I had no choice but to use the telegrams and letters to plug the gaps. It broke my heart. One of them was from Lou Armour, a full-time UCATT official and a lovely man. I felt like I was tearing him up.

I managed to fall asleep and woke just before dawn. I shifted and suddenly the whole floor began to move. It was a mass of cockroaches rippling like the surface of a pond. There were also these little brown things like earwigs and tiny white worms. And don't get me started on the rats – the prison was infested with them.

I screamed the place down and hammered on the door until the screws arrived.

'I'm not staying in here,' I told them. 'You have to move me.'

'For a few fucking cockroaches,' one of them scoffed.

'A few million.'

The cell was just next to the kitchens and the cockroaches were breeding in the warmth and invading the cells.

From then on I waged a running battle against them. I cut plastic bottles with my razor blade and used them to cover the legs of the bedframe, but the bedding was already crawling with parasites. I tried to keep my clothes off the floor, but shook the roaches out of them each morning.

One day I finally cracked and started shouting and swearing. The screws ignored me for a long while, but finally the officer in charge, Mr Ayres, came to my cell. There were hundreds of dead cockroaches on the floor.

He could see I was distressed. He told me to get my things and moved me to cell No. 8 on the second landing. I wasted no time. Some other poor bastard was going to get No. 37, which was wrong, but I didn't care. I couldn't spend another night like that.

Still exercising every day – fifty push-ups and a hundred sit-ups – I figured I might lose a bit of weight if the food didn't improve. A lot of the inmates wanted to exhaust themselves and sleep their sentence away. At night the screws brought round 'the liquid cosh', which was some sort of sedative or sleeping draught. Although I longed for a good night's sleep, I only took the drink once. I could see what it did to others – the dull eyes and hundred-yard stares.

Monday to Friday I sweated in one of the workshops assembling cassette tapes. With my hands I was crap. My fingers were too big. After the first week my wages came to the princely sum of 42p. Talk about slave labour! I scraped together all my money and had just enough to buy a battery for my radio and two letters.

The radio had quickly become my best friend. I listened to documentaries, news bulletins, comedies and classical music on Radio 4. I also borrowed books from the prison library and went to Sunday services where I had long theological discussions with the prison chaplain.

My parole date had been set and if I stayed out of trouble I could be home by April 1975 – a year and two months away. My only other hope was the application to appeal, which had been lodged immediately after the trial. On Friday 11 January I wrote in my diary:

This is it, the day that really matters. I have mixed feelings. I know that we should be granted an appeal. I know that we should be allowed bail. But after my experiences so far, I have fears for the impartiality of the Judge who hears the application.

Later that day I added:

Great news! We have been granted leave to appeal. I heard it at one o'clock on Radio 4. Our bail application will be heard on 1 February.

Marlene could only visit me once every four weeks. I had to send her a visiting order, which she took to the Social

Security office and collected a petrol allowance or a rail warrant to cover the cost of the journey.

The visiting room at Stafford consisted of bare tables and hard chairs. We weren't allowed to hug or kiss, because the screws thought visitors might be smuggling drugs, mouth to mouth. The most we shared was a cup of tea, longing looks and a quick squeeze of the hand.

As much as I missed the boys, I had no worries about them. Marlene would never have let anybody hurt them. She was like a lioness protecting her cubs. Even so, it broke my heart when she told me that Clifton had lost the power of speech and become very withdrawn since I went to jail. He had barely spoken a word in seven weeks.

A young fella sat at a nearby table with his girlfriend or wife leaning towards him. He gave her a little kiss and his hand reached under the table. Suddenly, the screws flew across the room, seized the table and wrenched it back.

Everyone turned to look. The young woman was pregnant and the lad had his hand on her tummy, feeling the baby kicking. It touched me that. The screws didn't apologise. They righted the table and told them to sit further apart. He had nothing, this lad, but they couldn't allow him this one small pleasure.

Marlene brought news of the campaign. The Shrewsbury Independence Fund had been set up by building workers and was supported by the Socialist Workers Party. John Carpenter and John Llywarch were speaking at meetings around the country rallying rank and file trade unionists.

Three and a half thousand people marched through the streets of London on Tuesday 15 January to demonstrate against the sentences. Similar protests were held in Liverpool, Edinburgh and on Teesside.

Arthur Scargill became one of the most strident

campaigners, speaking from every platform about our plight. In many ways the miners took the lead, along with dockers and building workers, to help raise funds to support our families.

Even Marlene, as shy as can be, spoke at meetings and joined the protests. I'll never forget picking up a newspaper and seeing a photograph of her marching at the head of a demonstration, arm in arm with building workers.

I didn't always get to see these stories. The prison authorities censored my newspapers, cutting out anything that related to Dezzie and me. Some mornings my paper would be full of holes, but the other prisoners would keep the stories and pass them on to me.

The authorities had also decided to separate Dezzie and me, putting us in separate blocks because they were worried we might start inciting trouble among the inmates. This was paranoia, but impossible to counter. From then on I saw him only briefly, snatching a few minutes here or there when the screws weren't looking.

Eventually, I made a formal application to the Assistant Governor asking to see Dezzie so we could discuss our appeal. He didn't want to grant permission, but I threatened to take the complaint to the Home Office.

Every concession, however small, had to be won like this. I criticised the wages. For six weeks running I had received only 30p because the workshop screw had been writing down the wrong hours. I was also angry about my circumstances. I had never been in trouble before, yet they put me into a prison with some of the most violent criminals in the system. Daily I was mixing with drug addicts, pushers, sex offenders, IRA and UDA prisoners, terrorists and killers; the dregs of society. This was wrong.

*

Friday 1 February

No breakfast, just bread and butter. I'm taking no chances after the cockroach incident. My stomach is upset because I only go to the toilet about once every six days. I can't bear the filthy smell of a single toilet that is used by about thirty people. And I'm sick of trying to use it in the space of ten minutes. It is barbaric.

We were banged up in the cells at 10.30 this morning because some of the screws have got some business to do. No exercise period again. I went to classes in the afternoon. I'm doing my 'O' level maths and English.

Later, back in my cell, a lad brought me the news. It had been on the radio. Our bail has been refused.

Everything now hinged on the appeal hearing set down for 19, 20 and 21 February in London. Our defence would argue that instead of leaving it up to the jury to decide if there had been a conspiracy (the crux of the case) Mr Justice Mais had intimated very strongly that there had been. He had also permitted inadmissible hearsay statements to be given in evidence and put the most adverse interpretation on ambiguous statements and actions.

As the appeal hearing drew nearer, the prison administration seemed determined to break me. The Governor, for no reason, ordered that I be returned to my old cell, with the cockroaches and bedbugs. He also dismissed my complaints about the workshop and my wages.

I was so angry that I contemplated withdrawing my appeal, but instead decided to make a formal application to be classified as a political prisoner. I knew that would ruffle a few feathers.

Two days later I managed to get an appointment with the Governor. He sat behind a big desk, completely clear of paperwork, with pens and pencils lined up in a neat row on the blotter. His shirt had perfectly ironed creases and the knot of his tie was tucked right under his Adam's apple.

I stood before him, with my hands behind my back, as though standing at ease, with a prison warder on either side of me.

'You seem to be making a lot of complaints, Mr Tomlinson.'

'I'm not trying to be difficult.'

I told him about the rats and cockroaches; how I hadn't been able to sleep and had been getting these blinding headaches.

He couldn't have been less sympathetic.

'What do you know about a demonstration this Saturday?' he asked.

'I don't know anything.'

'What? Are you telling me you haven't heard any rumours?'

'No.'

He looked disappointed.

'I don't think you fully understand how this works,' he said. 'If you want me to help you then I expect your cooperation.'

'But I don't know anything about a demonstration.'

It was the truth, but he didn't believe me. Two days later, on Saturday morning, a guard woke me early and told me to get washed and dressed. I had to pack my things and move quickly, taking only what I could carry.

I was taken to a cell in the punishment block, separate from the main prison population. It had a bare concrete floor, a table, a chair and a mattress on the floor.

'Why am I here?'

'You're being held under rule 43-1.'

'What does that mean?'

'You're being separated from other prisoners for their protection.'

'What am I going to do to them?' I asked incredulously.

The door had already swung shut and his boots echoed on the floor as he left.

I refused breakfast and ate nothing all day. For weeks I had suffered headaches, but this one grew even worse. The cell was tiny and airless, with a small window high on the wall. That night, when the lights went out at ten o'clock, I understood the true meaning of pitch-black darkness. Not a chink of light came from anywhere. For the first time I was scared.

I slept for two or three hours, tossing and turning. In the morning I waited to see if anyone would come and take me to the Sunday service. Maybe they wanted to separate me from Him as well.

Nobody arrived and I spent the morning pacing the cell, wishing my headache would go away. Late in the afternoon the Governor arrived. The screws told me to stand at the rear of the cell.

He stepped inside the doorway and looked as though a smell disagreed with him.

'Why am I being punished?' I asked.

'You have an attitude problem.'

'What do you mean?'

'You don't have the right attitude, particularly towards me. Is there anything you want to tell me?'

'What about?'

'Things that may be planned.'

I shook my head. For some reason he had me down as an

agitator and imagined I had planned some jailhouse protest or work-to-rule. With no explanation, he spun on his heels and the door clanged shut again. I spent another night in the blackness, praying for the morning.

The next day they let me exercise for ten minutes in a small private yard surrounded by high walls. It took thirty-five steps to complete a full circuit. It gave me an inkling of how a goldfish must feel swimming round and round in a bowl.

I had been in total solitary confinement for forty-seven hours. How long would they keep me here? I wrote:

Monday 11 February
Each morning, waking from the pitch black. Stark reality. The lights go on. I turn on the radio and listen to Radio 4. The latest news is of the struggle between the miners and the evil people who purport to govern.

The heavy bolt slides and the door opens. I go for fresh water both to drink and to wash in. I am not allowed to lie on my bed. The mattress is stood on its side with the blankets, sheet and pillows folded and placed over it. There is just the hard wooden chair or the stone floor to sit on for the next twelve hours.

On Tuesday the Governor visited me again and after four days in solitary he said I could go back to my old cell. Again, there was no explanation.

'I hope you've learned a lesson,' he said.

The lads on the wing seemed genuinely pleased to see me back. A couple of them lent me some magazines and I had my first meal for three days. The workshop had been on a go-slow ever since I went into solitary. People I barely knew had stood up for me.

Unfortunately, I had now become a marked man and the screws found dozens of ways to obstruct and irritate me. I had to fight to get every new razor blade. Apparently, they were frightened I might shave my beard off and try to walk out of jail looking like somebody else. Give me a break!

Even those around me suffered. A young con, Harrison, had a couple of cassettes planted on him in the workshop as a punishment for having spoken out about me. He was put on report and lost four days of privileges. Worse still, it would affect his parole.

Not all of the screws were like this. Every so often I encountered one who had a sense of humour or at least a sense of humanity. Mr Smith was a nice old guy, tough but fair. I kicked off about there being no bread one day and went back to my cell in disgust. About half an hour later, the cell door opened and a loaf of bread came flying through the air and hit me on the back of the head.

'There! Ya crying bastard!' said Mr Smith, laughing at me.

On 18 February, I woke early, packed my gear and was taken to reception. Dezzie was already there. We stripped and changed into our civilian clothes. Immediately, I felt different. Clean. Free. For the first time in months we could laugh and chat, unafraid of being stopped or overheard or having to run the gauntlet of the screws.

We travelled to London in a mini-coach, handcuffed all the way. They wouldn't even undo the cuffs when the coach stopped on the way for Dezzie to use the toilet.

We spent that night at Brixton prison, going through the same dehumanising progression of stripping naked in front of a dozen screws and being made to have a bath. It was great to see Mackie again. He told us all about his open prison –

plenty of recreation, extra visits, £1.35 a week and endless other privileges. I was glad for him.

They put us into a large single cell with three beds. The place was filthy but none of us cared. Our nightly cup of tea had dirt and floating bits of crap, but that was positively hygienic compared to breakfast. We were given a small spoonful of beans and a tiny sausage.

'I'll never eat all that,' I joked to the screw.

'Is that all for me?' echoed Dezzie.

The screw didn't crack a smile.

Afterwards, we were handcuffed, taken to the prison courtyard and loaded in a minivan with blacked-out windows. At the Appeal Court they kept us separate and led me through endless stairs to holding cells.

At 11.30, I emerged from beneath the courtroom into the dock. Turning my head I caught sight of Marlene in the gallery, along with our David, John and Rita Carpenter and loads of friends.

The panel of three Judges who had initially been appointed to hear the appeal had been altered. Lord Chief Justice Widgery, the most senior Judge in Britain, now headed the line-up. I knew straight away that something was up. The big guns had been rolled out.

Much of the day was taken up with legal arguments, as our lawyers pointed to the failings of the trial Judge. Lord Chief Justice Widgery didn't seem overly sympathetic. My heart sank. The legal argument and submissions continued for three days and then the appeal was adjourned until Monday 4 March when the Judges would announce their decision.

There were handshakes all round and then Mackie was taken back to Ranby Open Prison by taxi. Dezzie and I were handcuffed to each other and taken by minivan to Wormwood

Scrubs in Shepherd's Bush. It was my fourth prison in two months and the eighth for Dezzie.

Our new cell was filthy. Excrement, urine, dirty clothing, books and papers littered the floor. An old fella lay on the bed with his fly open, looking as though he'd just had a Barclay's Bank (wank).

'I'm not having this,' I said to Dezzie.

'Me neither.'

We apologised to the old lag and went to find the landing screw. He laughed at us.

'I been timing you,' he said. 'You lasted exactly two minutes. I thought you'd stick it for a couple of days.'

The landing screws had been taking bets on how long we'd last.

After a discussion we were sent to a cell on the top landing and this time our cellmate was a young lad doing time for drug offences. Although I've got no time for drug dealers, he wasn't a bad kid. Recently married, he had a photograph of his young wife who was beautiful. They had lived up north, but the prison authorities had moved him to Wormwood Scrubs, which meant his wife had to travel two hundred and fifty miles to visit.

This one particular screw whose job was to scan the incoming mail used to make a point of reading this kid's letters and quoting sections back to him. At the same time he used to wind him up, telling him how all his mates were probably screwing his wife.

A bit later I was dozing on my bunk when I heard a low moan. I turned and saw the young lad sawing away at his wrist with a razor blade. There was blood everywhere. I dived on him and Dezzie pressed the alarm bell. Blood spurted out like it was coming from a water pistol. I held on to his wrist, putting pressure on the wound.

The screws took the kid away to hospital and we mopped the floor. Two hours later they brought him back, stitched and bandaged. They threw him into the cell and one of them wrote on the noticeboard outside, 'Scratched wrists'.

How heartless! Some of these warders were more institutionalised than the prisoners and I doubt if they could have done any other job.

Sharing a cell with Dezzie made the time pass more easily. We had a few laughs, did crosswords, answered the radio quiz questions and listened to the trains rumble past Wormwood Scrubs.

We tried to stay out of trouble, but it was hard keeping quiet when conditions were so bad and the sense of injustice at our confinement burned so strongly in both of us.

On 28 February, we asked to see the Assistant Governor at the Scrubs.

'We're not happy with the conditions or the way inmates are treated,' I told him. 'We want to be transferred to an open prison and to be granted political status.'

He began mumbling about due process and regulations, but I interrupted, 'To show our determination, we have started a hunger strike.'

His eyes went wide and filled with doubt. This had shaken him up. Straightaway he agreed to let us go before the Board of Visitors. He also gave us the petition forms and notified the authorities of the hunger strike.

Giving up food wasn't such a huge sacrifice. Most of it I wouldn't have fed to pigs. I had no idea what physical effect it would have on me – apart from losing weight of course. I just realised that food was one of the few things I still had control over because they couldn't *make* me eat.

The impact of the decision was almost immediate. The

screws were suddenly more polite and even friendly. The prison doctor gave me a medical and made a note of how much I weighed.

Next morning we fronted the Board of Visitors – a panel of ordinary members of the community. I went in first and politely explained that I wanted to be reclassified as a political prisoner.

'I have been forced to mix with gunmen, gangsters and rapists, yet I should not even be in jail. My trial and conviction were political decisions . . .'

The chairman, a lady, treated me with the utmost respect and explained that she could do nothing until after the appeal process had finished.

Dezzie took a different approach with the Board. He attacked the fact that he had been shunted between eight different prisons in barely two months. How was his wife supposed to visit him? She couldn't be sure what prison he'd be in from one week to the next.

'We are politically hot property,' Dezzie said. 'Every time our case is mentioned by people the word "politics" comes up, yet we're not supposed to use the term . . .'

At this point the Governor interjected and said the issue would have to be put to another Board of Visitors because our appeal decision was imminent. If the appeal failed we were to be transferred back to HM Stafford, he said.

In the meantime, on doctor's orders, we were moved to single cells; mine on the ground floor and Dezzie's on the first landing. The cells were neat and tidy, with fitted cupboards, writing space and even a nice little display area for photographs. The bathroom was tiled with three or four hot water taps, clean toilets and urine stalls.

On the fifth day a male orderly did a urine test to see how my body was being affected by the lack of food. Strangely, I didn't feel very hungry, but I was tired and struggled to concentrate. Instead of going on exercise, I saved my energy.

On Monday 4 March, we were back in the Appeal Court to hear the verdict. The legal boffins argued, joked and acted out the pantomime. Finally, Lord Widgery read from a prepared statement. The charges of conspiracy and unlawful assembly were upheld. The affray convictions could be appealed.

There were more legal arguments and formal applications for bail. After a straight rebuff, we went back to the Scrubs. Elsa Warren sobbed in the gallery. Dezzie could only wave.

The next day the story broke in the papers about our hunger strike. The *Guardian* described us as 'looking pale and worn' as we sat in the dock, flanked by three policemen. We had gone six days taking nothing more than cups of tea.

On Wednesday morning we were transferred to HM Stafford and given another medical. I weighed 172 lbs and had lost 30 lbs since entering prison. We were taken to the hospital block and put in different cells. Dezzie was on the first landing, while I was on the ground floor. A piping hot meal arrived, but remained uneaten.

The hospital orderly was a big fella from Devon or Cornwall. He didn't wear a screw's uniform, but had a surgical jacket like a male nurse. The first time I met him, he put his face about an inch from mine and said, 'Oh, you're the hard case, are you?'

'I've never won a fight in me life.'

'Ah, well, we'll see how tough you are when I grease up a tube and shove it down your throat.'

'Yeah, I'm not looking forward to being force-fed, but you're gonna have to do it. I'm not in here for hurting anyone, you know.'

'Aren't you frightened?'

'Of course I'm frightened. I want to go home.'

He delivered a piping hot breakfast. A piping hot dinner. A piping hot evening meal. Then he even brought something for supper. Nothing passed my lips except for the mugs of tea.

Mr Smith came to visit me.

'What are you doing, Tomo?' he asked.

'I'm not eating, Mr Smith. I've had enough.'

'What are you trying to prove?'

'That I shouldn't be here.'

Later that same day, I had a visit from Mr Greenwood Jones, my English teacher. 'Don't do this,' he said. 'You'll damage your kidneys and who knows what else.'

'I have no option.'

'Yes, you have. Give it up.'

From then on I had regular visits from people trying to talk me around, including the Methodist priest, Salvation Army chaplain and the Assistant Governor.

The cell door was locked every night and opened in the morning so I could slop out. The door had a hinged flap with a latch, which allowed the guards to check on me.

One night, just after supper had been untouched, the latch opened and a newspaper was shoved inside. It was a godsend. I scoured every column inch, desperate to combat the boredom. There were stories about our hunger strike and delegates at the TUC conference had called for our immediate release. In other news Liverpool were through to the semi-final of the Cup. Things were looking up.

The next night another newspaper came through the latch. I couldn't get to the door quickly enough to see who it was. I wanted to say thank you.

It took a couple of weeks, but I finally caught him. It was the same hospital orderly who had threatened to shove a greased tube down my throat. Bless him.

I had stopped being hungry after the first few days. Mind over matter. I can understand how Bobby Sands, the IRA hunger striker, managed to starve himself to death in 1981. If you don't feel hungry, you don't have to eat.

At one point the doctor came in and said, 'You may as well tuck in; Warren has been eating for the last three days.'

He had told Dezzie the same thing. Neither of us believed him.

By day fourteen, my weight had fallen to 162 lbs. I tried not to think about what was happening to my body. The doctor enjoyed telling me how my digestive acids would eat through my stomach lining and my kidneys would suffer.

There were noises outside my cell at teatime. Directly opposite me, a little chap was being held in what looked like a padded room. He was dressed in special pyjamas, like a silver judo suit, and didn't have a proper bed. Every so often he lost the plot and started screaming the place down, ranting and raving about the Communists trying to kill him. He was Hungarian. God knows what he'd been through.

Next minute the doctor came running, along with the orderlies. They held him down and gave him a sedative. To their credit, they were very gentle with him.

Saturday 16 March
A visit from Mia. She looked great. She didn't bring the children with her – the round trip was too far for them.

Mia was a bit upset about the hunger strike, but she didn't try to talk me out of it.

John Carpenter drove her up. He told me about the demonstrations and rallies. People are coming from all over the country for a march in London next

Wednesday. Some of the Scottish lads are paying £14
for the return trip. They're expecting a thousand
people.

The protest drew three times that number, according to
headlines the next day. The crowd had marched on
Parliament and managed to get a meeting with various MPs
and the Secretary of State. A committee of MPs had agreed
to investigate our circumstances.

Fearing for our health, the protestors took a vote and then
appealed for us to end the hunger strike. Later that day a
telegram arrived from the House of Commons. The Assistant
Governor already knew the contents when he brought it to me.

'You're supposed to start eating,' he said.

'No, I want to see Dezzie first.'

They let us meet in the hospital courtyard. I had a blanket
over my head with a hole in the middle like a poncho. I was
naked underneath. My hair was well past my shoulders and
my beard halfway down my chest.

Dezzie was already in the yard when I arrived. He looked
OK, although his hair was the colour of a battleship.

He took one look at me and said, 'Fucking hell, it's Ben
Gunn.'

I looked like a pirate out of *Treasure Island*.

We embraced each other and shuffled around the yard,
stretching our legs.

'So what's the story?' he asked.

'We got to come off.'

'OK, when?'

'We'll make it in forty-eight hours.'

Dezzie nodded and scratched his unshaven chin. He
stared upwards at the grey sky. 'Hey, Rick, I couldn't wish to
have done time with anybody else.'

I had to turn away to hide my eyes. It was one of the finest compliments I had ever been paid.

The prison doctor looked relieved when I told him the news. It had been twenty days since I last ate and I had long ago stopped dreaming about food. I could honestly say that I wasn't hungry.

Less than twenty-four hours before I was due to eat again, I started getting pains in my stomach. The cramps slowly grew worse until I lay doubled up and drenched in sweat. I knew something terrible had happened. What had I done to myself? At the same time I didn't want to ask for help because it meant being indebted to them.

Finally I could stand it no more. I rang the bell. The big orderly came in.

'What's the matter?'

'I want to go to the toilet, but I can't. How can I be wanting to go to the toilet? I haven't eaten anything in three weeks.'

He said something about my stomach ingesting body fat and gave me two tablets. Laxatives.

'I'm going to leave your cell door open so you can reach the lavatory. It should only take a few minutes. You'll be fine.'

Half an hour later nothing had happened. If anything the pain had become worse. I lay on the floor, clutching my stomach, rocking back and forth.

He came back. 'Have you been?'

'No.'

'Bloody hell! I'd better give you another two.'

I managed to swallow the tablets, despite the pain. It wasn't just cramp. This was complete agony. My body was slick with sweat and I shook uncontrollably.

Another half an hour passed. The orderly grew worried.

'I shouldn't do this,' he said, handing me another two tablets.

I crawled to the lavatory, but couldn't sit down. Tears ran down my cheeks as I stood, braced against the side of the cubicle. Blood leaked down my legs.

Finally it moved. One lump. It was higher than the height of the toilet. I had to break it up to flush it away.

I crawled back to bed, changed my underwear and fell asleep for eight hours. It was the longest I had slept in four months of imprisonment.

Our hunger strike ended on the twenty-second day when I ate two pieces of toast. I had lost two and a half stone in weight since the trial. I don't know how close I came to being force-fed, but I was strong enough to walk out of the hospital cell and back into the general prison. The lads gave me a huge welcome. They banged plates and mugs against the railings, sounding me in like a returning soldier.

11

Free the Shrewsbury Two!

Among the notes from the lock-up are some of my letters to Clifton and Gareth. Many have drawings of cartoon characters and little stories to go along with them. I tried to make the stories as political as possible, just like in George Orwell's Animal Farm, *because I knew the guards doing the censoring would go bonkers.*

I never told the boys about prison. Instead I wrote about working on a farm and described how I could see animals out of my window.

'Every day the farmer feeds the chickens and collects all the eggs and sends Dezzie and me some for our breakfast. And tomorrow he's going to let us take the donkey's dinner out. The donkey eats grass and drinks buckets and buckets of water . . . When I get home I'll take you and your Mum for a ride and we'll have a picnic on a farm and play a big football match . . .'

A lot of the letters are like that. I make it sound as though I was in some enchanted place, with mountains in the distance and huge fish in the rivers just waiting to be caught. I also promised wonderful presents when I finally came home.

The cartoons were drawn by a little fella called Royston Dowd, who was a brilliant artist. We shared a cell for a while in Leicester Jail. Royston was a hermaphrodite, with women's tits and a baby's nudger. He was only tiny, almost bald, with glasses, and he was always running down to the showers when the blokes were washing.

Despite what you might think, Roy was fine in jail. Ultimately, he became the 'wife' of a real hard case, doing his ironing and fetching his meals.

He happily took the piss out of himself and whenever 'God Save the Queen' came on the radio or TV he would stand up and wave.

There was this real handsome young lad who had spent most of his life in borstal. Roy took a real shine to him because this young fella had the biggest nudger I have ever seen in my life. It was bloody unfair. He obviously had my share and someone else's as well.

Roy's eyes used to light up every time this kid went for a shower. He flirted outrageously with him, making the lad nervous as hell.

At about half past nine every night, this kid would bring in a bucket of tea from cell to cell and we'd dip our tin mugs into it. I always put a couple of spoonfuls of cocoa in the bottom of my cup because it made the tea taste better.

Roy and me were sharing a cell by this stage and every night without fail, when the door swung open, Roy would be bent over, spreading his arse. The young lad would go mad.

Finally one night he lost his cool and threw a whole bucket of tea over Roy, scalding his tender bits. He spent the next week walking around like John Wayne.

While lawyers continued lodging objections and appeals, the union rank and file maintained their rage. A demonstration was organised outside Stafford Prison to 'Free the Shrewsbury Two'. The Governor cancelled all staff leave, which made me about as popular as footrot with the screws. I didn't blame them.

Some forms of their victimisation were subtler than others. Prisoners taking educational classes were normally allowed to have the cell light on for an extra half an hour. Mine was always turned off. Either that or the screws would come and get me an hour late so I missed entire classes.

In the machine shop no matter how many hours I grafted, I was always the lowest paid bloke. This one week, I worked my bollocks off and the overseer gave me 37p.

'Can you check your figures?' I asked.

'No.'

'Can I see them?'

'No.'

'Then I'm asking for a labour change.'

He laughed, knowing full well that my request would be denied.

The conditions in the workshops were appalling, with no windows or ventilation or toilets. Anyone who complained was put on report and lost remission time. The same thing happened if anyone criticised the food. The Governor was supposed to 'test' the food every day and sign a consent form. I seriously doubt if one morsel passed his lips, particularly given the personal hygiene of some of the people serving the meals. It reminded me of a workhouse in a Dickens novel.

I came down for tea one Sunday night, all the way from the third landing, and stood in the queue and when it got to my turn I felt sick.

'I'm not eating that,' I said. 'Look at it.' The pork chops were encased in grease and full of gristle.

The whole wing stopped. Nobody took a step forward.

'C'mon, move along,' said the prison officer on duty. He wore chef's trousers and a white half coat, with a screw's hat. I didn't budge. No one moved. One of the screws went to find an assistant governor, Mr Turnbull.

'What's the matter, Tomlinson?'

'I'm not eating this shit.'

'What's wrong with it?'

'Look at it.'

'If you've no appetite, you can move along.'

'I wouldn't feed that to a dog. Look at them chops – you can't see the meat for the grease. The spuds are full of eyes and the cabbage isn't cooked.'

At that moment the dopey prison officer in the chef's trousers reached down, put his hand in the mashed potato and then into his mouth. A moment too late he realised his mistake. He had just broken every rule of prison hygiene – including the unwritten one that no prisoner was going to eat something a screw had shoved his hands in.

I looked at Turnbull and he looked at me. We both knew what it meant.

'All right, I want you back in your cells,' he said.

'What about our tea?'

'It'll be sorted out.'

He ordered the prison canteen to prepare hundreds of cold meals – proper salads with a nice bit of chicken, crisp lettuce, eggs and fresh bread rolls. They were brought across the yard on trolleys, twenty meals at a time, and distributed to the cells. It was one of the best meals I had eaten at Her Majesty's pleasure.

Late that night, when the lights were out and most of the cons were sleeping, I had a visitor in my cell. The Governor arrived, wearing his trousers over his pyjamas.

'I have a favour to ask you, Tomlinson,' he said.

'What's that?'

'Give me my prison back.'

'I don't have your prison.'

'You know what I mean.'

He left quietly, having delivered his message. Right from the beginning he had marked me down as an agitator, who would 'unionise' the men and cause trouble. Now he believed he had the evidence.

I hadn't asked anyone to support me in the canteen. Nothing had been organised or prearranged. I simply stood my ground. Others chose to stand with me.

From then on the authorities tried even harder to keep Dezzie and me apart. Our only means of communication was by passing letters at church, via other inmates.

I could put up with a lot of aggravation, but sometimes the pettiness and vindictiveness pushed me over the edge. Chatting to a con one day, who had a message from Dezzie, I suddenly felt a screw nudge me in the back.

'Move along, Tomlinson,' he said.

I just exploded. 'Is mine the only name you know?' I screamed.

This triggered a stand-up row, with all the other cons stopping to watch. Another screw jumped in and started slagging me.

'Can't your mate defend himself?' I asked.

The cons all laughed, but this only made things worse. I knew they were going to put me on report, but I didn't care. I was sick of their games and petty regulations.

A formal charge was delivered to my cell.

NOTICE OF REPORT

Name: Eric Tomlinson
Prisoner Number: 573143.

A report has been made against you by officer Mr Butcher that at 1300 hours on 24 March 1974, you committed an offence under paragraph 18 of rule 47 – i.e. refused to leave G dormitory to proceed to your place of work when ordered to do so.

Your case will be dealt with at adjudication

tomorrow where you will be given every opportunity
to make your defence. If you wish to reply to the
charge in writing you may do so on the back of this
form.

I retaliated with my own complaint against the prison
officer. Mr Smith counselled me against it. By morning there
would be a dozen screws swearing blind they witnessed
everything. I had no chance of winning and risked a worse
punishment.

The following morning I stood in the Governor's office,
with my arms behind my back. I explained that certain prison
officers were victimising me. My mail was being delayed or
not delivered at all. Rapists, blackmailers and child
molesters could talk freely with each other, but I wasn't
allowed to speak to Dezzie.

The Governor half cautioned and half threatened me that
it was a serious offence to slander prison officers. He then
described how the dispute process worked, binding me up in
red tape.

'There are other issues,' I said. 'The toilets are filthy and
there's never enough hot water. There are no brushes to clean
the dirty chamber pots. I have to use my own bloody nailbrush.
The underwear we get issued by the laundry is stained with
excrement and God knows what else. The workshops are like
bloody iceboxes with bare concrete floors . . .'

Halfway through I realised there was no point in
continuing. The Governor had not conceded a single point.
This was like a battle of wills and he wasn't budging an inch.

OK, well two could play at that game. From that moment
I made a conscious decision that things would be different. In
trade union terminology, it was 'work to rule' – I would give
them respect, but nothing more.

From then on I never once shut my own cell door. Screws would shout up from below, 'Shut the door, Ricky.'

I'd say, 'You know I can't do that.'

I made them climb three flights of stairs and shut it for me.

In the workshop, I agitated for bonuses and better conditions. All along they had feared I was going to unionise the prisoners; why should I disappoint them?

If anything, Dezzie was doing it even tougher. He was two-up in a cell with a fella who didn't wash. He also wasn't sleeping well and had health problems. The major difference between the two of us was that Dezzie had always been intense and dour. The injustice of his imprisonment ate away at his guts like an ulcer. By comparison, I let my sense of humour keep me sane. I laughed like a drain and I never got tired of my own company.

Without the same safety valve, Dezzie swallowed the liquid cosh every night, hoping to sleep his sentence away. Ultimately, I believe this is what harmed his health – all those sedatives washing around in his system.

In May 1974 the authorities grew sick of trying to break us and decided instead to try and bribe us. Dezzie and me were transferred to an open prison, HM Sudbury, in Derbyshire.

This was the soft end of the prison system, totally different from a closed nick. There were no armed robbers, sex offenders or violent criminals. Instead it was full of white-collar crims: bent lawyers, corrupt public servants and Jeffrey Archer types. The class system is alive and well, operating at an open prison near you.

Rather than being locked in cells, the accommodation in Sudbury consisted of long Nissan huts with about ten beds lined up along each side in dormitory style. Old-fashioned coal stoves kept the huts warm in winter and there were rooms off each end for the bathroom and toilets.

There were no high walls or razor wire fences. Open countryside surrounded the prison. And instead of being locked up twenty-three hours a day, we could wander about, playing football and cricket or using the gymnasium.

Although we had come from different ends of the political spectrum, Dezzie and me were both working class and the same sort of things made us laugh and moved us to tears. I enjoyed his company and would have trusted him with my life.

Dezzie truly believed that the trade union movement would get us out of jail, but I didn't share his confidence. I knew that we had been abandoned. The union leadership wanted us to go away. We were an embarrassment. More importantly, we were proof of their weakness and gutlessness.

The Labour Party had narrowly won office as a minority Government in February 1974. Surely this would make a difference. A lot of Labour MPs had expressed support for us and were putting pressure on the Government to intervene.

The decision to send us to Sudbury was possibly evidence of this. Roy Jenkins, the new Home Secretary, had approved the transfer. Unfortunately, nothing could be done to alter the outcome of our appeal or the Judges hearing the case.

Because of the large number of transcripts involved and the complexity of the case, the judgement wasn't expected until at least October 1974. In the meantime our lawyers had made yet another bail application.

Sudbury, Derbyshire
Dear Mia,
    Thank you for the two letters you sent this week
they were superb. I need those little happy letters
like an addict needs his opium or cocaine. The
human warmth in them chases away the sadness,

drabness and despondency that thrives in this place.

We had a nice surprise this week – a new book all about trade unions is being published. It is called *Spanner Bright* and the author has sent Dezzie and me autographed copies. It will add nicely to the collection of material I want to put together for the boys so they'll be able to read for themselves what really happened in 1972 and understand why we had to make a stand rather than accept 'the deal' by the prosecution.

Tonight on the radio I have been listening to a recording of Pablo Casals, the world's greatest cello player. The music is fantastic, really beautiful. I wonder if Clifton or Gareth will be interested in the classics. I hope so. So much depth of feeling. It's a funny cruel world when you stop to think. Even today I never associate anything nice or beautiful with the working classes, be it music, good books or poetry. There is still that feeling that it is too good for the masses. I look forward to the day when this will no longer be the case.

I often daydream about what the boys will do when they're grown up. I have all sorts of ideas and hopes for them. Plans and expectations have a funny habit, however, of stopping them making their own way in the world. Anyway, whatever they decide to do, at least they'll have a better start than I had . . .

Goodbye my queen.

Love Rick.

Marlene had been my rock. She had stood by me through the trial and imprisonment, never questioning me or asking me to sacrifice my principles.

A lot of the other guys had pictures of their kids all over their walls, but I always put mine away. I didn't want to be reminded of what I was missing. Time passed slowly enough already.

At one point Marlene sent me some new snapshots but the screws withheld them.

'There's a limit of two personal photographs,' I was told.

'What do you mean? There are guys here with dozens of pictures of girlfriends, wives, kids, families . . .'

'You're only allowed to have two. That's the rule,' said the screw, who was the spitting image of Charles Hawtrey.

I knew he was making trouble. What other explanation could there be?

'I want them photographs of me lads,' I said, unable to hide my anger.

'Are you threatening me?'

'No, I'm just telling you.'

He laughed and walked away.

Every Sunday morning at Sudbury the Governor came round for an inspection and we had to stand at our bunks, dressed in clean gear, with polished shoes and wearing the prison tie.

This time when he walked along the rows of men he did a double take when he reached me. I was standing at attention, wearing only a prison tie and a pair of Y-fronts.

He looked me up and down. 'No shirt, Tomlinson?'

'Oh, yeah, I got plenty in me locker.'

'I'll be back at four o'clock to see you dressed.'

'No, I won't be dressed.'

'You will.'

'No, I won't. Not unless I get me photos.'

The Governor's face turned pink and he marched out. The senior screw, a little weasel of a man with metal-framed glasses, pushed his face close to mine.

'Four o'clock we're coming,' he said.

'Oh, aye, and when you come back at four o'clock I'll be wearing nothing but a plastic flower tied to me nudger.'

'Why's that?'

'Because I want me bloody photographs.'

The Governor didn't come back. Within an hour I had my snapshots, which I looked at fondly and then put away under my bed.

The cottage in Coedpoeth needed a lot of work and some of my mates from the building trade like Tony Ledgerton, Peter Murtach, Lol Grace and Roger Mullen got together and started fixing up the place. Doors had to be cut to bastard sizes because the roof sloped and the electrics had to be re-wired. They built a staircase and replaced some of the windows.

Marlene gave me updates of the work in her letters and brought me a copy of the plans so I could toss in some ideas. While the work was underway she moved out of the cottage to a rented house in Plas Madoc.

Dezzie and I were back in solitary when I heard a morning news bulletin on the radio. Overnight a house in Plas Madoc had burnt down and two young boys had died. I felt my guts drop out.

At that moment I heard the door open at the end of the hut and footsteps approaching. I had never been so frightened in my life. They were coming to tell me that Gareth and Clifton were dead. I was sure of it. The footsteps stopped outside the cell. I looked up at the chief screw. He had brought me a newspaper – a rare act of kindness.

I told him about the fire and he offered to make a phone call, just to make sure the boys were safe. I will always be grateful for that.

*

The communal huts at Sudbury had a more relaxed atmosphere than most prisons because you didn't have to worry about gangs or bullies or turf wars. These were gentleman thieves or small-timers, rather than hardened crims.

Ironically, I even met a couple of fellas who had been hired by building employers to break the 1972 strike. They were part of an unofficial anti-picket force, which the prosecution at our trial claimed didn't exist. These lads had been paid a pittance to break the strike and the blood money was never enough to feed their families so they took to stealing and finished up inside.

In the bed next to me was a disgraced detective from the northeast called Bennett. He was serving three years for becoming a little too friendly with a few of the local hookers. Instead of arresting them, he ran a scam where the girls picked up clients and Bennett burst in on them and blackmailed punters instead of charging them.

He used to follow Dezzie and me around like a puppy. I don't know if he was spying on us or not, but we were careful about talking in front of him.

The most pampered cons at Sudbury were two senior public servants, who had worked for a large city council and taken bribes when handing out contracts worth millions of pounds. One of them was a right little shite. He'd been given the job of the prison postboy and walked around with this bag over his shoulder delivering the mail. He had his own chequebook and had the screws doing his bidding because he could pay for anything he wanted. The other guy seemed like a reasonable bloke and we had some good discussions about politics and religion.

Another prisoner, who we christened 'Unicorn', had only a strip of hair on the back of his head, pulled forward to look like a horn. The rest of his scalp was totally bare.

I asked him one day what had happened and he described living in a caravan park when a fire broke out in the neighbouring van. There were two toddlers inside so he opened the door and ran through the smoke until he found these kids. As he carried them out, a piece of the plastic ceiling melted and dropped on his head. He ripped off the molten plastic, but his hair came with it, leaving him permanently scarred.

Unicorn was a smashing lad. He wasn't angry or bitter about what had happened. 'The main thing was the kids were OK,' he said.

'How did you finish up in here?' I asked.

I expected the usual hard luck story. Every second fella in jail claimed to be innocent. Unicorn was different. He described how he and his brother-in-law decided to rob a building site because they were sick of having no money. The payroll was delivered on a Thursday afternoon by armoured van and the clerk spent all evening making up the pay packets. These were kept in the office safe overnight, before being handed out on Friday.

The lads broke into the office with some welding gear, including a huge acetylene bottle that took two of them to carry. Taking turns they began burning the handle off the safe, but every time they made a cut the metal would melt and fill up the hole. This went on for hours.

'Shhhh,' said his brother-in-law. Out the window they saw headlights coming towards them. They waited ten minutes but the headlights were still getting closer. They figured they should wait it out, rather than try to sneak out under the glare of the lights.

As the hours ticked by, they fell asleep. The police found them in the morning, snoozing peacefully, both looking like Al Jolson with blacked-up faces. The light outside the window had been a canal barge.

I cried with laughter when Unicorn told me this story. Most people would have been too embarrassed, but he didn't care. Some of the other stories I heard were fantasy league stuff, like guys claiming they had a million pounds stashed away, waiting for them when they came out. I met more millionaires in jail than on the outside.

Unicorn said to me one day, 'I'm off tonight. I'm getting out of here.'

'Oh yeah,' I thought. I didn't believe him.

He had his supper and the next thing he was off across the fields. All the screws were chasing him, but he was far too quick. I don't know what happened to him after that, but I hope he finished up OK.

The appeals process was taking so long that the Judges finally granted us bail on 3 June 1974. We were free men, at least for a few months and hopefully for good.

I walked out of HM Sudbury on a lovely sunny day, eager to get home. Billy Burns, a mate, came to pick me up and drive me back to North Wales. Marlene had been visiting me once a month, but I had barely seen the boys since Christmas. Now I wanted to make it up to them.

Clifton came barrelling up the front path and almost bowled me over. Gareth was more circumspect, trying to work out where he'd seen this big hairy bloke before.

There were celebrations in Wales and Liverpool. Anyone would have thought I'd been pardoned. Mam fussed over me like the prodigal son and vowed to feed me up. She was in her mid-fifties and still living in Elmore Street. Albert was on the building sites and Ronny worked for a bookmaker. David had always done his own thing. All were married by then and had their own families.

I had visions of doing lots of stuff with Clifton and Gareth, catching up for lost time, but our financial situation changed these plans. Marlene had been surviving on donations and charity, but now I needed to find a job.

My solicitor wrote to me on 8 July:

Dear Ricky,
    You will know how delighted I was at the outcome of the bail application. I feel sure that Mr McHale will have given you sober warning of what might happen in October (with the appeal) . . . May I plead with you as I have done with Des to keep out of trouble between now and then . . .

Mackie had served his sentence and been released, which left only Dezzie and me. We had become known as 'the Shrewsbury Two', but this notoriety didn't translate into job offers. The opposite happened. Local employers wanted nothing to do with us and a lot of the big construction companies had put us on a blacklist.

The C&A department store in Liverpool was being refurbished and Tony Ledgerton was a shop steward on the site. Using false names he managed to get us hired as joiners' labourers. It meant travelling fifty miles to work each day, but at least I could feed my family.

Over the next few months I bumped into a lot of people who shook my hand and wished me luck. Even some of the scabs who had fled from the sites that we picketed offered me words of support. One of them, a bricklayer, picked me up when I was hitchhiking home from work one day and ran me right to the front door of the cottage.

Like me, Dezzie had bought a little cottage that needed renovating. I spent a few weekends in Hennlan, North Wales, helping him lay the floor and plaster the walls and ceilings.

This one particular Saturday, Dezzie had hired an electric cement mixer and had sand and cement delivered to the cottage. He had the task of mixing while I laid the cement screed, ready for the tiler.

After plugging in the mixer, he followed instructions and mixed rough sand and cement.

'Tip it just there,' I said.

He lifted the mixer but couldn't take the weight. It toppled over, still spinning round and round. We sat on the floor laughing helplessly. The job should have taken us only four hours, but instead took all day because we were both so unfit.

During the week I had to be up and out of the cottage by half six in the morning and often I wouldn't be home until the lads were in bed. Most husbands and fathers were in the same boat.

As the months went by, I stopped thinking about the appeal and what the Judges might decide. A part of me thought that whatever happened the ridiculously harsh sentences would be shortened or waived. We were more trouble than we were worth.

At the same time I couldn't shake the sense that it was far from over. Dezzie still believed the trade union movement would rise up, destroy our enemies and carry us to freedom. He had complete and utter faith in this despite the fact that UCATT had published a leaflet after the trial disowning the Shrewsbury pickets and trying to justify why it refused to grant us legal aid.

UCATT admitted the prosecutions had been politically motivated, but argued that the trial at Shrewsbury had not been an attack on picketing in general. Swallowing entirely the lies and exaggerations of the prosecution, it said that no trade union 'could support its members committing acts which are obviously of a criminal nature and which are contrary to the union's instructions'.

Trying to appease the rank and file, the union described the jail sentences as 'excessively harsh' and made all sorts of noises about appealing to the Home Secretary and setting up a hardship fund for our families. Bollocks! Why would anyone trust them?

After five months of freedom, a telegram arrived:

Eric Tomlinson,
Surrender bail 9.45 a.m. Thursday 24 October, 1974.
Court 4. Court sitting at 10 a.m.
                    Registrar of Criminal Court of Appeal.

The Criminal Court of Appeal had reviewed the transcripts and studied the legal arguments. Now I was going to discover if I had been punished enough, punished unfairly or was being sent back to prison.

A lot of the evidence against us had been discredited and even Conservative commentators, like the former Home Secretary Robert Carr, thought our sentences had been harsh. Responding to a question by Germaine Greer on *Question Time*, he said the Shrewsbury pickets deserved to be convicted but he thought the sentences 'should have only been six months'.

Sitting next to Dezzie I listened to the Judges outline their decision. It was accepted that the trial Judge had exaggerated in his summing-up to the jury when he painted a picture of a nation on the verge of anarchy during the building strike. The charges of affray could not be justified by the evidence and were quashed.

In the next breath the conspiracy charges were upheld, along with the sentences. Leave to appeal to the House of Lords was refused. We were going back to jail.

The decision seemed especially cruel. Having reorientated myself with freedom and having got to know my children again, I now faced another sixteen months in jail and Dezzie another two years.

The Tory establishment had done itself a disservice. It had shown its anger and vented its spleen by making our sentences too harsh. If they had given us six months each the issue would have died away. We would have been in and out before there could have been any public outcry or campaign. Now they were really asking for trouble.

12

The Ragged Trousered Philanthropists

The light mist looks like falling silver tinsel in front of the lights and the technicians are scrambling to cover the cameras. That's the problem with filming in Liverpool. You can never guarantee the weather.

We're doing the final episode of Nice Guy Eddie, *a BBC series. I play this overworked, underpaid private investigator, Eddie McMullen, who has five domineering women in his life – a mother, a wife and three daughters.*

Eddie isn't an Inspector Morse or another Frost. He's a complete one-off; a fat, affable gumshoe, doing dog-eared work like serving writs, chasing unpaid bills and checking up on straying partners. After the pilot episode one critic described him as having the physique of a bag of builder's gravel and a nose like the last satsuma in the bowl. That sounds like me.

This is the first time that a TV series has been written completely around me, which is very flattering, but also pretty daunting. I really want to get things right.

I can't bear to hear actors moaning about wanting to get home because the day's shoot has overrun. In the building game we sometimes laid floors from eight in the morning until 6 a.m. the next day. Acting is a piece of piss compared to that.

In the film and TV industry you get treated like a lord. Someone picks you up and takes you to work. Someone takes you home. If it's cold someone is standing by with a blanket or an overcoat.

Mostly we're filming around the dock area, over in Birkenhead and on the ferries – the usual places that people associate with Liverpool – but there's a lot more besides that. I thought I knew everyone in Liverpool, but Tom Harnick, the location finder, knows more people and more places. He rooted out some incredible locations, good, bad and ugly.

A lot of the storylines of Nice Guy Eddie *are true. Tony Smith, a private eye and former policeman, is the technical adviser. And one of the writers, Johanne McAndrews, is a Scouser with an amazing ear for dialogue.*

Every time I do one of these location shoots, they hire me a massive Winebago with a kitchen, a double bed and a lounge. But they can't guarantee me the same Winebago two days in a row, which means I have to pack things up each day. That's why I've brought my own this time. It's a motor home that once belonged to Geoff Hughes (who used to be Eddie Yates in Coronation Street*). I've christened it the 'Minibago' because it's smaller. Each morning Albert picks me up from home and we drive to the set. Then we plug it in, get the kettle on and I'm happy as a sandboy.*

Last week we filmed a big boxing scene at the Adelphi Hotel. Needing lots of extras, I called in my old mates and even Rita got to dress up for the cameras. Out of ninety-odd people in the scene, I must have known half of them.

Another scene could have been taken straight out of my life. Eddie's Mam gets a gob on because he promised to come round and fix her boiler. A few years back when I won the Comedy Actor of the Year award, I rang Mam from London and told her how I'd just beaten Paul Whitehouse and James Nesbitt, two guys I really admired.

She considered this for perhaps half a second and then said, 'Oh, aye, so when are you coming round to fix my leaking tap?'

There's no chance of getting above yourself in this family.

Clifton didn't ask for me at first. He held it all back until about a week after I went back to prison. Then he started wetting the bed for the first time in years. Gareth would run to the front door of the cottage whenever he heard someone coming, expecting it to be me.

Marlene decided not to bring them to visit . . . not for a while at least. The separation had been painful enough already.

The appeal decision caused another wave of protests across the country. A thousand building workers walked off the job in Liverpool, as well as six hundred in London and a similar number in Manchester. Labour MPs like Dennis Skinner were asking questions in Parliament, putting pressure on the Home Secretary Roy Jenkins. Labour had consolidated power with a second general election win in October 1974, but this only succeeded in raising Dezzie's hopes of a pardon.

As before, we made a conscious decision that we weren't going to soldier. We refused to do shifts in the workshops or to close doors or to make our beds. Why should we make their lives any easier? Once you did that you became institutionalised.

The next step was to refuse to wear clothes at all. I took them off and dropped them in a pile on the floor. A screw came along and ordered me to get dressed. I refused. He sent for a more senior prison officer, who then sent for the Assistant Governor. Word passed right up the chain of command, but it made no difference. Dezzie had done the same thing and we were both threatened with lost remission time.

So be it. I didn't care if I served every single day of my sentence. They could do what they wanted, but I wasn't soldiering. I shouldn't have been there. I had done nothing wrong.

Without clothes we couldn't be left with the general prison population or allowed to have any visits. We were put into solitary confinement at Sudbury until the Governor could decide what to do.

His first decision was to send us back to HM Stafford, handcuffed in the back of a van. Again we were taken to the segregation cells, which were beginning to feel like a home away from home.

Dezzie was two cells away but we could still talk to each other. There was a four-inch pipe running between the cells, which must have been part of the hot water system. By speaking directly into the pipe we could hear each other clear as a bell. Some nights I'd be crying with laughter at some of the stories we told each other.

They tried everything to force us into clothes. First thing of a morning the screws would drag out the mattress, table and chair, leaving the cell completely bare. Then they threw a bucket of water on the floor so we had to sit on cold, wet concrete all day. The bedding wouldn't come back until six in the evening.

We were dragged up on charges for ridiculous things like insubordination, answering a screw back, or being late for something. Breathing would have been enough.

The routine was always the same. I marched into the Governor's office, still naked, flanked by two prison officers.

'Name?'

'Tomlinson.'

'Number?'

'Can't remember.'

He went fucking mad because he had to look up my number.

'OK, you're 573143.'

'Yes.'

'You'll remember it next time.'

'Of course.'

'What is the number?'

'I can't remember.'

They almost had to peel him off the ceiling. The charges system was supposed to keep prisoners in line, but mostly it was a joke. The screws could make up any story they wanted.

One morning Dezzie said something to one of them, who immediately bellowed, 'Right, Warren, Governor's office.'

'Fuck off!' said Dezzie.

'You're up before the Governor.'

'Fuck off!'

Nothing happened. He simply refused to go. I thought for a while they might muscle up and physically carry him to the administration wing, but instead they left him alone.

Next morning, Dezzie heard the key in the lock. The door swung open and there was the prison Governor, sitting at his desk. They had carried the desk into solitary and set it up outside Dezzie's cell door, hard against the brickwork. I had tears running down my face when he told me the story down the pipe.

In the early days they wouldn't let me have a radio in solitary and I had to write my diary on toilet paper. Later they relented and let me have a pen and proper paper.

Mr Smith, my favourite prison officer, came knocking at my cell door one evening.

'Can you do us a favour, Rick, and help this lad out?'

There was a young Scot who wanted to write a letter to his wife, but he couldn't read or write. He was embarrassed but relieved that someone could help him.

From then on it became a regular thing. Fellas would come to me with their letters – either to read them or write them. A lot of them were Scots, who were hard as nails and always getting into fights with each other.

One day this big gruff Glaswegian came in. 'Will you do us a letter, Rick?'

'Yeah, OK. Who is it to?'

'Ma wife.' His accent was so broad I had to listen hard to understand what he was saying.

'What's your wife's name?'

'Marie.'

OK.

'Have you got any kids?'

'Yeah. I got two wee girls.'

OK.

'How long have you been in now?'

'Six months.'

OK. So I started off.

Dear Marie,

    This six months away from you has been the longest six months of my life. I didn't realise what I had until I hadn't got it any more. I miss being there with you. I miss seeing the kids, kissing them goodnight. I know I haven't been the best husband in the world. I am going to try to change because I don't want to hurt you any more . . .

It was me! I was writing the same things that I wrote to Marlene. Finally, as I reached the end, I asked, 'Do you want me to say, "Love and kisses" or "Love and miss you"?'

This Glaswegian grabbed me by the throat, lifted me off the floor and pinned me against the wall.

'Are you being fucking funny?' he growled.

'How do you mean?'

'Are you taking the piss?'

'What do you mean?'

I suddenly realised that he couldn't say the words. He had never used words like 'love' and 'kisses' before.

'Don't you love your wife?' I asked.

'Aye.'

'Don't you want to hug your kids?'

'Sure.'

'Well, why don't you say so?'

He couldn't look at me.

'Well, I think it's about time. Whether you like it or not, I'm putting it down. They need to be told.'

A fortnight later he came back to me with the reply from his wife. He wanted me to read it to him.

She had written:

I cried when I read your letter. Those things you said
were lovely. Let's see if we can make a new start
when you come out. I've always said I loved you.
Now I know you love me too . . .

The big fella was choking back tears, but I knew not to look at him otherwise he would have had to kill me.

'OK, there you go,' I said, still not looking at his face.

'Aye. Good.'

I found it sad that these big tough men couldn't say they loved their wives and girlfriends. I didn't expect them to cry – not floods of tears anyway.

Like me they had learned to bottle up their sadness and cry on the inside, because you can't afford to show any sign of weakness in prison.

Some of the letters I read were heartbreaking. I told lads

that their wives were divorcing them or their girlfriends had run off with someone else. I felt their pain. Getting out and being reunited with loved ones was the incentive that kept most cons from going crazy.

Although separated from the main prison population, I still managed to make friends. A black fella called 'Tall Boy' used to give haircuts to the prisoners and he would come down to the segregation cells and collect me. I got to sit in the queue for an hour, chatting to other cons. When it came to my turn he'd say, 'That's it for today, Rick. I'll have to do you tomorrow.'

The next day he would come down and get me out again.

Tall Boy was in for drug offences and he said to me one day, 'How about we go into business when we get out of here?'

'What do you mean?'

'Well, I know all the users in my neighbourhood. I'll sell them the gear and then you'll walk in and pretend you're a detective and take it back off them. We can sell the same stuff over and over.'

He was dead serious and couldn't understand why the idea didn't appeal to me.

Although people looked out for themselves in prison, there were still examples of charity and kindness. One of the Scots guys who worked in the kitchens asked me if I had any tobacco. I told him I didn't smoke, but I had a little bit of cash set aside and I bought him some from the prison shop.

He was made up and wanted to do something for me.

'Do you like meat?'

'Yeah, I love meat.'

'I'll get you some hot meat from the kitchen.'

'OK.'

A few days later I found a makeshift package on my bed.

Unwrapping a green towel, I discovered the biggest joint of beef I had ever set eyes on. It was enough to feed a bloody army. Now I had a problem. The joint was too big for me to eat and wouldn't fit through the window. I had nowhere to hide it, so ate as much as I could and then tore off chunks, throwing them away. It was my first decent feed in months, but I spent the next three days on the lavatory with blocked bowels.

9 February 1975
HM Leicester
Dear Mia,

As you can see from the address I have been transferred to Leicester. I was moved on Tuesday shortly after sending you my last letter. I am settling in OK if that's possible. I don't know for sure where Dezzie is. The radio said he was in Lincoln but I think he went to Liverpool.

They're determined to split us up, hoping to divide and conquer, but it won't happen . . . I'm still refusing to wear prison clothes. The only sad part about this is that I won't be able to see you or the boys until my sentence is completed . . .

I got your photographs with me so I'm not so lonely. I look at them whenever I'm a little down in the dumps and it cheers me up . . . Have you had any luck with getting Clifton into school? Write and let me know. Please write as often as you can. Anything to help pass the time . . .

It made a big difference being split up from Dezzie. Even though we'd been in solitary for nearly three months we were still 'together', supporting each other.

Now I had to rely on second-hand information to find out

how he was doing. Elsa wrote to me a few times and said that Dezzie was also missing our chats through 'the hole in the wall'.

Leicester Prison was another nineteenth-century jail, dirty, overcrowded and crawling with vermin (and I'm not talking about the cons). It has the highest prison walls in the country and a facade like the battlements of a medieval castle.

It was supposed to house about 220 prisoners but more than 300 were crammed into the same space, usually two-up or three-up in a cell. The one advantage of my clothing protest was that it guaranteed me a cell to myself, even if it was back in solitary.

John McVicar, the armed robber who was tagged public enemy number one by Scotland Yard during the sixties, was in Leicester. I used also to see Harry Roberts, a notorious cop killer, who shot three unarmed officers in a quiet street in Shepherd's Bush in 1965. Roberts used to play lawn tennis with a few of the real hard cases. Meanwhile, McVicar would sit with his back to the railings, only ever wearing a pair of shorts, always reading something. None of these guys ever had to work and they seemed to be able to wear whatever clothes they wanted.

The cell next to me was occupied by Mick King, a fairground fighter who hit people first and asked questions when they were unconscious.

Now and then, Eddie Clayton, one of the nicer screws, would open our cell doors and let us play chess. I wasn't very good at the game, but Mick was even worse.

The games went something like this. Mick would make a move and take his finger off the piece. I then reached over and took his queen, at which point he grabbed my hand and crushed it in his fist.

'I hadn't took me finger off,' he growled.

'OK, Mick, sorry, I thought you had. Carry on.'

Eventually, Mick won the game, sometimes without losing a piece.

Because I refused to wear clothes, I couldn't go and collect my food from the canteen. Mick would go for me, bringing back a meal on a tray. One morning he came down and hurled the tray across my cell sending sausages rolling everywhere.

'What's the matter with you?'

'You're a fucking nonce, you!'

'*Me?*'

'Yeah, you! Buttons just told us what you're in for . . . interfering with young girls.'

'That's rubbish.'

'Well, that's what he said.'

I had never met this Buttons, but I discovered that he worked in the kitchens.

'Don't bother bringing me dinner down,' I told Mick. 'I'm going up for it.'

Then I went to Eddie Clayton. 'Can I have me prison clothes? I'm going up for tea.'

He looked surprised and pleased. I think he figured I'd given up on the protest. That evening, I walked into the canteen and took my place in the queue.

All the food was in metal trays and saucepans. The screw on duty was a Welsh guy, Taffy. He saw me coming and made himself scarce.

'Who around here is called Buttons?' I asked.

'I am,' said a guy ladling the soup.

'Are you?'

In a heartbeat, I had dropped my tray, reached across and grabbed his head. I forced it down until his nose was almost touching the scalding soup.

'My name is Ricky Tomo. I shouldn't be in here. I did nothing wrong. So why are you telling people I molest kids?'

He was blubbering, 'I'm sorry. I'm sorry.'

'You will be fucking sorry.'

'I was being stupid.'

I could feel the steam on my forearm. 'From now on you tell the truth. I'm not in here for anything to do with kids. Remember that.'

I let go of his head and he fell backwards. Then I composed myself, took off my clothes and walked back to my cell with them bundled under one arm. About two minutes later Mick came in with a tray of food. He gave me a wink and got off.

Lock up any group of men in a confined space and you're asking for trouble. And that's even before you take into account different personalities, histories and the racial element. No matter how hard I tried not to step on anyone's toes, eventually it happened.

I had a falling out with Mick, although I can't remember exactly why. As I've said, Mick only knew one way of settling a disagreement.

'I'll see you in the lavatory in the morning, Tomo,' he said.

That night I lay in bed listening to him punching the concrete wall of the adjacent cell, getting ready for the morning. Maybe he was trying to psych me out. It worked a bloody treat.

Eddie Clayton came to see me.

'Tomo, don't fucking go there.'

'I got no choice, have I? If I don't go I'm a coward and if I do go I'm gonna get pasted.'

Mick had a fearsome temper and fists like frozen legs of lamb. What could I do?

At 8 a.m. the cell doors were unlocked so we could slop

out. Mick's door was first and he strode to the toilets where he waited for me. Eddie Clayton slid open the bolt and pushed my door. He peered inside and burst out laughing.

'I hope it bloody works on him,' I said as I danced out on me toes, wearing just a pair of boxer-style underpants. I had a sock on each fist stuffed with paper to form enormous boxing gloves.

'Where's this fucking fella looking for a fight?' I said, as I danced up to Mick, looking like Jake La Motta without the muscles or the conditioning. He laughed so loud I thought he was going to swallow his tongue. Then he waved me away and by that afternoon we were playing chess again.

HM Leicester had a wonderful Governor called Norman Hill, an ex-bricklayer with hands that were gnarled and twisted from years spent on building sites. He must have been about sixty and he broke all sorts of protocol by walking about the prison on his own.

Normally the Governor travelled mob-handed with an escort of guards or the chief officer. Norman had his own set of keys and wandered around in everyday clothes. He used to drop in to solitary and we'd chat about politics and the rights and wrongs of the world.

'You shouldn't be in here,' he said to me one day.

'I know.'

'I'm not talking about solitary, I mean in prison.'

'I know what you mean.'

He was a lovely, gentle man, passionate about the working class and the difficulties we faced. He knew that I once supported the National Front and still had very right-wing views.

One day he came in and said, 'Have you read this?' He

handed me a book, *The Ragged Trousered Philanthropists* by Robert Tressell. 'They call it the building worker's bible. You should read it.'

After the first page I couldn't put it down. It tells the story of a group of builders and tradesmen in the fictional English town of Mugsborough in the early 1900s. Their working conditions are appalling, but nobody complains because they're too frightened of losing their jobs and having their families starve or finish on the street.

Tressell captures perfectly how these workers are exploited, demoralised and discarded by employers who care for nothing except profits. The book had been written in 1910, yet despite two world wars, various Labour Governments and the so-called welfare system, nothing has changed.

No other book, before or since, had such an impact upon me. I could picture the scenes Tressell had written because I had been there and seen injured workers too frightened to seek help in case they lost their jobs. And I had seen people forced on to the dole queue because an employer wanted to make the bottom line look better.

Up till then I had always held pretty right-wing views. I had grown up in a Conservative household and dabbled with the National Front. Now my politics began to change. It wasn't a Paul of Tarsus conversion; there was no blinding light on the road to Damascus. I simply began to question everything I had previously believed.

Since going to prison not a single letter of support had come from anyone from the 'right'. Yet there had been hundreds of telegrams, letters, cards and messages from people from the 'left'. They knew about my former involvement with the National Front, but didn't care.

At the same time, one of our strongest supporters had been the Socialist Workers Party – an organisation I used to attack – which had raised money, organised campaigns and helped look after my family.

Norman Hill relaxed the regulations and allowed me to see Marlene as long as I wore clothes during the visit. Sometimes she brought the boys with her. Clifton had started school and Gareth was now talking. Although they recognised me, they were always nervous at the start, clinging to Marlene's skirt and sneaking me smiles.

My admiration for Marlene had continued to grow. Apart from looking after the boys, she continued to campaign to 'Free the Shrewsbury Two'. Demonstrations and public meetings were being held around the country. Marlene spoke at many of them, as did our David, sometimes reading statements from me that had been smuggled out of jail.

Through my lawyers I made a direct appeal to the Home Secretary to exercise his prerogative for clemency. Roy Jenkins refused the application.

Marlene then wrote to him complaining about my transfers between prisons in the dead of night, without any warning.

He replied, 'I am sorry if this makes it any more difficult for you, but for the present at least your husband will have to remain in solitary because he refuses to wear prison clothes . . . It is not the usual practice of the prison authorities to notify relatives when a prisoner is transferred. This is left to the prisoner himself.'

Meanwhile, the BBC had commissioned a documentary on the Shrewsbury trial, which was sure to keep the issue in the news. At the same time Labour MPs, including the Minister for State and Industry, Eric Heffer, had called for a full-scale inquiry into the Shrewsbury pickets.

April 1975
Leicester Prison
Dear Mia,

I hope you all arrived home OK and that both Clifton and Gareth enjoyed their visit. Gareth has changed so much it took me by surprise . . .

I always feel a bit down in the dumps after seeing the kids but they both look well and they're both coming on lovely. I don't know if I'll be able to send you a birthday card. I think they have to be ordered here, I'm not sure, but I want you to buy yourself something nice and special and pretend it's from me.

Can you arrange to come on your next visit by yourself? I know it means coming by train but we haven't been able to speak to each other on our own for months. Think about it and let me know. It would be nice to have just a few minutes on our own. Before I forget, happy birthday for the thirteenth. Just remember to look after yourself and my two great boys. Don't go short of anything. Keep smiling. I'll see you soon.

Love Rick.

My protest continued. Periodically the lay prison governors would arrive to check on conditions and the welfare of prisoners. These were ordinary people from various professions, who always seemed rather intimidated by their surroundings as they inspected the cells.

'Are you sorry for what you did?' one of them asked me, as I sat naked in my cell.

'What do you think?'

They laughed and carried on.

Another day a priest visited.

'Isn't it about time you thought about your family, Rick?' he asked. 'All you have to do is say you're sorry and you can get out of here.'

'I can't do that, Father, because I haven't done anything wrong. *You* know that and *they* know that.'

The priest then told me there were seven political prisoners in British jails, including Dezzie and me. My eyes went wide. He was the first person to admit that we were political prisoners.

I began racking my brain trying to think of who the others could be. There were the Price Sisters – Irish girls who went on hunger strike. The disgraced MP John Stonehouse was also in jail, but I don't think he counted.

20 May
Leicester Prison
Dear Mia,

The weather in the past few days has been great and the sun in a place like this gives far more than just a bit of warmth, it seems to chase away the invisible gloom that is never very far away . . .

There is not a lot to report from this end. Things just keep moving along and each day they have stolen from me is a day nearer to the end of this farcical sentence. Tomorrow I am going to petition the Home Office again to be reclassified as a political prisoner. They refused my application last time, but I think certain information that has come to light must add extra weight to my arguments . . .

The time is passing slowly and every day brings my release closer, but the anger and hatred I get towards the cowards who imprisoned me grows daily. There is no way they can ever be forgiven, nor will we ever let them forget . . .

My first opportunity for parole came in June 1975. Given the amount of trouble I had caused and my failure to admit guilt or express any regret, I had a snowball's chance in hell of being released.

Ironically, one of the Sunday newspapers did a story claiming that I was a model prisoner, wearing clothes, weaving baskets and being an all-round good egg. Maybe the authorities had planted these stories so they could justify giving me parole.

I spoke to Marlene and told her that I wouldn't apologise for something I hadn't done.

'I'd rather stay here forever than give in to them.'

She didn't waver. 'Do what you think is best.'

I don't remember going in front of a parole board. The panel of experts met in some distant room and made their decision based on what they read in my file. I was summoned to the Governor's office and Norman Hill broke the news to me.

'Your parole has been refused.'

'OK.'

As I turned to leave, he said, 'Look, I can make a phone call right now and get this reversed. That's all it takes.'

'I don't want you to.'

'Don't you want to get home to your family?'

'Of course.'

'Then just say you're sorry.'

'I can't do that.'

I realised then how much they *needed* to get us out. And I'm convinced if the powers that be could have turned back the clock, they would never have brought charges against the Shrewsbury pickets. We had become a public relations nightmare – particularly for a Labour Government.

I wrote to Mia and told her the news.

I don't feel disappointed so I hope you don't. It just
means you and the boys will be going on your
holidays to Blackpool without me. Make up your
minds to have an extra special good time.

A few weeks later I had a visit from Alan Abrahams, Peter
Carter (a left-wing activist) and Billy Jones, who had all been
with me on the picket lines. Alan had become a full-time
local official with UCATT.

Having asked for my clothes, I dressed and sat across the
table from them in the visitors' room, catching up on the
latest news. I could see something was troubling Alan.
Finally he coughed up.

'You're going to have to come off the protest.'

'What do you mean?'

'We want you to come out.'

'No way.' I looked from face to face. Surely they weren't
serious. What about the truth? Our struggle?

'Dezzie isn't well. He's not sleeping and the liquid cosh is
messing up his head. His feet are bad, but they won't let him
wear surgical shoes. He can barely walk . . .'

'He should come out.'

'Yeah, but he's too proud. He won't come out while you're
still in here.'

'So what are you saying?'

'If you do the rest of your time, Dezzie won't last the
distance. He's got an extra year on you.'

I had tears in my eyes. 'I can't do it.'

Alan's voice softened to a whisper. 'We're ordering you,
Rick. This is what you have to do. It's the only chance we
have of convincing Dezzie to come out.'

It broke my heart, but I agreed. The heaviest burden was not
being able to tell Dezzie the truth. If he knew I had sacrificed

myself for him, it would have broken him completely: he was too proud.

I wrote him a letter and explained that I was coming off the protest for the sake of my family. As well as wearing prison clothes, I would start to soldier. There were tears on the page as I wrote the words.

The letter that came back was full of vitriol. Dezzie accused me of being spineless and a turncoat. I had sold out.

Although bitterly disappointed, I kept reminding myself of his failing health and how much we had been through together. If not for that, I would have stayed in jail forever. They would never have broken me. I honestly believe that.

A fortnight later I started wearing clothes and Norman Hill arranged to move me upstairs. He asked if I minded sharing a cell with Royston Dowd, the hermaphrodite who drew a lot of wonderful pictures on my letters to the boys.

Roy was the landing cleaner, which meant our cell door was left open most of the day, but I didn't take much advantage of this. Instead, I kept to myself and wrote my diary.

Walking along the landing one day, I saw a fella coming towards me with long grey hair, sallow skin, rimless spectacles and perfectly manicured fingers. We were about to pass when he stepped in front of me and kissed me on the lips. I think he expected me to push him away or give him a thump, but I pulled him towards me and kissed him back.

'How do you do? I'm Sacha de Houghton,' he said, in a beautifully rounded, upper-crust accent.

'I'm Ricky Tomo.'

'Oh, I know who *you* are,' he said, raising one eyebrow.

'How's that?'

'You're a personality, dear boy. A breath of fresh air.'

Sacha should have been talking about himself. He looked like Bamber Gascoigne with his luxuriant grey locks and we could spend hours talking about politics, art, painting and classical music. My knowledge had been newly obtained, reading books and listening to Radio 4, but Sacha had been classically educated at expensive schools and university.

'What are you in for?' I asked him one day, as we walked around the exercise yard.

'Robbery.'

'What sort?'

'The Sheriff of Nottingham, I stole all his paintings.'

Quite clearly, Sacha wasn't your ordinary, common variety con. He told me that he came from a famous Catholic family who, like the Duke of Norfolk, had supported Rome during the Reformation.

Some of the screws seemed to resent the fact that he was smarter and better educated than they were. On the landing one morning we were walking past a particularly surly screw and Sacha put on his best sergeant major voice.

'Come here, boy.'

The screw jumped to attention and took off his hat. Then he realised what he'd done and his face turned purple.

'You're charged. You're both charged,' he bleated.

Sure enough, next morning Sacha and me were outside the Governor's office waiting for our hearing. We had each filled out a form giving our version of events. An Assistant Governor chaired the hearing. I went in first and my statement was read back to me.

'Is that correct?'

'Yeah.'

'I wish to warn you, Tomlinson, that you have made malicious remarks about one of my prison officers and if these prove to be false it will increase whatever penalty I give you.'

'Yeah.'

Sacha was summoned next. The Assistant Governor looked at his statement and glanced at the screws standing on either side of him.

'What is it you're trying to say?' he asked Sacha.

'I've written it all down.'

'Yes. Well . . .'

'Aren't you supposed to read it back to me?'

The Assistant Governor looked lost. Sacha had written his entire account in Latin, which the Governor obviously couldn't read, let alone send to the Home Office. Instead he dismissed the charges, mumbling something about a misunderstanding.

'When I leave here, I'm going to America,' Sacha told me afterwards. 'I'm taking a YP (young prisoner) with me and we're going to set up an antique business. The Americans love that sort of thing.'

Jails are full of fantasists so I wasn't sure whether to believe him. I knew he'd met a handsome young lad from the YPs' block, who was also nearing the end of his sentence, but the idea of them jetting off to America and starting a new life seemed like a pipe dream.

About a month later Sacha came to me to say goodbye. I shook his hand and wished him luck. I was going to miss our discussions. Later that day I was chatting to a screw.

'What did you make of that Sacha de Houghton?' I asked.

'Oh, he's bloody mad.'

'Really? So he was just bullshitting when he said he was off to America to set up a business?'

'No, he was telling the truth,' said the screw. 'I booked the plane tickets for him.'

A buzz went round the block one day as everybody was ordered into the cells and locked away.

Roy explained breathlessly that they were bringing in a special prisoner – a real hard case called Martin Frape who had originally been sentenced to fifteen months but had been inside for eleven years.

'What did he do?'

'Tried to cut a guard's throat.'

The next day the cell door was opened so Roy could go and clean. Most of the other cons were banged away. A screw called Murphy was on duty. Martin Frape came down the stairs from the next landing. He was an ordinary-looking guy, very wiry and full of nervous energy. He asked Murphy if he could have a pillow.

'Here you are. We got plenty,' I said, handing him a pillow. Roy was always picking up extra stuff while doing the cleaning.

'And I want a po [a piss-pot],' said Frape.

'Yeah, we got a spare one of those.'

Murphy took the pot from me and threw it under the table-tennis table.

'Go and get it,' he said.

Frape's eyes bulged with a murderous look.

'Here, I'll get it for you,' I said, getting down on my hands and knees and crawling under the table.

I handed him the pot and he nodded thanks before walking away.

I looked at Murphy in disbelief. 'Why did you wind him up like that?'

He gave me one of his horrible grins. I could never understand the logic of some screws. Give them a set of keys and a uniform and the sense of power went to their heads.

Most of them had enough sense to leave Frape alone. He was allowed to wear his own clothes and given a plum job in the prison gymnasium, where he could lift weights all day.

Pretty soon Roy was doing his ironing and making his bed like a proper little wife.

Early in July 1975 I received a letter from the Home Office informing me of my release date. It was obvious they wanted me out. Despite all the time and privileges I had lost during my protest (and my refusal to say sorry) they were rushing me to freedom.

On Friday 25 July I stepped through the wicket gate of Leicester prison and became a free man. Well, not completely free – a paroled prisoner.

There were cheers and hugs of welcome. About thirty friends and family had come to greet me, including Marlene, who seemed a little overawed by all the media attention. Photographers, TV cameras and reporters jostled to get close to us.

I wore a pinstripe suit, had a bushy beard and hair tumbled over my shoulders. Next to me were Paul Foot, the left-wing journalist and commentator, along with Jim Nichol from the Socialist Workers Party and Peter Carter. There were no union officials from UCATT or the TGWU. Having abandoned us at the outset they didn't dare show their faces.

It was eight o'clock in the morning and people were eager to talk to me and shake my hand. I didn't make many decisions for myself in that first hour. Like a wheelbarrow I went where I was pushed.

'I am bitter about my conviction, but I do not consider myself a martyr,' I told the reporters. 'I was a victim of a political situation. The important thing now is to get my mate Des Warren released.'

Someone else asked if I regretted what I had done.

'No, not at all, I would do the same again.'

When asked about the conditions inside, I didn't hold back,

attacking the harassment and humiliation, the transfers to different jails, the appalling food, slave wages and demeaning jobs. At the same time, I kept focusing on Dezzie. My decision to come out would only be meaningful if I managed to get him out as well.

On the drive back to North Wales I felt mixed emotions. On the one hand I was thrilled to be going home to the cottage and the boys and my old life. Yet at the same time I realised that things had changed. I wasn't the same person who had gone to jail. My politics had changed. I was better read, better informed and better able to understand how the world worked.

The country had also changed. Now we had mass unemployment, widespread strikes, punk rock, angry students and a grocer's daughter from Grantham had started her bid for power.

I had no time to enjoy my freedom. Within days I started a whirlwind tour of the country, campaigning for Dezzie's release. I slept on floors, sofas and spare beds, speaking at meetings and marches.

I shared platforms with some wonderful speakers. Paul Foot impressed me with his wit, sharpness and the facts he had at his fingertips. He could set out the problem and the solution, while being entertaining at the same time.

Arthur Scargill was the personification of power and passion. The miners had been magnificent in supporting us, making sure Marlene and the boys didn't go hungry and even sending them on the odd holiday.

I first met Arthur at the TUC conference in Blackpool in September 1975 and have since stood alongside him at public meetings and on various picket lines. During the national miners' strike in 1984 he gave me an NUM badge that I wore proudly. Some time later, when I was in London for an audition, a homeless guy ran after me and said, 'Do us a favour. I don't want any money, but can I have that NUM badge?'

I wanted to keep it, but this guy was living in 'Cardboard City'. I gave him the badge and a few quid.

The 1975 TUC conference was a fiery affair. I went along to campaign for Dezzie and put a rocket up the trade union hierarchy for abandoning us. I watched from the gallery as Mick McGahey, the Scottish miners' leader, attacked the TUC for not doing enough. He called for a general strike to free Dezzie.

Then a spokesman for the Electricians Union, Tom Breakell, stood up and opposed the motion. He claimed that people like Dezzie and me were guilty of 'gangsterism'.

I leapt to my feet, yelling in protest.

'What do you know about Dezzie Warren? Do you know how long he's been in prison? How long has he got to stay there? When are you going to get off your fat arses and do your job?'

The place was in uproar. People wanted to hear me speak, but the members of the general council wanted me silenced. On either side of me, along the row of seats, the bouncers closed in. Crying with frustration, I kept pleading for a chance to speak. There were boos and protests from the floor. How could they do this? It was more proof of how gutless the union hierarchy had been.

They threw me out. An old guy who they bundled out with me was also crying. We sat on the front steps, weeping together.

Dezzie's health continued to deteriorate, but he refused to accept the chance of parole. I wanted to write to him and visit, but I couldn't bring myself to look into his eyes and see the disappointment. At the same time there were things happening in his private life that he knew nothing about. I couldn't have lied to him, so it was best that I stay away.

He eventually served thirty months of his three-year sentence. The authorities didn't give any warning of his release. They threw him out of the back door at midnight, so there would be no TV cameras or journalists.

Dezzie had made it clear that he didn't want to speak to me or have anything to do with me. Later he wrote a prison memoir, *The Key to My Cell*, in which he said some hurtful things, but I didn't blame him because he didn't understand what really happened.

It was more than a decade before I saw him again. I knew that Elsa had divorced him and, like me, he had struggled to get work in the building game. By then I had a little casting agency in Liverpool, providing extras for TV shows and films. Arriving at the office one morning, I found a note that had been pushed under the door.

'Dear Rick,' it said. 'Des Warren is really ill. I'm sure he'd love to see you.'

There was an address in Chester, but no telephone number. I drove over that afternoon and knocked on the back door. Someone shouted, 'Come in.'

Dezzie was lying on the floor, crippled by Parkinson's disease. His arms were permanently bent and his chin locked against his chest. He needed a big thick rope to pull himself up.

He looked at me. 'Hi ya.'

'Hi ya.' I put my arms around him.

'It's been eleven years, seven months and sixteen days since we last spoke,' he said.

I had tears in my eyes.

13

Nailing the Coffin Down

The Minibago has become a talking point on the set. All the facilities guys keep dropping round to get the guided tour. They've also taken a real shine to our Albert who is looking after me.

Practical jokes are commonplace and Albert is good for a laugh. I mention to him that the BBC drivers are normally dressed up in a jacket, white shirt, a tie and a chauffeur's hat. He goes to the wardrobe department and next morning he arrives looking like Morgan Freeman in Driving Miss Daisy.

We reach the set and Albert jumps out of the Minibago, tucks his cap under his arm and opens the door for me. All the facilities guys are dumbstruck.

Next morning he wears a full butler's uniform and delivers my tea on a silver tray. The day after he's wearing a pith helmet and a safari suit. People just fall about laughing.

Albert always has a cup of tea waiting for me when I finish a scene. One morning he leaves the lid off the electric jug and boils it dry. I get back from make-up and find the jug has melted into the letter 's' while Albert has been outside chatting with the lads.

I call him in.

'I'm awful sorry, Rick,' he says.

'That's OK. Here's twenty quid. See if you can get us another one.'

While he's out I put a 'For Sale' sign up in the window of the Minibago: 'Electric kettle. One previous owner. Apply within.'

In the other window I put up a 'Situations Vacant' sign: 'Wanted: Personal assistant to look after Nice Guy Eddie.'

By the time Albert gets back all the lads have put in applications and I'm organising job interviews. One fella has written: 'I have twenty years' experience in show business and I have never burnt an electric kettle . . .'

That's the nice thing about working in Liverpool. I know most of these people. I started in the business with many of them. Sometimes there are ten or fifteen mates sitting outside the Minibago, telling jokes and drinking tea. Some of them are caterers and some clean the bogs.

I hate the word 'star'. And I hate being on jobs where people are in awe of the actors and are too scared to talk to them. That's what's nice about having Albert around. When everyone's trying to tread softly around me, he'll lean out the door and shout, 'Hey, Bollocks! I made you a cup of tea and you've left the bloody thing. Make your own in future.'

He's priceless.

What I valued most about being free were the simple and everyday things like being able to have a bath and not having to share a toilet with sixty other blokes. There were no cockroaches. I could turn off the light when I wanted. I could step out of the door and inside again. Out and in . . .

Having been released, I always figured I would pick up where things left off, working as a plasterer, playing the banjo and raising my kids. The reality was delivered very bluntly every time I walked on to a building site looking for work.

I was blacklisted. The bigger, organised sites put my photograph on the window of the site office as though I was some sort of outlaw. I don't know if this was legal, but I could do nothing about it.

Dezzie suffered a similar fate. He went as far as changing his name by deed poll and disguising himself by growing a beard and dying his hair ginger. He walked on to this site wearing an overcoat and a scarf wrapped around his neck. Before he reached the foreman's hut, a couple of the lads shouted out, 'All right, Dezzie? How ya doing?'

He turned around and went home again.

I started doing bits and pieces – odd jobs and favours for friends – anything to earn a few quid. My only guaranteed income was working as a compere at weekends for some of the clubs and pubs.

I did Saturday and Sunday nights at the Croxteth and Gilmoss British Legion Club, better known as 'The Croxy', where Albert was the concert secretary; and on Sunday afternoons I worked at the Cantrill Farm British Legion. This usually involved telling a few gags, singing a song and introducing the other acts.

During the week I spent my time renovating the cottage. I built two bathrooms and an extension for a dining room. And when I couldn't get tilers to do the slate roof because it was so steep I did the job myself, perched on a ladder.

Clifton had started school in Pennagettly, a little village nearby. He and Gareth were totally different personalities. Gareth was good with his hands and always making things with a hammer and nails, or digging holes in the garden to make a cubby house. He was a real boy's boy. Clifton could run like the wind and excelled at any sport he tried. People used to say they looked like me. Clifton had dark skin and dark eyes, while Gareth was blond and fairer.

I always imagined that our family was complete, which is why it came as such a surprise when Marlene fell pregnant again. She had no idea until she was six months' gone. At first I wasn't thrilled with the idea. A year out of prison, I still hadn't managed to get steady work. How would we cope? Marlene was in her late thirties, quite old to be having another child in those days.

On Christmas Day 1977, the cottage was strewn with torn wrappings and the boys were showing off their new toys. I had spent what little money we had on gifts for them, just like my Dad had done for us. Marlene was heavily pregnant, but fussing in the kitchen, preparing a turkey and cutting up vegetables.

She went into labour just before midday. Charlie Clifton took her to the hospital while I stayed to look after the lads. The vegetables had been cut up and prepared, but I had no idea how to cook them. For Christmas dinner we ate a roast turkey, bread and butter and choc ices to finish.

The moment I set eyes on our Kate I fell in love. She was a gorgeous little thing, with brown eyes and fair hair. The boys weren't jealous. From the outset Marlene told them, 'Now this is your little sister. You have to look after her, OK?'

They were quite chuffed about that; the added responsibility helped them grow up a bit faster and take care of each other.

These were hard times and we were living on the few quid I made working the clubs on weekends. One Sunday afternoon at the Cantrill Farm British Legion, I bumped into Georgina Smith, a nice old stick, who you still see doing TV commercials and other bits and pieces.

She knew I was skint because I couldn't stay for more than the one drink.

'Have you ever thought about doing extra work?'

'Acting?'

'Well, nothing quite so grand. They pay twenty-six pounds a day, including travelling expenses.'

'For doing what?'

'Standing around mostly. They put you in costume, tell you where to stand and when they finish filming you get paid.'

I'll have some of that, I thought.

Nobody could work in film or TV without an Equity card and you couldn't get one of those unless you were a bona fide show business act. I went to see Eddie Ross, the local secretary of Actors' Equity.

'I've been working the clubs,' I told him.

'I know, I've seen ya,' he said, helping me fill out the application.

I arranged to have some photographs done and before long I had my first job in a series called *Fallen Hero*. Del Henny, a tremendous English actor, played a rugby league star forced out of the game by injury, trying to come to terms with his new life.

They wanted some kids in the scene, so I took Clifton and Gareth with me for the day. This meant I got a chaperone's fee as well as my own payment. The boys were made up, peering out the windows of the bus as we drove from Manchester to a location in the countryside.

Our scene was filmed on a canal bank where I had to sit with the two lads pretending to be fishing, while Del Henny acted in the foreground. It took an hour to set up and less than a minute to film. At the end of the shoot we boarded the bus to go back to Manchester. As we were about to leave the first assistant came on board.

'There's a lady who wants an autograph,' he said to Del Henny.

'I'll do better than that,' he replied, getting off the bus and walking down the front path to where an elderly lady stood at her kitchen door. Del stayed talking to her for about ten minutes and then apologised to everyone for keeping the bus waiting. I thought it was a lovely gesture.

Over the next three years I did loads of walk-on-walk-off parts. I was a bather on a beach, a drinker in a pub, a passer-by with a hat, a passer-by without a hat, a peasant, a farmer and a Polish shipyard worker.

When Granada filmed *Brideshead Revisited* in 1980, I was hired for a location shoot at Castle Howard in Yorkshire. Hundreds of extras were dressed as farm workers, peasants and villagers for a funeral scene where we had to walk slowly behind a team of horses pulling a gun carriage with a coffin draped in a Union Jack.

As we stepped off the buses the wardrobe ladies began sorting people into groups and organising costumes and make-up. The fella in front of me had a big bushy moustache.

'You'll have to have that off,' he was told.

He looked crestfallen. 'I've had this for twenty years.'

The wardrobe mistress shrugged and handed him scissors and a razor. Then she turned to me.

'You'll have to lose the beard.'

'I can't do that. I'm halfway through another job. They need me beard for continuity,' I lied.

She regarded me dubiously and turned to her assistant.

'Dress him like a seafaring captain. He'll look OK.'

Having spent hours getting put into costumes and made up, we stood in a rough line while the director, Charles Sturridge, did a quick inspection. The big fella next to me, newly shaven, kept fingering his naked top lip self-consciously.

Sturridge came along the line, paused in front of him and

said, 'That's marvellous, but can we put a false moustache on this chap?'

The poor lad didn't know whether to laugh or cry.

Everything was being set up for the funeral procession, with the sun setting in the background. This meant we had only one chance to get it right. As we stood behind the horse-drawn carriage, we were given a signal: 'Two minutes to action.'

An old woman, who must have been eighty plus, came hustling down the hill in her peasant clothes, determined not to miss out.

I yelled out to her, 'Hurry up, love, they're waiting to nail down the coffin.'

Everyone fell about and the old dear went bonkers. Suddenly, the flag went up and the cameras rolled. The horses started up the hill and we walked behind with our heads bowed. It was a beautiful scene.

I enjoyed working as an extra and I didn't think twice about hitchhiking all the way to Manchester at five in the morning for a job. The film and TV industry fascinated me, but even more so the actors who brought the scripts to life.

Working as an extra on a TV drama called *Secret Orchard* I watched a scene that featured Freddie Jones and Judy Parfitt on a pier. She pushed him along in a wheelchair and they both had long, emotional speeches which were filmed in one take.

'I would never be able to do that,' I told myself. 'How do they remember all them lines?'

The nearest casting agencies were in Manchester and Leeds because that's where the TV companies were based. In about 1978 I began to wonder if a local agency would guarantee more work for local people. It might even be a paying concern.

I borrowed four hundred quid off my old mate Colin Walker, who had worked on the boat. Eddie Ross from Equity showed me the ropes. First I needed an agent's licence and the proposal had to be publicised in the *Stage* newspaper, giving people an opportunity to lodge any objections.

Apart from Colin's seed capital I had no other money so everything had to be done on a shoestring. I paid a couple of months' rent for a single room office in Camden Street, Liverpool. Then I had the phone connected and bought a few bits of second-hand furniture – a desk, a chair and a four-drawer filing cabinet.

From the moment the application became public I was inundated with calls from people wanting to sign up. Many of them were mates I'd worked with over the years in the pubs and clubs. I got them to send me eight by ten inch photographs which I separated into categories – men, women, age, colour, expertise, etc . . .

I couldn't commute back and forth to Coedpoeth every day; the fares were too expensive. Instead, I began sleeping in the office, keeping blankets and a pillow in the bottom drawer of the filing cabinet. At night I lay the cabinet on the floor and put a couple of blankets over the top, trying to keep clear of the mice and cockroaches.

It took six weeks for the licence to be approved. Eddie Ross helped me devise a name for the agency – ART Casting, which stood for Advertising Radio and Television.

In the meantime I had been sending letters to the BBC, Granada, Yorkshire TV, and the smaller independent production companies, publicising this new agency and boasting of its fresh talent.

I sat in that office every day waiting for someone to call. Boredom set in and finally desperation. I kept inventing new filing systems for the photographs and staring at the phone.

Eight weeks later, on a Thursday afternoon, I had a call from Yorkshire TV. A lady called Ruth Boyle wanted to see some photographs of young girls for a shoot the next day.

'Fine. OK. I'm right on it,' I said.

How was I supposed to get her these photographs in a matter of hours? I didn't have a fax machine or enough money for a courier or motorbike messenger.

I sent Colin Walker on the train. He went to Leeds with a half dozen photographs and put them in Ruth Boyle's mailbox before catching the train home again. One of the girls got the job. She was made up.

ART received 10 per cent of her fee, which was only three quid for a day's filming and didn't even cover the cost of Colin's train fares, but at least we were up and running.

From these humble beginnings, the agency became a thriving little business and over the next fourteen years it provided thousands of extras for TV soaps, feature films and drama series. Although it never made much money, it gave me enormous satisfaction because people valued the work. There were also loads of laughs and wonderful memories.

When the American mini-series *Jenny's War* was filmed near Leeds, ART provided the extras. It was about an American mother, played by Dyan Cannon, whose son is shot down and captured by the Germans during the Second World War. She goes into occupied territory to help him escape.

The director needed guys to play POWs, so I sent a whole bunch of my mates along. The shoot lasted nearly a month and they used to meet up at Camden Street every morning at six and board a hired coach to take them to the location. It was at the height of the miners' strike and every day, without fail, the police stopped them.

'Where are you going?'

'We're prisoners of war.'

'Pull the other one.'

'We're in this movie.'

'No you're not. You're pickets.'

They had to talk their way through every time because the police were so paranoid about anyone joining the strike.

When the filming had almost finished the first assistant director announced, 'Look, we only need a few of you tomorrow because it's all going to be close-up work. There'll be a few extra lines for some of you, which means extra money.'

He went round and picked people he wanted.

'You and you and you . . .'

He came to Jackie Hamilton, the famous Liverpool comedian, who had been marvellous keeping the lads entertained on the coach trips. He missed Jackie out.

'I'm awful sorry,' he said later. 'You've been bloody marvellous, Jackie, but I just can't use you.'

'Why not?'

'Well, to be honest, you're supposed to be a POW . . . all skinny and haggard from months without decent food. Look at you! You're fat, red-faced and you've got a boozer's nose.'

'I know,' said Jackie. 'But I only got captured yesterday.'

Some of the extras had previously worked on another American project called *Fall of Eagles*, about the overthrow of the Russian royal family in 1917. Some of the crowd scenes were filmed at the Liverpool Town Hall, which doubled as the Imperial Palace in St Petersburg.

The extras had to dress up as Russian peasants and the director came over and explained the scene.

'Now, the Czar is going to walk out on the balcony. When he does I want you to start jeering and booing him. You hate this guy. He's living in luxury while you're all starving. Give it plenty of feeling.'

He got the thumbs up from his technicians and yelled, 'Action.'

The Czar appeared on the balcony and we gave it everything, shaking our fists, jeering and yelling abuse.

'Cut! Cut! Cut!'

The director appeared again. 'That was great,' he said. 'There's just one little thing. Can you try to say "Death to the Czar" and not "I'll knock yer bloody head off if you come down here, ya bastard"?'

At lunchtime, when the crew broke for lunch, it was a short walk to the Adelphi Hotel where meals were provided. Along the way Jimmy Wilde passed an old tramp sitting in a pub doorway.

'You wouldn't have a few bob for a sarnie and a cup a tea?' he asked.

'Tell you what,' said Jimmy. 'You look like one of us in them rags, so why don't you come along and we'll get you a hot meal.'

The old tramp was made up as he sat and ate with the rest of the extras.

The next day they broke at lunchtime and headed off to the Adelphi again. The same tramp sat in the doorway.

'Any chance of another meal?' he asked.

'OK, aye,' said Jimmy.

The tramp whistled and about forty homeless guys came out of the woodwork. There were so many of them that real extras got lashed out of the dining room and didn't get fed.

It took twelve months before ART began to pay its way. At times I had as many as a hundred extras working on the same day and we earned a reputation for reliability and professionalism.

The workload meant I often didn't get home more than

once or twice a week. The rest of the time I stayed with Mam or slept in the office.

Being away from home didn't seem unusual. My marriage had always been like that – even when I worked on the building sites. Marlene seemed happy to stay at home and raise the kids while I earned the money.

Of a weekend I compered at the Croxy Legion, which had become another home away from home. Dressed in a dinner jacket and dicky bow, I would bounce on to the stage, tell a few gags and then introduce the singers and comics booked for the evening.

'Ladies and gentlemen, we have three acts tonight and it gives me absolutely no pleasure to introduce the first of them because let me tell you they're crap! You won't have seen anything as bad as this in your life . . .'

This became a running gag. Before the second act, I'd say, 'OK, we've had a few complaints about crowd trouble. Let me warn you that if any of you misbehave I'll be bringing that last act back on again.'

I also used to recreate the glory days of the Blue House, by dragging people out of the audience for improvised comedy skits, using props and sound effects.

During the 'childbirth' skit old Elsie, a bingo seller, played the mother-to-be. We hid the two dolls up her front and lay her on a decorator's table, while I went to work with the hammer, chisels, saw, pneumatic drill, etc . . .

Suddenly, the table collapsed and Elsie hit the floor. The dolls shot out of her and went flying through the air, landing in the laps of the audience. There was mayhem.

Thankfully, old Elsie wasn't hurt. She became the talking point of the club for the next month and used to tell me off for being so awful. At the same time her eyes were bright with pride.

The Croxy had a barmaid called Annabelle who was one of the most beautiful women I have ever seen. She lived on the outskirts of town and often the chief club steward, Jimmy Dowd, would give her a lift to and from work.

I knew Annabelle was married, but I had never met her husband. One night she asked if I had my van.

'Maybe you could give us a lift home?'

'Oh, aye.'

We stayed behind for a drink and then I drove to her place. Pulling up outside, she made no effort to get out of the van. Instead she seemed to want to talk.

We chatted away and it grew late. I began thinking to myself, what am I supposed to do here? Does she want me to make a pass at her? If I put a hand on her and she screams we'll both be embarrassed.

I must have sat there for over an hour wrestling with this dilemma until finally Annabelle said goodnight and went inside.

The following night I was back at the club and she asked me if I planned to have a drink after the show.

'Yeah. I normally have a couple.'

'There's a club I want to go to. Will you take me there?'

The club was in the south end of Liverpool in the black quarter of the city. There were only about twenty people there, but the atmosphere and music were great. Later I drove Annabelle home and we finished up kissing. One thing led to another and we began seeing each other. Mostly I took her to mates' houses where we could snatch a few hours together before I dropped her home in the early hours of the morning.

One particular night I didn't have the van, so I caught a taxi back with her.

'Do you want to come in for a minute?' she asked.

'Are you sure?'

'Yeah.'

Carrying my banjo, I followed her into the house. Her husband appeared at the doorway and he eyed me up and down as Annabelle introduced us. He was a big bastard.

We made small talk for a few minutes and then he apologised.

'I'm potato picking in the morning, Rick, so I'll have to excuse meself and get some sleep.'

'Rick might be staying,' said Annabelle.

'OK. I'll put the little 'un in bed with us. Rick can have his room.'

My God, they've got a kid! I felt awful. I didn't want to stay, but Annabelle insisted. The cab had gone and the buses weren't running until morning.

Her husband went to bed leaving us alone. Annabelle sat on the settee. I had an armchair opposite. She reached over and ran her hand along my leg.

'No, this isn't right,' I whispered, glancing at the bedroom door.

'Oh come on,' she whispered.

I shook my head. She lifted her top and showed me her breasts.

'Tell me what you think of me.'

'I think you're lovely.'

'How lovely?'

'I think you're one of the most beautiful women I've ever seen,' I whispered. It was the truth, but I wasn't trying to get her into bed. I was trying to keep her quiet.

'You're a sight to behold, you really are. None of the other women at the Croxy come anywhere near you.'

At that precise moment the bedroom door swung open and her husband came charging out, bare-chested and wearing just a pair of dungarees.

'You bastard! You bastard! You're trying to give her one.'

I'm dead. He's going to kill me, I thought.

Before I could say anything Annabelle leapt to her feet.

'How dare you talk to a guest in our house like that! How dare you!'

Picking up the gist, I stammered, 'I'm sorry, Annabelle, but I've never been so insulted in my life. Don't ever invite me here again.'

Grabbing my banjo, I headed for the door. I could feel my sphincter opening and closing with fear. Outside, I ran as fast as I could down the street until I reached the bus stop.

It was two in the morning and the first bus wasn't due for another four hours. I fell asleep standing up, bloody near freezing to death. The bus driver woke me. He recognised me as 'Hobo Rick'. At that hour I had no place else to go except Mam's.

The following weekend I was back at the Croxy, waiting to go on stage. All day I had been thinking about Annabelle. What was I going to do? She was married. She had a kid.

When she didn't turn up for work I grew even more concerned. Maybe her husband had hit her.

Next minute she walked in. Thank God, I thought. Then I saw *him* right behind her. Three other couples arrived with them. All the lads were big and heavy. I'm in trouble here, I thought.

In the dressing room backstage my mind worked overtime. What was I going to do?

Albert put his head in the door. 'Rick, you're on.'

I emerged from behind the curtain with a little mincing walk.

'Darlings, darlings, my little angels,' I said, giving them a little curtsy. 'Your little flower is here again welcoming you all. Now I want you all to be upstanding for "God Save the

Queen" and I'm not talking about me, I'm taking about the *real* Queen.'

It got a few laughs and kicked the show off nicely. I studiously avoided looking at Annabelle the entire night. Instead I contemplated how quickly an ambulance could get me to hospital.

The show finished and I tried to sneak out without being noticed. As I crossed the lounge, weaving between drinkers, I felt a tap on my shoulder. It was Annabelle's husband.

'I want to talk to you.'

This is it. Here it comes.

He held out his hand. 'I'm awfully sorry, Rick. I didn't realise you were gay.'

It took a split second to understand what he was saying. My disbelief turned into a weak smile.

'Well, I don't like it to be known, generally,' I said, shaking his hand.

'Yeah, well, I'm sorry I went off at you like that. I'm a jealous bastard at the best of times, you know.'

'Yeah.'

'Look, you're quite welcome to stay with us any time you want to. I mean that. I really enjoyed the show.'

'Aye. Brilliant. Thanks.'

Being away from home so much was a recipe for misbehaving, but I should have learned my lesson after Annabelle. Instead I stumbled into another affair with an old flame.

Nancy was about a year younger than me and had lived in Lance Street when we were growing up. Although small, she had a tremendous figure, even at the age of twelve. Back in those days we did a bit of fooling around and almost went the whole way before Nancy panicked and said no. That was fine by me. I respected her wishes and we stayed friends.

She had grown up and married a cracking fella, Dougie, and the two of them would come into the Croxy of a Saturday night to see the show. She was still a fine-looking woman and the two of us could dance up a storm.

One night after the show Nancy stayed back for a drink. She asked if I minded walking her home. She only lived a few hundred yards from the club.

This began happening regularly. Dougie would leave early, kissing Nancy on the cheek and telling her, 'Goodnight, love. Rick'll see you home.'

On one of these nights, as we left the club, she put her arms round my neck and said, 'Do you want to do the honours, Rick?'

'Are you sure?'

'Yeah.'

So I did just that. It was a knee trembler in a back alley. We were both a bit old for that sort of thing, but it was nice just the same. Afterwards, I dropped Nancy home.

'I'll come down and see you tomorrow,' she said.

The next day she arrived at the ART office in Camden Street and we ended up making love on the desk.

As much as I liked Nancy, I had real pangs of conscience. Dougie was a smashing bloke. I didn't want to be sneaking around with his wife.

'Don't worry. He knows,' she said.

'How could he know?'

'Because I told him.'

'You did what?'

'I told him. He knows I'm here.'

She could see me struggling with this and laughed. What on earth was happening?

Sure enough, the next Saturday, Dougie raised a glass and said, 'All right, Rick, how yer doing?'

'Good.'

'Will you make sure Nancy gets home tonight?'

'Sure.'

This went on for months until I heard that Dougie had been rushed to hospital, riddled with cancer. He knew all along that he was dying and couldn't fulfil some of his husbandly duties. That's why he gave Nancy permission to see someone else, as long as he approved of her choice.

We gave Dougie a great send-off and after that I didn't see Nancy for a while. When she finally came into the club one night, I asked, 'How are you fixed?'

'I'm good, Rick. I'm seeing someone.'

'Good for you.'

She married the fella and I know she's still with him because she sent a condolence card to my Mam's funeral.

Although pleased for Nancy, a small part of me felt a sense of loss. As much as I loved Marlene, there wasn't that same spark between us. We didn't laugh any more or stay up late talking about the kids. With so much else happening in our lives, we had forgotten each other.

14

Roland's Workshop

It is early July 2002 and a documentary maker called Peter Taylor has phoned me. He's working on an exposé of MI5 and prominent people who were put under surveillance during the seventies. Under the thirty-year rule a lot of secret files are now available and guess what! There's one on me.

I love conspiracy theories, but I never thought I'd be in one of them. Back then I was a hairy-arsed building worker who went on strike for better conditions. It is hardly the bloody Profumo affair!

Peter wants to interview me about the contents of my file but at first I have doubts. Then he tells me about some of the other well-known people who were also labelled as subversives. He mentions Arthur Scargill.

'Is Arthur going to be interviewed?'

'Yes.'

'Let me talk to him. I'll get back to you.'

I call Arthur and ask him if Peter Taylor can be trusted.

'As far as you can trust anyone,' he says.

A few days later I meet Peter at the Crown Plaza Hotel on the waterfront in Liverpool. He has a small production team, with a cameraman and sound engineer. We order some tea and find a quiet room for the filming. At first we talk politics and I tell Peter that I used to be a member of the National Front. It takes him by surprise.

'We weren't skinheads or thugs. They were just ordinary guys worried about their kids and their country.'

'So what happened? Why did your views change?'

'It didn't happen overnight. I grew a bit older, educated myself. Politics is in the gut. I know what's right and what's wrong. I know when someone's getting a raw deal.'

'Does your past embarrass you?'

'I don't give a monkey's. What's done is done.'

He asks about the trial, my two years in prison and campaigning to free Dezzie. He's obviously done his homework because he knows I was kicked out of the TUC conference in 1975.

'Did you know that Special Branch has a file on you?' *asks Peter.*

'When we were on strike there were always rumours about us being watched and how we should be careful what we said, but we used to laugh about it.'

'Would it surprise you to know that you were under surveillance?'

'Now it doesn't surprise me – knowing what I do. But at the time I would have been shocked. I didn't regard myself as the sort of person MI5 would be monitoring.'

'Do you know what you were classed as?'

'No, I don't.'

'Well, I have a report here and I have spoken to an MI5 agent and he has described you as a political thug prone to violence.'

I laugh.

'Why are you laughing?'

'Because it's so bloody stupid.'

'Were you a subversive?'

'Subversive. My arse. I love England and the people in it. My father cried when the old King died. I had a boat called the British Heart *and we painted it red, white and blue. I love this country more than the Special Branch guy who's branded me a thug . . .'*

It makes me angry to think stuff like this has been on file for all those years and I've had no chance to redress the lies. And it just goes to show how an untruth can get repeated over and over until somehow it becomes a fact. The MI5 agent interviewed for the documentary quoted from the same court transcripts, based on the same dodgy statements, made by the same police officers and lumpers during the trial. Not one of them had identified me as having thrown a punch or caused any criminal damage, yet I still finished up being labelled a thug and subversive.

This talk of spies and surveillance has started me thinking. Were there any clues that I missed? Not long after I went to jail someone broke into the cottage and took some letters and photographs, but nothing valuable. Why would anyone bother?

And then years later, when I had the casting agency in Liverpool, there was another break-in. I came to work one Monday, unlocked the door and discovered that someone had cut a hole through the ceiling. My desk and filing cabinet had been rifled, but the only thing taken was an index book listing the names, addresses and details of people on my books.

At the time this didn't strike me as being sinister, although the police dismissed any suggestion it might be kids mucking about.

The previous Friday I had been on the set of an Irish production called Iris in the Traffic – Ruby in the Rain about the troubles in Northern Ireland. The drama was filmed in Liverpool using semi-derelict houses, because it looked so much like the back streets of Belfast.

The show starred a couple of young Irish kids and I got talking to their chaperone, who belonged to the peace movement.

'Are you Ricky Tomlinson, one of the Shrewsbury Two?'

'Yeah.'

She was really interested in the case so I offered to send her a booklet on the trial and posted it a day later.

Maybe I'm seeing shadows or maybe there was a link. Peter Taylor says that MI5 had a whole section dealing with break-ins and dirty tricks. I was a 'subversive' according to the files and we know they kept tabs on peace campaigners. Makes you wonder.

The advertisement in the *Stage* said: 'Auditions: Wanted Equity Members with Trade Union Experience.'

That's me, I thought. I wrote off a letter, but made sure to use a false name on the application because in a lot of places I remained on a blacklist.

A letter came back granting me an audition in London. I had to make my own way there, but they offered to reimburse my travelling expenses. According to the letter, I had to be at London Weekend Television, on the South Bank, for three o'clock on Wednesday afternoon.

A mate of mine, Tony Gates, was hoping to get work as a bricklayer on the Barbican site in London so we decided to pool our resources. Together we had just enough money to put petrol in my old post office van. I had no idea if the van could make it as far as London, but neither of us could afford the train.

We set off, allowing ourselves loads of time. The van didn't let me down. It chugged along in the slow lane, rattling gently and occasionally backfiring in anger.

We arrived in north London and came off the motorway near Brent Cross, where there was a huge sign at the side of the road saying 'Welcome to London'.

'Right, we're here,' I said to Tony, as I parked behind the sign.

I had only been to London three times before, once in the back of a prison van, once in a bus that went as far as Wembley for the Cup Final and once for a National Front demonstration. I had never driven myself and in the case of the prison van there were no windows.

Tony and I separated and agreed to meet up at the offices of LWT when he finished his interview for the Barbican job. I began walking, figuring the South Bank couldn't be far away. I walked . . . and walked . . . and walked.

Four hours later, having been lost half a dozen times, I arrived at the Thames, hobbling on blistered and bloody feet. The foyer at LWT was full of fellas about my age and I recognised their type immediately. Many of them were full-time union officials in collar and tie, carrying briefcases.

'There's nothing here for me,' I told myself.

They called my name and I went up in the lift. The casting lady, Nicky Finch, showed me to an office where a good-looking young bloke sat on a desk with his feet on a chair. I thought to myself, Mam would clip you round the ear and say, 'Get ya feet off the furniture.'

'My name is Roland Joffe,' he said, glancing at my application form. 'And your name is?'

'Eric Johnson.'

'What sort of work do you do?'

'I used to be in the building game. I'm a City and Guilds plasterer.'

Roland put down the clipboard. 'What do you think about the police?'

'I don't like a lot of 'em.'

'Why's that?'

'I don't trust them.'

'Is that from personal experience?'

I shrugged.

Swinging his legs on to the floor, Roland walked around me and then returned to his desk. 'Do you know what hard times are?'

'Yeah.'

'I don't think you do.' His voice had a sharp edge. 'I don't think you know what it's like to be hungry. I don't think you've ever had to really struggle . . .'

I could feel my hackles rising. Who was this pretty boy in his Cuban-heel boots and black leather bomber jacket? How dare he lecture me on what it's like to struggle! I bet he's never missed a meal in his bloody life. His jacket is worth more than my entire wardrobe. I just walked eight fucking miles to get there.

I lifted up my foot and put my finger through a hole in the bottom of my shoes.

'And I suppose you think that's fucking nail varnish,' I said, showing him the blood. 'You can stick this job up your arse!'

I stormed out, along the corridor and down the lift. Tony was waiting for me in the foyer.

'Come on, let's fuck off,' I said.

We were halfway down the street when he asked, 'Did you get the expenses, Rick?'

Shit! We had no money to get home.

I went back and the receptionist sent me upstairs. I knocked on the office door and asked for my expenses.

'How much is the train fare?' a woman asked.

'Twenty-two pounds.'

She turned to another girl. 'Give him twenty-five pounds.'

Just then Roland Joffe walked back into the room. He followed me down the corridor, trying to convince me to come back.

'I know who you are,' he said. 'You're Ricky Tomlinson. You were in jail.'

'I don't care what you know.'

The lift doors closed and I caught up with Tony. I was

fuming all the way home in the van. What a waste of time! At least Tony had better news. He had a start on the Barbican site from the following Monday.

About a week later I was in the ART office when Roland Joffe's secretary rang.

'Roland will be in Oldham next Saturday and he wants you to do a workshop for him.'

I thought the request was pretty odd, but I called Tony Scoggo, hoping he might come with me. On Saturday morning we threw all our tools in the back of the van and drove to Oldham. The sun was shining and we had the windows down. It was a good day to be working outdoors.

We arrived at the address, which was basically a small hall rather than a house. The place was full of people who were milling around. I went up to a girl who seemed to be taking names.

'Listen, love, can you tell me where I should be? I'm here to build a workshop for Mr Joffe.'

She looked at me and laughed. Scoggo nudged me in the ribs.

'I don't think it's that sort of workshop, Rick.'

'What d'ya mean?'

I looked around and saw chairs lined up and a few faces I recognised. One young lad, Frankie Clarke, was a writer from Liverpool.

'Have you come to the workshop, Rick?' he asked.

'Yeah, kid. Should be a laugh,' I said, feeling embarrassed.

Roland Joffe arrived and began handing out photocopies of a story from the *Guardian* newspaper.

'I want you all to read this and we'll talk about it,' he said.

The story concerned a group of people on a council estate, who were facing a large rent increase. The tenants were kicking up a stink because the place was run-down and falling apart.

'OK, I want you to pretend that you are residents of a housing association,' said Roland. 'You live in this block of flats and they're trying to put the rent up. You don't want to pay any more. You don't think you should have to. That's why you're in this hall. You've called a meeting to decide what to do.'

He stepped to one side and I glanced at Scoggo, who looked back at me. The silence became drawn out and people shifted on their seats.

Finally, someone behind me says, 'Well, I don't think it's right they're putting the rents up.'

'It doesn't seem fair,' says someone else.

People nodded and a woman piped up, 'I don't know what we can do.'

Jesus, what a sorry lot this is, I thought. It's bloody scandalous them putting up the rent. Jumping to my feet, I bellowed, 'Well, I'm not fucking having it! I don't care what yous want to do, but I'm not paying a penny more. Look at this place! That's supposed to be a playing field for the kids out there. There's not a swing or a goal post on it. There are no fucking amenities, the lifts are always broken and you wait six weeks to get a window fixed. Fuck the rent! I'm not paying it!'

Scoggo was suddenly on his feet beside me. 'I'm with him. If he's not paying the rent, neither am I.'

Next thing people were shouting, 'Hear! Hear!' Others were applauding and shaking their fists.

'They're quick enough asking for their fucking money, aren't they?' I said. 'When was the last time this place had a coat of paint? When were them drainpipes unblocked? When did you see grass in that playground? No wonder the kids are getting all sorts of colds. The place is wet and the stairways stink . . .'

I just went on and on, getting people fired up and debating what we should do. Eventually, Roland said, 'OK, that's enough for today. Thank you for coming.'

Scoggo and me headed for the door. Roland intercepted us and took us to one side.

'I'm doing a film for TV, could you manage a couple of lines?'

'Oh, aye, yeah, I'd be made up.'

'OK, I'll be in touch.'

The casting director called a few days later.

'We would like to offer you a part in a film called *The Commune*. Will you accept one thousand seven hundred pounds for the role?'

'How many people do I have to kill?'

She started laughing.

'And Tony Scoggins is also being offered a part. We'll pay him one thousand four hundred. Is that OK?'

'That's brilliant.'

I phoned Scoggo straight away. He thought I was joking at first. This was a vast amount of money for both of us.

Almost immediately the phone rang again.

'Look, I'm awfully sorry, but the play has been cancelled,' the woman said.

'Why?'

'The TV company has pulled out. Roland wants to let you know that he's very sorry and that your cheques are in the post.'

'But we didn't do anything.'

'He's insisting that you still get paid.'

I didn't learn until much later what had happened. Jim Allen, a working-class playwright from Manchester, had written the script for *The Commune*. It was always going to be controversial because of the subject matter – a working-class uprising triggered by urban decay and mass unemployment.

LWT had initially agreed to go ahead, but got the jitters and cancelled the project because the material was too sensitive. Furious at this, Roland had insisted that all the actors chosen for the play should receive their agreed fees.

The money was a complete godsend, but disappeared as quickly as it arrived. Just when our finances seemed to be improving, something would happen to put us behind again. In this case the drive shaft of the van snapped a couple of days after getting back from Oldham. It broke right down the middle and I abandoned the van beside the road.

Mick McNally helped me buy another van. Mick had been a barman on the big ocean liners and had grown rich on the tips from wealthy Americans. Slim, with thinning hair and a pale complexion, I could always picture him in his tuxedo and dicky bow behind the bar.

Back on dry land he bought a little social club in Huyton called the Fur and Feather, which had been started by pigeon fanciers and still had bird lofts out back.

The club really struggled at first, but I offered to organise the entertainment, running the bingo and booking the acts. We soon had the place jumping of a Saturday and Sunday. The organ player in the band was selling his van and Mick lent me the money. I paid him back each week out of my wages.

Two months after my abortive acting debut, I had another call from Roland Joffe.

'Could you get up to Newcastle to do an audition?'

'Oh, aye. When?'

'Tonight.'

I phoned a friend to look after the office and drove to

Newcastle. Roland met me at a house in the suburbs. Nobody else was there except a woman he introduced as Val McLane. Later I discovered she was Jimmy Nail's sister and a cracking actress.

'I want you to pretend you're married,' Roland said. 'Val here is a local councillor and she's spending more and more time at council meetings and less time at home, leaving you to look after the kids. It's late in the evening. The kids are in bed. She's still not home. You're feeling angry and frustrated. You're fed up. Any minute now she's going to come through that door. What are you going to say to her?'

Val went outside and Roland squatted in the corner of the room, seeming to fade into the wallpaper. I sat at the table waiting . . . and waiting . . . What's going on here? I thought. When is she going to come in? This is ridiculous.

Suddenly, I heard a key in the lock.

'Where the hell have you been?'

'At a council meeting.'

'It's after ten o'clock. What's going on at them bloody council meetings? The kids were waiting up for you. They wanted to say goodnight. Don't they matter to you any more?'

We had a full-scale, stand-up row, with Val giving as good as she got.

She was screaming at me, 'Why don't you get a job? At least I'm out there doing something, instead of moping about all day crying into me teacup.'

'There *are* no fucking jobs.'

'How do ya know? Ya stopped lookin' months ago.'

In the end Roland stood up and said, 'OK, that's it.'

I was standing in the kitchen physically shaking with rage. It took me ten minutes to calm down.

Roland grinned at Val. 'I think he'll be perfect, don't you?'
She nodded and gave him a wink.

The same film that LWT had cancelled two months earlier was now back in pre-production. The BBC had picked up the option and changed the title to *United Kingdom*. Instead of being given 'a few lines' Roland wanted me to play a lead role.

'How are you going to get home?' he asked.

'I think I'll fly. I'm high as a kite.'

Filming began in 1979 at a run-down block of flats in Newcastle. Just as in the audition, I play an unemployed working-class bloke, married with four kids and living in a tenement block. Val McLane is my wife and a local councillor. When the council jacks up the rent, the tenants refuse to pay and barricade themselves in the flats. The riot police are sent in to break up the dispute. Colin Welland is the Chief of Police.

I didn't have preconceived ideas because this was all so new to me. The fact that nobody showed me a script or rehearsed scenes beforehand didn't seem strange. Roland operated on a different level. He wanted every scene to be as spontaneous as possible, which meant allowing dialogue to arise from the situation rather than rehearsing it in advance.

Later I learned that a lot of classically trained actors find it difficult to improvise, whereas someone like me could do it naturally because the words just came out of my head.

The thought of learning a script terrified me and I knew I couldn't put the same emotion into a scene if I kept worrying about remembering the dialogue word for word.

Before each scene Roland would give us each a piece of

paper with a few ideas or a few lines. Then he explained what was supposed to happen and left the rest to us.

A lot of the time I wasn't even aware of how cleverly he manipulated me to get the performance he wanted. The day before I had to make a big speech, he took me for a walk along the river and we chatted about the scene. He was very subtly putting arguments into my head.

The next day he gave me a few words as triggers. When the camera rolled all of his ideas came flooding out in my speech, yet sounded completely spontaneous.

Apart from Colin Welland, the cast included Bill Patterson and Peter Kerrigan – all wonderful actors. They were staying at a big fancy hotel, while I was put in a little bed and breakfast.

'I don't want you mixing,' Roland told me. 'I can't risk you suddenly calling each other by your real names during filming and messing up the scene. And I don't want you becoming friends because you're supposed to be on opposite sides of the barricades.'

This discipline was maintained throughout the four week film shoot. We weren't allowed to use our real names in the canteen, wardrobe, the make-up trailer and even after filming had finished for the day.

Some nights I stayed with a local family so I could get to know the kids who were playing my children in the film. This proved really important because some of the scenes were harrowing.

In one particular moment in the film, the youngest lad is caught stealing and the police bring him home. After they leave I go off at the lad, tearing strips off him. Val McLane is yelling at me, 'It's your fault. You were supposed to be looking after him. It's not him that should be getting locked up – it's you!'

The young lad runs into the kitchen and I follow him. The camera is rolling and Roland is crouched in the corner.

'Listen, you don't think I'd let the police do anything to you,' I say to the lad, who is sobbing his eyes out. I give him a hankie to wipe his nose. 'Do you know the last time I done this? It was when I was wiping your arse when you was a little baby.'

He laughs and cries at the same time. Roland shouted 'Cut' and I looked up to see the cameraman and the sound engineer with tears in their eyes. That's when I realised we had done something special.

Once the final scene had been filmed Roland let the cast socialise with each other. This prompted a three-day bender in which we attempted to empty the cellars of Newcastle's finest pubs.

Back in Liverpool, I kept working in the clubs and running ART. In the meantime, *United Kingdom* was edited and Roland organised a special screening for the cast, crew and selected friends. I had a job working as an extra for Granada that day and afterwards caught the train from Manchester to London. Albert travelled down from Liverpool with Peter Kerrigan. Still dressed in my working clothes, I met them at the cinema.

Albert looked like a tailor's dummy he was so dead smart.

'You can't go in looking like that,' he said.

'Why?'

"Cos you look like a scruff.'

'I been working,' I protested.

At that moment Roland arrived wearing an old pair of faded overalls. His wristwatch had broken so he had strung it around his neck on a tattered piece of string. I looked at Albert and laughed.

Colin Walker, who had lent me the money to start ART,

was working as an electrician in London and I invited him along to the screening.

As the first scene flickered on to the screen, I saw myself twenty foot high and thought I was like a fairytale giant. Yet within minutes I was totally lost in the story as all the different scenes came together and I understood the nuances of the plot.

Halfway through, Colin nudged me and whispered, 'This is *your* film, Rick.'

'What do you mean?'

'This is *yours*.'

Broadcast as the BBC Play for the Day in 1981, *United Kingdom* won critical acclaim. A lot of very nice things were said and written about my performance, which was flattering. One newspaper managed to confuse me with Bill Patterson. He phoned me up and apologised.

'You deserve the praise,' he said. 'Nobody can take that away from you.'

Despite the plaudits, the BBC has never reshown the drama, which is unusual. Perhaps this is further evidence of the controversy it caused. A few years ago Roland tried to buy it back from them, but was again turned down.

Soon after the broadcast Roland invited me down to London to stay with him for a few days. He lived in a beautifully restored period house in Chelsea with amazing tapestries and paintings on the walls.

As he gave me the guided tour, I noticed a beautiful bronze statue of a hand, which looked as though it was emerging through the floor. I could almost picture a giant in the cellar trying to get out.

'Who made that?' I asked.

'My grandfather.'

'He could make a few bob down the markets doing stuff like that.'

The Grants arrive on Brookside Close . . . From left to right: Damon (Simon O'Brien), Barry (Paul Usher), Karen (Sheila O'Hara), Sheila (Sue Johnston) and Bobby.

A night out with some of the cast of *Brookside*. From left to right: Michael Starke (Sinbad), Dean Sullivan (Jimmy Corkhill) and Louis Emerick (Mick Johnson).

Director Roland Joffe took a gamble and cast me in *United Kingdom* (1981). It was my first acting role.

With Robbie Carlyle in *Riff Raff* (1990), directed by one of my heroes Ken Loach.

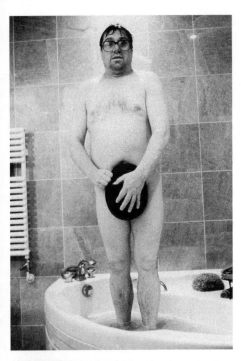

A classic scene from *Riff Raff* (in case you're wondering, I don't use a body double). Later, when I was living incognito above a boxing club in Liverpool, Ken Loach printed this picture in the *Guardian* under the heading, 'Have you seen this man?'

With Loachie at an awards do.

At the Berlin Film Festival, where I was nominated for Best Supporting Actor for *Riff Raff*. From left to right: David Putnam, Sally Hibbon, myself, Glenn Close, and my two Liverpool mates Jimmy Coleman and Georgie Moss.

Stealing a sheep with Bruce Jones in *Raining Stones* (1993).

Outside the Limelight Club with Scoggo.

Chloe the Garston Butterfly in 1964 –
a beautiful soul with a sad history.

The Red Triangle Boxing Club
where I lived when I had no
arse in me kecks and was
being chased by bailiffs and
debt collectors.

A tense scene from *Cracker* with Robbie Coltrane and Geraldine Sommerville. After my history with the police, I now had to play one.

On the waterfront in Dublin filming Jimmy McGovern's *Dockers*. Mersey Docks refused us permission to film there.

Jim Royle in a characteristic pose. I didn't wash that shirt for nearly three years.

The Royle Family, clockwise from the top: Sue Johnston as long-suffering Barb; Craig Crash, co-writer of the show, as Dave; the wonderful Caroline Aherne, creator and co-writer of the show, as Denise; myself as Jim with 'baby David' on my lap; Liz Smith as Nana and Ralf Little as 'our Anthony'.

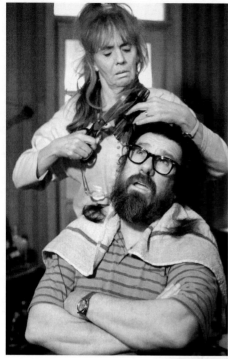

With Sue, playing husband and wife again.

With Caroline Aherne at the British Comedy Awards in December 1999. We had just won Best Comedy Actor and Best Comedy Actress.

Roland laughed. 'You're right. He was Sir Jacob Epstein.'

We came from different worlds. Roland had grown up around famous sculptors, painters, theatre directors and actors. I worked on building sites and market stalls. At the same time he was perhaps the first middle-class guy I truly respected because I knew he wouldn't give me any shit. He used to talk about all of the films he wanted to make and each of them contained a strong message about justice and equality.

A while back I was reading David Putnam's autobiography in which he recounts how he produced *The Killing Fields*, a shocking film about *New York Times* correspondent Sydney Schanberg and the atrocities of the Khmer Rouge in Cambodia in the mid-seventies.

Putnam knew the film was going to be controversial and had to be handled perfectly. He was looking for a director; someone new, who could tell such a huge story without losing touch with the human plight of the individuals involved. One night he switched on the TV and thought he was watching a 'fly-on-the-wall' documentary. A man and a woman were having a stand-up row. Putnam said he was riveted. He couldn't take his eyes off the screen. He thought this fella was going to kill her.

He was watching *United Kingdom*.

When the credits rolled, he made a note of the name Roland Joffe. He couldn't believe this director had managed to get such remarkable performances from newcomers like me. He contacted Roland and offered him the chance to direct *The Killing Fields*.

The casting agency had gone from strength to strength and I continued working the clubs. When I finally stepped down at the Croxy Legion they gave me a gold watch for long service along with a pullover, a book and other odds and ends.

A committee man, Nella Morgan, had told me earlier, 'We're going to lose you sooner or later, Rick. We think you're gonna make it.'

I remembered this when I was filming *United Kingdom*. Roland had told me to improvise a scene where I had to walk into a garage and ask for someone. So I went in and said, 'Has anyone seen Nella Morgan?'

Nella was made up. I had immortalised him on screen.

Despite the reviews and kind words, I had absolutely no expectation of it ever happening again. I didn't regard myself as being an actor. This had been a one-off.

Within weeks I was back in Manchester doing extra work. Scoggo had arranged to give me a lift home and we met at a bar called the Stables at Granada TV. Liz Dawn, who plays Vera Duckworth on *Coronation Street*, came over and asked what I'd been doing.

'I got a day's work.'

'Doing what?'

'As an extra.'

She looked horrified. 'You can't do that.'

'Why not?'

'You're an actor.'

She reached into her handbag and slipped a few quid into my hand. 'Here y'ar, chuck, get yerself a drink.'

Apparently, once someone had proven himself as an actor, he wasn't supposed to do extra work. Nobody had ever told me. I didn't have an agent and wasn't in a position to turn down a day's work.

Soon after that the director Phillip Saville came to Liverpool casting for Alan Bleasedale's *Boys from the Black Stuff*. He contacted ART wanting to see about ten people, including a couple of tough, careworn working-class women in their mid-fifties, as well as a few rough labouring types and someone who could play a bank manager.

Going through the files, I picked out some likely candidates and phoned them up. Phillip took a room at the Adelphi Hotel and I brought each person up to see him. When he'd been through the candidates, he said, 'Why didn't you put *your* name down, Rick?'

'I was asked to provide ten people as an agent. That's what I done.'

'What if I have a part for you?'

'That's OK.'

It was a small role, playing a doctor in the six-part series, but more importantly a lot of local people were hired as extras.

I loved the eccentricity of Phillip Saville. Every evening he would send a message to ART listing what extras he wanted for the next morning. It might be six burly docker types, or a clerk or a woman receptionist. Matching people up to the different roles was a challenge, but I got a buzz out of getting people work who really appreciated it.

Towards the end of filming we held the wrap party at the Adelphi Hotel because some of the main actors had finished their scenes and were leaving town. It was a Friday night and we filled the function room with actors, directors and assistants.

Bernard Hill had played Yosser in *Boys from the Black Stuff* – a tremendous character, brilliantly acted. Yosser came to represent the desperation of Britain's unemployed and his catchphrase 'Gizza job! I can do that' entered the nation's consciousness.

Unfortunately, Bernard had put a lot of people off-side, particularly the wardrobe lads and the make-up ladies.

Maybe he was having a tough time at home, but it still didn't excuse his rudeness.

The wrap party carried on into the early hours and everyone seemed to have a good time. Bernard had been talking with a girl and later I saw her sitting on the steps crying. I sat down beside her and asked her what was wrong.

She sobbed a little harder and I put my arm around her shoulders. Suddenly, Bernard appeared and grabbed her arm, pulling her angrily to her feet.

'Hey, come on, Bernard, there's no need for that,' I said.

'It's none of your business.'

'She's upset.'

'I told you to get lost.'

'That's about four times tonight you've insulted me.'

He held up his fingers and signalled five. I thumped him. It just happened. One minute he was standing and the next he was laying at my feet. He bounced up and we squared off but people jumped between us.

'See you in the morning,' I growled at Bernard, challenging him. Isn't it amazing how you go right back to your roots? That's the sort of thing I used to say when I got into fights outside the Grafton.

The phone didn't stop ringing the next morning. People had heard about the fight and were calling to get the drum. Phillip Saville rang and wanted to meet me at a well-known local pub, the Crack, at eight o'clock that evening.

'Don't be telling anyone you're going,' he said. 'We'll keep this between ourselves. We'll have a quiet drink and you can tell me what happened.'

I arrived a little early and bought a pint of mild, before finding a quiet corner. Five minutes later the door burst open and Phillip waltzed in wearing a white suit, white shoes and a white fedora hat. His cigar was about a foot long. So much for a secret rendezvous! He couldn't have been more conspicuous if he was stark bollocking naked.

After explaining what had happened he advised me to stay away from the set for a few days to keep a low profile.

The executive producer Michael Wearing called me the next morning.

'I've had Bernard Hill on the phone. He wants to sue you.'

'Does he?'

'I've told him it's got nothing to do with the BBC. It was at a private party at two or three in the morning. You were both pissed. That's the last comment we're making on the subject.'

'Fair enough.'

I didn't hear anything more about lawsuits and nothing else was said. I have always admired Alan Bleasedale and respected his work, but I have never been offered a part in anything else he has written. Maybe this is just a coincidence. In recent times the two of us helped promote Liverpool's successful bid to become Europe's Capital of Culture in 2008. Twenty years had passed under the bridge – long enough for any hard feelings to wash away.

The last time I saw Bernard Hill was about eight years ago, when I was down in London for a dubbing session. I wandered out of the studio to eat my lunch in the lovely little park in Soho Square. I was sitting there with a smashing actor, Paul Copley, when Bernard Hill walked over.

'Hi ya, Paul,' he said, ignoring me.

I held out the olive branch and said, 'Hello, Bernard.'

He didn't take it. Instead he totally blanked me. That's fine, I thought. Bygones don't have to be bygones.

The truth is I'm really sorry about the whole incident. I have very few regrets in my life. I don't even regret a lot of the wrong things I've done or the mistakes that I've made because at the time I thought they were right.

There was a time when getting into fights didn't bother me, especially when I was young, but nowadays violence terrifies me. I smacked Bernard because he was being a twat, but he didn't deserve that. I wish I could turn back the clock.

15

Dear Bobby Grant

Rita wants to get married. It must be about time. We've been together for ten years and if anything happens to me where would that leave her?

Nowadays, whenever we go to functions and she sees 'Rita Tomlinson' on the seating plan instead of Rita Cumiskey, she goes mad. And she hates it when I introduce her as my wife.

'Actually, I'm not his wife. He won't marry me,' she tells people.

It's not that I don't want to do the honourable thing. I love her and I want to spend the rest of my life with her. I just can't be arsed with all the fuss and hassle of organising a wedding.

Before Mam died she said to me, 'Are you gonna marry that girl?'

'Yes, Mam.'

'When?'

'When the time is right.'

'Well, don't you go and mess this up.'

She told all my brothers the same story, which puts it on a par with a dying wish. That pretty much settles things.

I'd like to be able to tell you that my proposal was incredibly romantic, featuring flowers, soft music and me on one knee. Unfortunately, I can't actually remember popping the question or Rita answering it. We just knew.

When it came to the wedding I told her we could either have something very small, with just our immediate family, or we had to go for the full monty. Anything in between means alienating friends who don't get invitations.

A small wedding would have suited me, but I've been married before in a church, with bridesmaids and all the bells and whistles. Rita had a little register wedding in Liverpool, with hardly anyone there. This time she deserves the best of everything and I'd hire St Paul's Cathedral if it would make her happy.

We're still trying to settle on a date. I favour next March, but that depends on whether they make another series of Nice Guy Eddie. Apart from the filming, I'd have to shave off my beard and Rita says she won't marry me unless half my face is hidden.

Her son Tony is coming home for Christmas from Australia and might not be able to get back again. That's why Rita wants to have the wedding in the first week of January. She wants Tony to give her away.

I keep joking to her that all these women are going to be heartbroken when they hear I'm getting married. Even now they're probably slashing their wrists. She rolls her eyes. 'In your dreams.'

It was Tony Scoggo who heard about the auditions for *Brookside*. He phoned up and asked if I wanted to come with him.

Phil Redmond, a well-known producer, had organised a casting session in Liverpool. He struck me as the sort of fella who could have been an actor himself. In his early thirties, he had a real presence, with long hair and striking looks.

After I'd waited my turn, he paired me up with Eileen O'Brien and wanted us to improvise a scene where we are shopping in a supermarket.

'Look at them adverts,' I said. 'Fifty per cent off! Fifty per cent off what? And when they say half fat how d'yer know how much fat that is? Might be half of nothing . . .'

This went on for a while until Redmond called a halt.

'Have you ever thought of being a scriptwriter?' he asked, which was a backhanded compliment.

Afterwards I had a cup of tea and a sandwich with Eileen.

'I haven't done very well,' she said, 'but I reckon you've got the job.'

A few days later I was called back for a second audition, this time opposite Sue Johnston, an established actress who had been classically trained. We got on like a house on fire and were cast together as husband and wife, Sheila and Bobby Grant.

Along with our 'children' Barry (Paul Usher), Damon (Simon O'Brien) and Karen (Sheila O'Hara), we were to become the main family in a flagship drama that had been commissioned by the soon-to-be launched Channel 4.

Sue Johnston was an only child but you wouldn't know it from meeting her. She grew up in Prescott on the outskirts of Liverpool, where her Dad had been a plumber. She went to drama school from a young age and had been working almost constantly since then.

It had been almost ten years since I'd had a regular income and here I was being offered a twelve-month contract. Instead of having to scrape money together to pay the bills Marlene and I could clear our debts and put a little aside.

Our finances had been so precarious we had just decided to put the cottage up for sale and borrow a few grand from the bank to buy a much smaller house in Wrexham.

Having signed up for *Brookside* we immediately took down the 'For Sale' sign and stayed in Coedpoeth. At the same time I arranged to rent the parlour house in Wrexham to a couple of university students.

The first episode of *Brookside* went to air at 8 p.m. on 2 November 1982. More than a million people watched the show and the gritty storylines were applauded for breaking new ground. We had some wonderful writers like Jimmy McGovern, Frankie Clarke, Chris Bernard, Alan Swift, Kaye Mellor and Andy Lynch, to name just a few.

Phil Redmond wanted the storylines to be issue-led and to tackle social problems such as unemployment, crime and poverty. The language was very uncompromising and triggered a barrage of protests.

Mam had always been a bit of a prude and she was horrified to hear me swearing. She couldn't watch *Brookside* in the living room. Instead she used to stand in the hallway and watch the TV through the crack in the door.

Redmond agreed to tone down the language, but the publicity quickly helped us pull an audience of over two million. Phil can take most of the credit. A local boy made good, he had grown up on a council estate in north Liverpool and gone on to become a successful TV writer.

One of his cleverest moves with *Brookside* was to ignore the traditional studio and instead buy ten houses in a cul-de-sac in West Derby. Six of the bungalows were turned into sets for the soap, while the others became a production office, canteen, wardrobe department and editing suite. Apart from saving money on costs, he made a killing on the real estate.

The audience figures continued to climb and I was soon getting recognised in the street and receiving fan mail. One particular woman didn't like the way Bobby Grant treated Sheila.

'Dear Bobby Grant,' she wrote. 'You ought to be ashamed of yourself . . .' and she ended with, 'PS You've got the biggest squarest head on television.'

I pinned the letter up on the noticeboard where it gave everyone a laugh.

The Grant family was the focal point of the show in the early days. Bobby was a typically working-class guy who had moved his family on to a middle-class estate in the hope of bettering their lot. He was a shop steward and later became a full-time official of the union.

The fact that I appeared on TV and was photographed by magazines and newspapers didn't matter to me. Acting was making me a good living and I had no right to complain about being in the public eye. In my entire career I have only twice refused an autograph and I regret doing it now.

The kids were pretty impressed at having a famous Dad but I don't think it bothered Marlene whether I worked on the building sites or on TV. Later she told me she would have preferred me to be a plasterer. She wanted a husband with a nine-to-five job, with a regular income, who would be home for his supper at six and out every morning by seven.

She had never embraced the show business scene. This wasn't because of shyness. Marlene can strike up conversations with complete strangers, which is something I can't do. She just didn't feel comfortable around TV people and preferred to stay at home.

The students who were renting the parlour house in Wrexham stopped paying rent after the first three weeks. Having borrowed money from the bank we relied on the rent to cover the repayments.

I went round to see them. Hazel was a member of the Socialist Workers Party and seemed like a nice girl when she signed the lease.

'We're not paying,' she said.

'Why not?'

'We don't think it's worth it.'

'It's a fair rent. You said so yourself.'

She shrugged. 'I've changed my mind.'

'Well, you have to leave.'

'We're not moving,' she said brazenly.

'Hang on. You can't stay if you're not paying any rent. I'm paying off a bank loan.'

'That's not our problem.'

'Listen, I'm trying to sort out my life,' I told her. 'You know where I've been. I'm only just getting back on my feet . . .'

'I don't give a shit. We know our rights.'

'What about my rights? I can't subsidise you.'

She laughed.

The guy sharing the house with her was a martial arts expert, something which Hazel enjoyed pointing out to me as she slammed the door in my face.

Marlene and I talked about what we should do. The tenancy laws were a joke. If we went to the police it would take months to get a court order and another four weeks for them to comply. If they ignored any ruling, it would mean another trip to court and even more delays. Meanwhile, I had the bank demanding payment. My first cheque from *Brookside* had been enough to clear our other debts.

Taking matters into our own hands, we went back to the house and knocked on the door. As it partially opened, I threw my shoulder against it and Marlene flew inside. Hazel tried to run up the stairs, but Marlene tackled her and dragged her backwards out of the door by her feet. The big fella came out of the kitchen and squared up to me. He was about six foot four. I had a hammer in my hand and I swung it. Thank Christ I missed.

I must have looked totally psychotic because he took off out of the door. The snow was about knee-deep and he slipped and slid all the way down the path. By then I didn't care if he was the heavyweight champion of the world. I wanted a piece of him.

Eventually he reached the road and took off with Hazel running after him. I called them every name under the sun and told them not to come back.

Marlene was almost in tears when she saw the state of the house. Paint had been smeared on the walls and garbage left rotting in the kitchen. Stuff had been broken or gone missing. A specially boxed bottle of whisky that had been given to me by the Scottish miners when I campaigned for Dezzie had disappeared from the basement, along with some other things.

To prevent them returning, we had to occupy the house, but I couldn't bring my kids into such filth. We were in the process of cleaning up when the police arrived.

Hazel and her boyfriend had made a complaint. Because of the ridiculous tenancy laws *we* finished up getting charged and ordered to appear in court.

Paddy Rush offered to babysit the kids, having already helped me change all the locks and fix up the bedrooms of the parlour house.

A local solicitor represented us at the hearing. The Judge listened to both sides of the case and admitted that his decision might not seem fair.

'As much as I have doubts about the tenancy laws, it is clear that people cannot be allowed to take the law into their own hands.'

I could see Hazel and her boyfriend smirking.

'You will vacate the premises and let these people return.'

'I won't,' I said.

He acted as though I might not have understood. 'You will vacate these premises and let these people return.'

'I won't.'

'Mr Tomlinson, I am going to ask you one more time. If you fail to obey this court I will hold you in contempt and send you to jail.'

'I'm sorry, Your Honour, but I won't let them into my house. You should have seen the state of it. Filth from one end to the other . . . mattresses on the floors . . . I had to lash everything out and burn it . . .'

He turned to the court constable and ordered him to lock me up. As I left the court, I heard him asking Marlene the same question. She, too, refused and finished up in the cell next to me.

What is it with me? Every time I appear in court someone locks me up.

The snow was so deep outside that they couldn't take me to Shrewsbury Jail or Marlene to the nearest women's prison. Instead we spent the night in the police cells.

Three days we spent in jail. Every morning a solicitor would come in and say, 'Are you prepared to apologise to the court and abide by the Judge's ruling?'

'No. We've done nothing wrong.'

Meanwhile, Paddy was at home guarding the kids. At one point the bailiff came round and demanded to be let in. Paddy opened the bedroom window and told him, 'You'll come into this house over my dead body.'

Paddy was only five foot two, but he was telling the truth. They would have had to kill him to get inside.

Although only in the next cell, I couldn't see or talk to Marlene. I worried about her. She had never been in jail before. She had three young kids at home. I wouldn't have thought any less of her if she had abided by the court order.

Instead, she stuck to her guns. Although there were times when we didn't see eye to eye on things, I had never questioned her strength, courage or loyalty.

I can understand why some people squat, particularly when you see derelict or empty houses and people sleeping in cardboard boxes. And I am outraged when I hear about Rackman-style landlords, who charge extortionate rents for places that have no heating or hot water or should be condemned. But this was different. I wasn't a slumlord taking advantage of people. I had barely enough money to feed my kids.

After four days the students gave up their fight. Maybe someone like Jim Nichol had a quiet word and asked Hazel why a member of the Socialist Workers Party was doing something like this to someone like me.

Whatever happened, the case was dropped and we were allowed to go home. I fixed up the parlour house and sold it pretty soon after that.

My other brush with the law during *Brookside* taught me an important lesson about fame being a two-edged sword. It was after a book launch in London for a Liverpool writer. I had arranged to meet up at Stringfellow's with Sue Johnston and Andy Lynch, one of the *Brookside* writers.

Andy and I turned up at the nightclub and there was a queue outside. As we approached the bouncers on the door, two northern lads waiting in the line said, 'Can you get us in, Rick?'

'Yeah, sure. Walk in with us. They'll think we're all together.'

The lads fell into step behind me with Andy bringing up the rear. The bouncers recognised me and waved us through. Once inside the lads disappeared and Andy took me upstairs where we could look over the dance floor from the balcony and hopefully see Sue.

Ten minutes later the young lads found us and gave us each a half of lager as a thank you. I didn't even get a chance to take a sip. A bouncer threw a coat over my head, before punching or kicking me unconscious. Andy didn't fare any better. Something blunt was driven into his side and scraped from his hip to his armpit. It caused a massive bruise and almost pierced his skin.

Within seconds we were both on the floor, being dragged out of the club. I'm seventeen stone and Andy is even heavier, but they must have done this hundreds of times because they had it off pat.

Thrown out the back door like bags of trash, I was still unconscious, but Andy screamed abuse and tried to fight back. A photographer just happened to be on hand to record the event and the pictures were splashed across the *News of the World*.

With me still out cold, Andy began to panic. Someone called an ambulance and I was taken to hospital where I finally came round as they wheeled me into the Accident and Emergency room.

I didn't find out what had happened until much later. The northern lads who had come in with us had gone to the bar and bought two halves of lager. They had no idea how much drinks cost at Stringfellow's. The barmaid asked for seven quid, but they only had a fiver on them. Instead of leaving the beers, they put the money on the bar and took them.

The barmaid told the bouncers, who spotted the lads just as they handed the drinks to Andy and me. Nobody bothered asking any questions. They figured we were freeloaders and threw us out as violently and publicly as possible. All this for the sake of two quid!

The next morning I contacted my old mate Jim Nichol, who had become a solicitor in London. He advised me to make a formal complaint to the police.

I told them what had happened and described the bouncer who hit me as the spitting image of the actor Paul Nicholas. Apparently this lad was well known as a thug and a bully, but the police had never had enough evidence to prosecute him.

A warrant was issued and within hours he turned up at the police station with his brief.

Before the case could reach court, Jim Nichol phoned and advised me to drop the complaint.

'Why?'

'He has statements from about ninety people saying you threw the first punch.'

'How could I throw the first punch? He put a coat over my head and I had a drink in my hand.'

'He obviously has a lot of friends.'

I had to swallow my pride, which I found very difficult. It was a good job this fella didn't come from Liverpool because he never would have knocked anyone else out – I can guarantee that.

We filmed two episodes a week of *Brookside* and worked about five weeks in advance. Most of the cast were guaranteed fifty-two episodes a year, but the Grant family were in as many as eighty. This meant long days, working from eight in the morning and often not finishing until midnight.

Whenever I worked late I stayed with Mam rather than drive all the way home.

Normally they gave us the scripts a week in advance. I made a point of waiting until the kids had gone to bed before studying.

When our finances improved, I bought a little static caravan at Kerfoot's Campground near Towyn in North Wales. Surrounded by open fields, it had a fairground and a little social club in the adjoining field. We used to drive up on Saturday, settle in and then go to the club of an evening for a few drinks.

Brookside had become the most popular show on Channel 4, pulling an audience of nearly eight million. At first the gritty realism won praise, but after a while the storylines began to rely more on shock than being true to life. Nothing was taboo – abortion, the Pill, Aids, marital rape, stalking, even incest.

From a practical viewpoint, *Brookside* taught me the mechanics and discipline of acting. Although never great with learning lines, I managed to ad-lib a lot of the time and get through.

ART provided most of the extras for the show, as well as some of the smaller parts. Scoggo had missed out in the initial auditions, but eventually played 'Mattie', my best mate in *Brookside*.

Coming up to Christmas a club singer called Brian Bowfield (best known as Hawk out of Jeff Hawk and the Plainsmen) asked if I could get him some work because he had no money to put anything under the tree for his kids.

Although a real good singer, Brian used to get his words mixed up. He'd say things like, 'I resemble that remark' instead of 'resent that remark' or mispronounce 'forensic' and say 'florensic'.

I managed to get him a little speaking part, but felt nervous the whole time. I quietly warned the rest of the cast, but didn't tell the director for obvious reasons.

We were filming on a Friday and Brian was playing a

plumber who had come to Brookside Close to fix a toilet for the Collins family. He had to say, 'There you go, Mrs Collins, I think you'll find that's OK. Any more problems just get in touch with me and I'll come back on Monday.'

Then he was supposed to walk down the path, get in his van and drive off.

Unfortunately, Brian couldn't drive so we gave him a few impromptu lessons beforehand in my Skoda at the back of the site.

It was getting late and the light had started to fade. This was the last scene of the day and had to be done in one take. With my heart in my mouth, I stood watching with Sue Johnston and a couple more actors. It had started sleeting and the crew were itching to get home.

The director George Spenton Foster yelled 'Action', and Brian came out of the house.

'There you go, Mrs Collins, I think you'll find that's all right. Any trouble, just give me a call and I'll come back on Monday and sort it out.'

'Thank you.'

He walked down the path, got into the van, started it up, found first gear and drove smoothly away.

'That's a wrap,' yelled George and everyone seemed relieved. The other actors looked at me as if to say, 'What were you fussing about? He was perfect.'

At that moment Brian arrived, beaming triumphantly, and announced, 'There you go! Eat ya heart out, Sir John Geilgoil.'

They reckon Kenneth Branagh knows every line of dialogue for every character when he works on a film. I have enough trouble remembering my own.

Simon O'Brien always amazed me by how he could

arrive at work, take a script out of his bag, ask what scene we were doing next and read it for the first time as he changed. He would be word perfect when the cameras rolled.

Brookside had a great cast and although I know it's a cliché we were one big happy family. Simon O'Brien and Paul Usher came to Kate's birthday one year. We normally gave her a party in July because her real birthday was on Christmas Day. Simon and Paul had become big heart-throbs by then and when word leaked we had a fan invasion. Police were needed to sort out traffic in the village and keep the crowd under control.

Another year I got Bill Dean, who played Harry Cross in *Brookside*, to put on a Santa suit and entertain the kids at Kate's birthday. On set we were always playing practical jokes on each other. Billy took delight in winding me up one day because he had big plans for the evening, while I had to spend the night studying my lines.

I slipped into the production office and got one of the girls to type up two pages of straight dialogue off the top of my head. As he was about to leave, she gave it to Billy.

'There's been some last minute alterations to the script. Can you learn this for the morning?'

Billy went home and spent all night rehearsing. Next morning he arrived on set.

'How was the party, Billy?' I grinned.

At that moment he realised it had been a wind-up. 'You bastard!'

When Simon O'Brien decided to leave the series, the writers came up with a suitably dramatic exit, having him stabbed to death.

When it came to the funeral episode, Simon had obviously finished his scenes and we all assumed he had gone home.

We came back from lunch and did the scene where the entire Grant family were standing around the coffin, with our heads lowered in prayer. There were tears and sobs.

The lid of the coffin slowly opened as though some vampire was looking for a feed. I jumped a foot in the air and the girls screamed.

'Gotcha!' said Simon, as he climbed out.

Being Bobby Grant guaranteed me loads of invitations to showbiz parties, premieres, book launches and charity gigs. When the film *Letter to Brezhnev* had its international premiere in Kirby, I agreed to be the master of ceremonies. Young Frankie Clarke had written the screenplay and his sister Margie was the star, alongside Alfred Molina. ART had done the casting for the smaller parts.

Albert and Ronny came with me to the premiere. We drove my old Skoda, which had a dozen sheets of plasterboard on the roof-rack and a bag of plaster in the boot.

As we reached the cinema I caught sight of all the TV cameras, the red carpet and the searchlights. Embarrassed, I drove straight past and parked the Skoda round the corner. I changed into my dinner jacket and arrived on foot.

Glamorous showbiz parties were a real eye-opener. I wasn't shy or uncomfortable, but neither did I embrace all the trappings. To begin with, I didn't like champagne and half the time I couldn't tell what I was eating when finger food arrived on trays. Is it cooked? Is it even dead?

Roland Joffe invited me to his fortieth birthday party in 1985, when he took over the Groucho Club in Soho, London, inviting friends from around the world. I had never been to a party like it. I recognised Jeremy Irons, Liam Neeson and David Putnam, but there were dozens of others I couldn't put names to.

Waiters dashed around with trays of champagne and a fella played a baby grand in the corner.

Roland had just finished working on *The Mission*, a wonderful film about Jesuit priests bringing Christianity to South America. He had called me to ask if I fancied a part, which was very flattering. It would have meant spending five months in South America working with the likes of Liam Neeson, Jeremy Irons, Ray McNally and Cheri Lungi. I would have gone in a heartbeat, just for the experience, but unfortunately Phil Redmond refused to release me from my *Brookside* contract.

The Groucho Club had an amazing carvery with all the trimmings. Rather than look like an idiot I confessed to the chef that I didn't know what half the stuff was. Looking pleased, he began explaining the different dishes and giving me little bits of meat to try. I finished up with a mound of food on my plate.

After dinner waiters began passing through the crowd with bottles of pink champagne, which I had never seen before. I noticed a fella standing on his own a few feet away. I nodded and raised my glass to him, as if to say, 'Have you got a drink?'

He held his glass up.

'Are you in the game then?' I asked.

Before he could answer there was a loud cheer and David Putnam walked past with Jeremy Irons and two others, carrying a huge birthday cake on their shoulders.

They set the cake down and a Marilyn Monroe lookalike burst from the top and sang a breathless rendition of 'Happy Birthday' to Roland. We all clapped and Roland made a generous thank you speech.

As he finished speaking, he caught sight of me and came over.

'I want you to meet someone,' he said.

He directed me a few feet to the same fella I had acknowledged earlier. He was small and thin, with his hair pulled back into a ponytail and a little goatee beard.

'Ricky Tomlinson, I'd like you to meet Robert De Niro. Robert, this is Ricky Tomlinson.'

I didn't have a clue. Honest to God. I had always pictured De Niro as this big, powerful brawler, like in *Raging Bull*. Yet in real life there is nothing of him.

Working full time on *Brookside* and doing public appearances and charity shows, I spent a lot of time away from home. This didn't seem any different. I had always worked away.

In hindsight, I should have spent more time with the kids, but instead I became one of them fathers that waltzes in, gives them a lot of laughs and then disappears again. I saw the best of them, but it was Marlene who was there when they were sick or lonely or frightened.

I know some women are going to read this book and call me a bastard for having affairs and spending so much time away from home. Maybe they're not far from the mark, but I can only tell you how I saw things.

Marlene and me were total opposites. She was happy to be a housewife, a homemaker and a really good Mum. I was a showman and a party animal, more at home in crowded bars, listening to live music and making people laugh. We were two different people and over the years we'd grown further apart. At the same time, I would never have divorced her. I had made a promise when we married and I believed in 'till death do us part'.

That's why it came as such a shock that day in 1985, when the mailman delivered a long narrow envelope. Marlene picked it up from the mat and walked down the hall, before dropping it in my lap.

'What's this?'

'Your divorce papers.'

Honest to God, that was the first I knew. I was gobsmacked. I didn't know what to say. She had already walked into the kitchen and started making a cup of tea.

'Don't you want to talk about this?'

'No.'

'How can you say that? We've been together twenty-four years. What about the kids? We owe them something. We have to try.'

'I have tried.'

There were dozens of reasons why Marlene could have left me over the years, but why now? The tough times were behind us. We had more money than at any time in our lives. We had a car, a caravan and enough to take the kids on little holidays.

The truth is, we didn't talk. We couldn't discuss things unless it related to the kids. This is all we had left in common.

Strangely, I didn't feel sorry for myself or angry. I was more worried about what Mam might say. Nobody had ever divorced in our family. Surprisingly, when I broke the news she didn't turn a hair.

'Whatever will be, will be,' she said. 'These things happen.'

Marlene is very single-minded and not the type to change her mind. For that same reason, I didn't try to talk her out of it. I still wanted to be a father to my kids and she seemed happy with that.

We continued living in the cottage on friendly terms until the divorce was finalised, although I spent more and more time in Liverpool. I can't remember how we broke the news to Clifton, Gareth and Kate. I know they took it pretty well.

They could see their Mum and Dad still talking to each other, rather than having bitter rows.

Years later Marlene told me the story about how she went to a solicitor and asked about getting a divorce.

'Does he knock you about?' he had asked her.

'No. He's never lifted his hand to me.'

'Is he a layabout?'

'No, he's a workaholic.'

'Is he good with the kids?'

'Yeah, he's great with them.'

The solicitor shook his head. 'Explain to me again why you are divorcing him.'

Unfortunately, when it came to the court proceedings, a different picture emerged. The grounds for the divorce were my unreasonable behaviour and I was portrayed as being a lazy boozer who spent no time with the kids. This hurt.

We were officially divorced on 27 August 1986. Determined to do the right thing by Marlene, even before the settlement we began looking for houses. I wanted to keep the cottage because I had spent so much time and effort fixing it up. Marlene wanted to make a fresh start in a place of her own.

Eventually, the choice came down to two, including a large detached house with four bedrooms in a village near Coedpoeth. It cost thirty-five thousand pounds and Marlene thought it was too much. She wanted the cheaper house but I convinced her that she needed the extra space. One of the bedrooms was almost twenty feet long and perfect for Clifton, who had become a very promising table-tennis player and could have a table in his room.

It cost me all I had, including money I had put aside for my tax bill. I arranged for some of my mates to tidy up the garden and move the shed. Later, when Marlene wanted the big bedroom divided in two, Albert put in the wall and door.

She sold the house quite quickly after that and bought another place only a few hundred yards from the cottage. This suited me because I was closer to the kids.

It was a strange feeling being single again after so long. A part of me felt abandoned and set adrift. When it came to looking after myself I was pretty hopeless. I couldn't cook and had never washed or ironed my clothes. I had gone from being looked after by my mother to being looked after by Marlene. I'm not fishing for sympathy here, I'm just telling you the truth.

Once the initial sense of shock had worn off, I threw myself into work. The sense of abandonment slowly gave way to feelings of freedom and excitement. I could do what I wanted. It was like a second chance.

Phil Redmond had given a lot of people their start on television, particularly youngsters from Liverpool who would never normally have had this sort of opportunity. Many of them went on to become great technicians, cameramen, sound engineers, editors and directors.

Most of the actors I worked with came from middle-class backgrounds and had gone to drama or stage schools. There were no openings for working-class kids because these schools were expensive.

In 1986 I bought an old stone church that had been advertised in the *Wrexham Evening Leader*. It was at Summer Hill about two or three miles outside Wrexham.

The church had been deconsecrated, but still had the pews and a pulpit. It cost about seven thousand pounds and I bought it outright with money I had made from *Brookside*.

The plan was to set up a drama school for local kids,

charging them only a few bob, and getting local teachers involved. I supplied the money and a mate, Billy Burns, put in the elbow grease.

Billy was a lorry driver by profession and very good tradesman. We took out all the pews and the pulpit, ripping up the old floors and putting in a proper dance floor, a stage and curtains. We also built toilets, while an office upstairs became a storeroom and changing rooms. Soon after it opened, the drama school featured on TV when Sir Harry Secombe came to Wrexham to film the show *Highway*.

We had some great kids pass through the doors and a few went on to become full-time actors or to do TV commercials. I used to get there once or twice a week and loved working with the kids. It didn't make any money, but that was never the aim.

Our Ronny had been running the casting agency, with the help of a secretary. We needed more space and Liverpool City Council offered me a derelict building on the corner of Mount Pleasant, facing the Adelphi Hotel. The windows were boarded up and the floors were either missing or covered in filth, but I could see the potential.

I agreed to refurbish the building in return for a five-year lease at a reasonable rent and a waiver on the rates for the first year. Albert and some of his building mates began work, initially refurbishing a couple of rooms for ART on the first floor.

Suddenly, I had this huge building at my disposal and my imagination ran wild. I could turn the second floor into a club and concert room, with a smaller private bar on the same level. And the top floor could become offices that I could rent out to writers and other creative people.

It was a massive task, which meant rewiring virtually the whole building, plastering walls, laying floorboards and buying furniture and fittings. Demonstrating my ignorance of such things, I didn't bother getting receipts or keeping a check on how much money it all cost. I had a dream.

The Limelight Club opened in 1987 and a lot of my mates from the pubs and clubs became regulars. Most of the time it was just a drinking club, with entertainment on weekends. We encouraged new musical acts and also drama, with a writers' group using some of the spare rooms.

Needing someone to manage the club, I took on a business partner, Pat O'Rourke, who had experience in running pubs and clubs. He was about my height, stocky with a goatee beard and glasses – a bit like a Scouse version of Rolf Harris. And although he didn't put any money into the Limelight Club, we had a gentleman's agreement on a fifty-fifty split.

The two of us became great mates and used to challenge each other to pool games, with the loser having to undertake some embarrassing dare such as hopping on one foot for two hours while serving customers. After one loss I spent an entire day in a short dress, black socks and shoes. Another time I threatened to make Pat walk the plank into the Leeds–Liverpool canal.

Being a 'face' on TV meant a lot of these stunts finished up in the *Liverpool Echo* and helped publicise the club.

Increasingly, I was happier at the Limelight than anywhere else – and that included on the set of *Brookside*. Although I had enormous admiration for Phil Redmond, I didn't always agree with his decisions. The show had won a huge audience because of its gritty realism and topical storylines but the cutting edge became dull as the storylines grew ridiculous.

It was a working-class soap, looking at working-class issues, yet during the year-long miners' strike in 1984–1985

the dispute was never mentioned in *Brookside*. Along with
Sue Johnston, I spent hours on the picket lines supporting
the miners. It was the biggest issue in the country and should
have been included in a show that prided itself on being
topical. To me this was a sell-out and many people agreed,
including Jimmy McGovern, who wrote many of the finest
episodes.

Similarly, when a district auditor expelled forty-seven
Liverpool councillors from office for refusing to set an annual
rate there were mass protests and demonstrations in
Liverpool. 'Better to Break the Law than Break the Poor' was
the slogan, but again it didn't warrant a mention in *Brookside*.

Phil Redmond, in my opinion, embraced Thatcherism and
as a result the storylines no longer pointed out working-class
poverty or Tory spending cuts. Instead the plots began
pushing the boundaries of credibility, with kidnappings,
buried bodies and what became known as 'slut-and-sleaze'
storylines.

Once you start along this road you finish up with ridiculous
plot twists like the Bobby Ewing shower scene in *Dallas*. As
a result, *Brookside* began losing popularity. After nudging
eight million, audience numbers fell away to half that
number.

I had been on the show for nearly five years and my
character Bobby Grant had gone through a lot of changes. He
had started off as a passionate, hard-working trade union
official, flawed but basically a decent bloke. Slowly his
reputation took a bit of a bashing with a marital rape and a
drinking problem, but that was OK. I knew it was difficult for
writers to come up with decent storylines.

People were spreading rumours that Bobby Grant was
going to be portrayed as bent and corrupt – someone who
would sell out his mates and his class. There was enough

union-bashing in real life without me portraying it on TV.

Although I made my feelings known, I didn't take things any further. Having been through a divorce, I had enough on my plate.

ART casting had launched some amazing people like Milandra Boroughs in *Emmerdale Farm*, Tricia Penrose from *Heartbeat*, Mary the Punk from *EastEnders* and Ziggy from *Grange Hill*. We gave local people work.

At the cottage one night I had a phone call from Phil Redmond. He asked if I'd come and see him right away. I assumed it must have something to do with *Brookside* so I drove forty miles to his Liverpool office.

'I'm interested in learning about the casting business,' he said, after offering me a seat.

'What did you want to know?'

'How exactly does it work?'

I thought he might want to buy ART or go into partnership, particularly when he said, 'There'll be something in this for you.'

He asked me what percentage the agency took; who looked after expenses; the turnover and staffing levels. Then, after about forty minutes of milking me for information, he shook my hand and showed me to the door.

Within weeks Phil Redmond had opened his own casting agency from one of the houses on the *Brookside* site. Called 'Mersey Casting', it provided all the extras for the soap and was run by Dorothy Andrews. Rather than having 'something for me', Phil had set up in direct competition to ART and took a lot of our business.

For all his undoubted talent and his working-class roots, Phil has always known where his last pound came from and made sure he held on to every one of them.

When I first started working on *Brookside* he wanted to pay actors three hundred pounds a week if they weren't used for more than three minutes on screen. I would probably have said yes, but Equity stepped in and told Mersey TV that people had to receive the full rate for the job.

None of us received travelling expenses and people were encouraged to say they were Liverpool-based. Members of the cast who lived out of the region had to pay for their own digs.

I remember a director being told he had to share one of Redmond's houses with another member of the crew. When he complained and asked for normal expenses, he was moved to the Adelphi Hotel. Shortly afterwards he was moved again – off the set completely.

Soon after production started Phil Redmond took the cast to one side and said, 'If we get the viewing figures up to two million we're all going to get shares in the company.'

Within a few weeks the figures were well over two million. Someone asked him about the shares and he said, 'No, what we need is to reach four million. Then we can all go forward together.'

Eventually we reached eight million on a minority channel, but there was never any mention again of shares in the company.

After the amazing success in that first year, I mentioned to Phil that I had always fancied going to the BAFTA award ceremony.

'It's about a hundred pounds a ticket,' he said.

'That's OK.'

He booked a table for *Brookside* and we each paid a hundred pounds. Only later, when I talked to other people in the industry, did I discover that production companies usually pick up the tab for nights like this. They pay for tables so they can showcase their stars. Given the success of *Brookside*, a few hundred pounds for tickets would have been small change.

When the new season started in February 1988 I overheard a couple of people talking about a Christmas party at Phil Redmond's house. It was news to me. I confronted one of the crew and discovered that I was the only member of the cast that hadn't been invited.

Normally, this wouldn't have worried me except for the fact that none of the others had told me.

Sue Johnston came and apologised. 'I didn't realise you weren't invited until I arrived and you weren't there. Then I didn't know whether to tell you or not. I thought it might make it worse.'

I liked Sue a lot, but it took me a long while to forgive her for that. We had always looked out for each other and had stood side by side on picket lines.

Poor old Billy Dean fared even worse. I lost my temper with him a few days later and said, 'Billy, if you were twenty years younger, I would have you.'

His eyes filled with tears.

Phil Redmond got wind of how unhappy I was and came to see me in the canteen. He made no mention of the Christmas party, but invited me for a meal at his place.

'Thanks Phil, but I'm OK as I am,' I said.

Up until then I didn't think I had a problem at *Brookside*. Yes, I often niggled about pay rises and proper expenses, but I wasn't a difficult actor and I prided myself in being totally professional in front of the camera.

Now I began putting two and two together. A few months earlier, Jimmy McGovern had come to me and said, 'Rick, do me a favour, just keep your head down.'

He obviously knew something was in the wind.

When my contract finally came up for renewal, Dorothy

Andrews came clean and said the company were offering me a three-month contract instead of the normal twelve.

'No, I'll go now,' I said straight off.

She looked shocked.

'We didn't mean . . . not now . . . ah, you'll have to wait . . . let me see . . .'

Up until that moment I hadn't been looking to leave the series, but now the decision came easily. It was obvious that Phil Redmond didn't want me on the show, but he also didn't want me just walking out.

Dorothy came back to me.

'How long will you do?' she asked.

'Nine months,' I told her. This would give me long enough to sort something else out. Financially, I was stretched after the divorce settlement and setting up the Limelight Club.

As it turned out, I didn't last nine months. Matters came to a head in April 1988 when I argued again over the slut-and-sleaze storylines and the demonising of Bobby Grant who had become a boozer, a whinger and a dinosaur.

In one particular storyline, Karen Grant, my daughter, had gone off to university and was living with her boyfriend. Sheila Grant, my staunch, never-off-her-knees Catholic wife, should have been doing her nut, but instead she was portrayed as being absolutely OK with this. It was Bobby Grant who ranted and raved like some moralising preacher.

'Why would I do that?' I said to the writers. 'I'm a left-wing firebrand trade unionist. I'm not going to give a damn about premarital sex as long as Karen is happy.'

Unable to get through to people, I put on my coat, walked off the set and drove home. All hell broke loose.

The next day I phoned the director, Norman Foster.

'Look, I'm coming in on Friday. You'll have to do what you

can to write me out of the series because I'm not coming back after that.'

I didn't want the job any more. I knew I was walking away from a regular income and a high-profile show, but that didn't matter.

The *Liverpool Echo* tracked me down a few days later and I told them the same story.

'Phil Redmond and I have always had an understanding that I would not do anything to betray the working class. I have had differences with some of the writers over the scripts for some time, but the other week everything came to a head . . . As far as I'm concerned they can send Bobby to America or even to the moon and I will go along with it, but if they try to make him do anything which betrays the working class I won't be playing the part.'

My fight had never been with Phil Redmond, although I didn't always agree with him. He is a towering figure in British TV, who has never been frightened about taking risks or trying something new.

From a personal standpoint he is enormously creative and a lot of people owe their careers to having been given a start on a Redmond production. At the same time, Phil has never received the critical acclaim of writers like Jimmy McGovern, Alan Bleasedale or Willy Russell, which I think disappoints him.

I left *Brookside* in 1988 and the show carried on successfully, as I knew it would. Sue Johnston stayed on for a while and then like most of the others went on to bigger and better things. Paul Usher is a regular in *The Bill* and Simon O'Brien does a travel programme.

The ratings of *Brookside* continued to slide and in October 2002 the audience had fallen to 400,000. Channel 4 moved the soap to Saturday afternoons, which pretty much signalled the end. Finally, in June 2003, it was axed completely.

Ironically, I read an interview with Phil Redmond in which he admitted that some of the storylines had gone too far. He wanted to return to the campaigning agenda, dealing with issues like the NHS and childcare. 'Things that engage and worry people in society,' he said.

16

The Limelight

I don't know whether it is because of Mam or the fact that I'm getting married again, but I want to find people from my past. I want to thank them for the memories and maybe even give them a few quid if they need a hand.

Girls like Margie King, Mary Jackson and Nancy gave me so many wonderful memories. I used to adore dancing with them and holding them close.

Just before Mam's funeral I bumped into Georgie Star, a local entertainer, and asked him if he remembered Margie King.

'That's not her name now,' he said. 'But I think she's living in Skelmersdale.'

'Can you get me a phone number?'

About a week later I called Margie, which took her by surprise. She had followed my career and had been a real fan of Brookside she said. We arranged to meet and George picked her up. As I waited at the bar of a local pub, a very neat, grey-haired old lady walked up to me nervously.

'Hi ya, kid?'

'Hi ya.'

'Are you having a drink?'

'I don't drink.'

'You don't mind if I have one?'

'No.'

We had a half hour chatting and we laughed at the same memories.

I reminded her that I once loved her.

'I know ya did,' Margie said. 'I loved you, too, and a part of me still does. But I'm not in love with you.'

I knew what she meant.

Even before this, while filming Nice Guy Eddie *I told Tony Smith, the private investigator who advised on the series, about Mary Jackson and he offered to help find her. Tony spent months on the case, searching through births, deaths, marriages, newspaper libraries, phone records, databases, you name it. He sent me updates on the search, but ultimately drew a blank.*

Don't get me wrong. Rita is the woman I love and I want to spend the rest of my life with her. But at the same time you reach a certain stage in your life where memories take on a greater importance. I just want to know what happened to Mary and be sure that she's OK. If she reads this, I hope she gets in touch.

Rather than travel back and forth to the cottage I spent most of my time in Liverpool at the Limelight Club. I had a room upstairs with a bed and a chest of drawers. Joffe, my bull mastiff, had the run of the place, including the rooftop yard which had railings around it.

The Limelight seemed to be ticking over, but I didn't take much notice of the books. Pat O'Rourke made sure the bills were paid and the bar was kept fully stocked.

Pat was married and had four stepdaughters. His wife Agnes worked at the Limelight and her youngest, Diane, who was sixteen, often came down to lend a hand. She had fair hair, a pretty smile and was a really good grafter, although I sometimes felt that her parents worked her like a navvy.

The club had a bistro licence and served breakfast from about ten in the morning. During a local postal strike I opened earlier and served up a full English breakfast for 75p.

Among the club regulars was Chloe, who came in most mornings for a spot of breakfast. Often she didn't have enough money for anything other than a cup of tea.

'Are you having anything to eat, Chloe?'

'I don't feel like it this morning, Hobo.'

'Look, I done too much bacon this morning. I don't want to waste it. How about a bacon sandwich?'

'Oh, go on, then. I don't want to see it wasted.'

Often we'd sit and talk about growing up in Liverpool. Chloe had been forced on to the streets as a prostitute at the age of sixteen. Dressed in a short skirt and fishnet stockings, she worked in all weathers, unable to go home until she had earned ten shillings.

She became known as the Garston Butterfly because she had two little tattoos of butterflies on her ankles. One night in the depths of winter, she had spent hours trying to find a customer, but the only ship in port was a Soviet freighter and those on board were more likely to be soldiers rather than merchant seamen.

Cold and tired, she climbed the gangplank and a young sailor shouted at her in Russian, pointing a rifle. He looked barely out of his teens. Chloe raised her hands in surrender and with a mixture of hand signals and broken English, she tried to explain that she just needed somewhere to lay down her head.

The soldier nodded and motioned for her to follow him. Here we go, she thought. He'll take me down below and he'll rape me. There'll be others – the whole crew. Maybe they'll keep me prisoner and set sail. They'll use me and then toss me overboard into the Atlantic. Nobody will ever know.

She followed him along the narrow passageways until he reached a cabin. Inside was a simple wooden bunk with a blanket, a table, a chair and a locker. On the table there was an ashtray, an empty beer bottle and the bottle-cap.

Chloe curled up on the bunk, facing the wall, and waited for the hands to touch her. Instead she heard the cabin door shut. She fell asleep and didn't wake until many hours later when the door opened again. The soldier held a finger to his lips and motioned her to follow. She carried her high-heel shoes so as not to make a sound as she retraced her footsteps and arrived at the gangway.

It was growing light as she stepped off the ship. She turned and saw the young soldier. He raised his hand and waved. Chloe opened her handbag when she finished the story and showed me a beer-bottle cap. She had taken it from the cabin and carried it with her for the rest of her life as a reminder of the nicest thing anyone had ever done for her.

Soon after we met Chloe's health deteriorated and I discovered she had cancer. Several times a week she travelled to Clatterbridge Hospital for chemotherapy.

Jimmy Culshaw, one of the writers living upstairs, came into the bar and I threw him the keys to my car and asked him to drive Chloe to the hospital. From then on I tried to organise a lift for her whenever I could. I also went to see her when she was admitted for a few weeks. She had lost all her hair and her skin was as white and thin as rice paper.

Chloe managed to pull through and the cancer went into remission. She would often come down and help me clean up the club or work in the kitchen. One particular night she took a turn for the worst.

'I don't feel so well, Rick. I'm going to go home.'

'Why don't you get your head down upstairs in my room? Just until you feel better. I'll run you home later.'

She went upstairs and I carried on working behind the bar until it grew late. Suddenly there was a dreadful scream and the sound of breaking glass. I raced upstairs and burst into the room. Chloe had used a chair to smash the window and had crawled out on to a balcony that was barely two feet wide. Four floors above the street, she clung to the edge.

I reached through the window and grabbed her, pulling her inside. She was shaking with fear.

'He was by the door,' she stammered. 'A big fella. He wouldn't let me out. He had a long coat and he was bald. He kept saying, "No. No. I'm waiting for Nellie."'

Nobody could have been in the room. Chloe had either been dreaming or had seen a ghost. Two days later, Nellie Grace, one of the regulars at the club, dropped dead unexpectedly.

I don't know who leaked the story to the *Liverpool Echo* but next minute I had a reporter on the doorstep wanting to know where it all took place. I took him up the back stairs and he suddenly went deathly white. I thought he was joking, but his skin had gone clammy and his hair stood on end. He had come to take the piss out of me and been scared senseless.

The *Echo* wrote a story about the club being haunted and this triggered even more interest. Among the calls was one from Maureen Singleton, who lived in nearby Preston. With short-cropped red hair, dark slacks and a long flowing coat, Maureen looked a lot like Anne Robinson. She claimed to know someone who could exorcise the spirit. Oddly enough I didn't laugh. When it comes to the supernatural I have an open mind and I also knew that Chloe was frightened of nothing, yet something had clearly terrified her.

Maureen introduced me to David Drew, who wore a simple suit and had ginger hair and a ginger beard. He wasn't some amateur mystic with a crystal ball in his front room. David had done big professional stage shows as a psychic. He went upstairs on his own and came back an hour later.

'This place is alive with ghosts and there's a couple here I can't move,' he said. 'I'll have to come back again.'

'How much do I owe you?'

'Oh, no, nothing.'

He visited the club three times, paying his own expenses and staying in a little hotel next door. On the last visit he concentrated on a bathroom upstairs. I could hear stuff flying everywhere and he came out covered in bruises with his clothes in a mess.

'How did it go?'

'Everything's fine now.'

I looked in the bathroom. The floor was littered with shampoo, soap and toiletries.

'What was it?' I asked.

He laughed. 'Everyone thinks that spirits are going to be headless horsemen or defrocked vicars.'

'So who was this?'

'A guy who shot and killed someone and then committed suicide. He wouldn't believe he was really dead. I had to convince him.'

As I said, I keep an open mind about these things. David later put on a show at the Limelight and proved to have amazing skills. He would take a ring or a necklace from someone in the audience and reveal details of their lives that he couldn't possibly have researched earlier. Some people were left in tears.

This wasn't our only unexplained phenomenon in the club. After clearing away glasses and cleaning up one night, I went upstairs and heard people talking in a room that I knew was empty.

Creeping downstairs, I got Pat O'Rourke, Agnes and Diane to come up and they, too, heard the voices. A bank operated on the ground floor and about a year earlier someone had been arrested trying to break in from the upper floor. I figured someone must be trying it again, having entered across the rooftops.

'Go and call the police,' I whispered to Agnes. 'Tell them not to use sirens.'

Meanwhile, I sent Diane down to open the front door and to show them in. The police arrived and tiptoed upstairs. There were four of them, all in uniform. They listened outside the door and we all heard the voices. After lots of hand signals and whispers, I slowly turned the key and they went charging in. The room was completely empty. Nothing. Nowt. I felt foolish.

'It's OK,' the senior policeman said. 'We heard the voices too.'

Nobody could ever explain what happened, but I have no doubts the building was haunted. The final proof came when I saw a ghost with my own eyes.

It happened on the beautiful old spiral staircase that rose from the lobby to the upper floors. The casting agency and my office were on the first floor. Further up the stairs was the Limelight Club and the small private bar, along with the toilets.

About midday one day, as I came back downstairs to the office, I noticed a woman with a baby in a pram, holding a toddler with one hand.

I said 'Hello' and carried on down the stairs. Suddenly, I thought, how is she going to get down the stairs with that pram? When I came out of the office she had already gone. Someone must have given her a hand, I thought.

The following morning I chatted to Albert Skinlen, a

mechanic who was staying in a small room above the club. Albert seemed upset about something.

'I'm not being funny,' he said, 'but whenever I come down these stairs I can't look over the edge. I have to keep my face to the wall.'

'Why?'

'Because every morning when I look over the banister I see a woman with a baby in a pram going down the stairs, but when I get to the front door it's locked. There's nowhere she could have gone.'

Albert had seen the same woman! I phoned Maureen Singleton who got in touch with David Drew.

'There shouldn't be anything there. David has cleared everything out. Are you doing any building work?'

'We've been ripping down some walls to build a drama school.'

'That's it. You've disturbed them.'

'Disturbed who?'

'Whoever the woman is.'

Fine, I thought. I can live with that. She wasn't doing any harm.

Owning and running a club is perhaps the ultimate male fantasy. The drinks are free, your mates are close and the laughs are plentiful. I worked well with Pat. I handled the customers and he handled the business side of things.

His stepdaughter Diane had now turned seventeen. Whenever I was doing an errand in the van she would ask to come with me. Sometimes we would stop and have a cup of tea and a sandwich on the way back. She must have had a little crush on me at the time, but I didn't realise. It was probably because I treated her more as a grown up than her parents did.

I began to notice that Diane would make excuses to spend time with me. She clearly had a soft spot, but I was old enough to be her father.

Finally, I stopped the car one day and said, 'Listen, kid, I think you're really great, but you shouldn't be looking at someone like me as anything more than a friend.'

She started crying.

'What's the matter?'

'I'm not a virgin.'

'What difference does that make?'

'You won't be the first. Someone has already done that.'

She dissolved into a flood of tears and explained the problems she had had when she was younger.

We talked for a while and after she calmed down I dropped her back at the club. She apologised for burdening me with her problems.

Soon after this things started going pear-shaped at the club. Despite having some big nights and full houses, this didn't translate into bigger takings. In fact, when the booze bills and VAT became due we struggled to pay them. At first I juggled certain payments, writing letters and making excuses. Later I began borrowing from people to pay debts that simply couldn't wait.

To make matters worse, I had bought Chloe's house from her for twenty-eight thousand pounds to help her out of her own financial hole. I borrowed the money from ART, but knew that it had to go back into the company to pay a tax bill the following year.

Chloe lived in a lovely little detached cottage with a little garden in a leafy lane in Grassendale, a nice area of Liverpool. Initially, I thought of living there, but realised it made more sense to find a tenant.

Pat O'Rourke left suddenly, leaving me with more

problems. Nothing had been put in writing about us both being liable for debts of the partnership, so I had to shoulder the burden on my own.

Trying to run the Limelight by myself only made things worse. I had never run a club before and knew little about stocktaking or bookkeeping. On the surface everything seemed fine, but in reality I was falling further into the red.

At home one night in the cottage, I answered a frantic knocking at the door. Diane stood shivering on the doorstep. She had been crying.

'What's the matter?'

'I've run away from home.'

'Well, you better come in and have a cup of tea.'

She sat at the table with her head resting in her hands, while I made some toast and poured the tea. I still had no furniture in the cottage except a small table, two dining chairs, a sideboard and a mattress.

'What are you going to do?'

'Can I stay here?'

'I don't think that's a very good idea.'

'I've nowhere else to go.' She started crying again.

I knew I should send her back to her family. The cottage had no furniture and I had barely enough money to put milk in the fridge.

Diane arrived at my lowest ebb. My marriage had failed. I was seeing less and less of the kids. Creditors were circling like vultures. We were both emotionally vulnerable, which explains what happened, but doesn't absolve me of guilt. As a forty-eight-year-old man I should have known better. She was only seventeen. Diane stayed with me that night and the next and the next. We were together nearly four years.

Pat and Agnes were angry, but their fury was nothing

compared with Marlene's. At the club one day I had a phone call from a mate. 'Rick, you better get home.'

'Why?'

'All your windows are smashed.'

Sure enough, every pane of glass had been broken at the cottage. Marlene had started at the outside and then moved inside. She had broken every plate, mug, cup and saucer, along with my banjos, a guitar and the TV set. A bronze bust of John Lennon (one of only six cast) had been hit with such force that it broke his nose and his glasses.

The only thing undamaged was a big jubilee sideboard that was so tall I had notched two or three of the ceiling beams to fit it in. Marlene had tried and failed to pull it over.

I don't know what she resented the most – the fact that Diane was only seventeen or that I had found someone else.

Despite the damage, nothing was ever said or done. I certainly wasn't going to make a complaint to the police. The next day Marlene came round and offered to help clean up the place. I told her I'd be OK.

Whatever warmth there had been between us now disappeared completely. She wouldn't talk to me on the phone and neither would she let me visit the house or see the kids.

On Christmas Day, Katie's birthday, she always got twice as many gifts as the lads. I went round to the house with a black bin bag full of presents as well as envelopes of cash that I had managed to save.

I knocked on the front door and no one answered. Marlene came out the back and walked along the side path. She took the sack of presents from me, went inside and shut the door. Katie was standing at the front window watching. It was awful. I can still picture her face now – the look of disappointment and sadness. She has always been incredibly loyal to her Mum, but I know she wanted to see me that day. She wanted us to be a family again, even if just for an hour.

Marlene went even further and took me back to court demanding an additional 'periodic payment' as part of the divorce. I couldn't believe it. Creditors were queuing up. My cheques were bouncing. How could she possibly think I had any money?

When the case reached Wrexham County Court I was ambushed with a building society statement for a small amount of money that I hadn't declared when we divorced. Honest to God, I had totally forgotten the account even existed, otherwise I would have used the money to help pay off my debts.

Marlene's solicitor accused me of hiding assets. He carved me up in the witness box and by the time he finished I wasn't even sure what day of the week it was.

When it came time for Marlene to give evidence she pulled a masterstroke. My solicitor, Neville Goldrein, asked her if it was true that she had only worked in paid employment for eleven months during our marriage. At this point, Marlene very carefully took a pair of glasses out of her handbag and slipped them on. The message was clear: her work as a seamstress had ruined her eyesight.

The Judge ordered me to find another twelve thousand pounds before 17 September 1989. It was laughable. I already owed tens of thousands of pounds to the VAT man, the liquor supplier, the bank and the council.

I took out a second mortgage on the cottage to raise the money for Marlene. At the same time I went to mates like Mick McNally and hit them up for loans.

Mick was the sort of bloke who was always talking about doing deals worth hundreds of hundreds of pounds. We had a long history and I knew he could trust me to pay him back.

'How much do you need?' he asked.

'Four grand.'

'OK, come with me.'

We went to the Allied Bank of Ireland in Castle Street and he withdrew the cash. I took it straight to the liquor supplier and paid the outstanding bill, which meant the Limelight could stay open.

Diane and I worked long hours at the club trying to keep it going. She celebrated her eighteenth birthday and we had a lot of laughs despite the hardship.

I didn't see the age difference as being an issue. She had always seemed so wise and mature. By comparison, I was a big kid. People might argue that I took advantage of her, but I don't see it that way. I thought the world of Diane and we had a strong, loving relationship.

I hope she thinks the same way. She had put up with a lot of stick in her life and had never really had a childhood. She was a little skivvy for everyone – including me.

In hindsight, the Limelight was in jeopardy right from the outset when the Government changed the licensing laws in 1988 – a year after we opened. Up until then, places with a bistro licence were guaranteed a good crowd of an afternoon when the ordinary pubs were shut for their compulsory break. Once the pubs could open all day, we didn't get the afternoon crowd, who stayed on till evening.

My problems were compounded when the city council suddenly decided to sell our building when the lease came up for renewal. I had spent tens of thousands of pounds on refurbishing the site, but now had to negotiate a tenancy agreement with a new owner, a big clothing retailer.

Instead of paying eighty pounds a week they wanted six hundred. With the help of Neville Goldrein we negotiated them down to three hundred, but it was still nearly four times

Beauty and the Beast. With my lovely daughter Kate.

On my 60th birthday (clockwise from left) Mam, Clifton, myself, Gareth and Mam's sister Liza.

With Doddy and Mam, celebrating Mam's 84th birthday.

In Sue Johnston's back garden with (left to right) the poet Adrian Henry, Brookside mate Dean Sullivan and the brilliant TV writer Jimmy McGovern.

With another great writer Alan Bleasedale and producer Col McKeown. Both Alan and I worked on Liverpool's successful bid to become European City of Culture 2008.

One of the greats – Sir John Mills. I doubt if there has ever been a nicer man.

Arthur Scargill campaigned to have me released from prison. We've been mates ever since (even though he forgot the date of my wedding).

With the lovely Rita, who has seen my best and worst but still agreed to marry me.

Give me a banjo and I'll give you a song. I began playing at seventeen, when it was just an excuse to pick up girls.

. . . with Sue Johnston . . .

. . . with Albert, who can sing right down to the depths of his boots, just like Dean Martin. I'm playing the banjo that was later confiscated by the bailiffs . . .

. . . having a ball on
Parkinson, with Michael
Starke (left) and Noddy Holder
(right). The audience wanted
an encore but we only knew
the one song . . .

. . . with Ally McCoist on the
John Daly Show in Dublin.

Master of disguise (not with a nose like mine) . . . with Sean Hughes in *The Greatest Store in the World* (1999).

Facing the media as *Mike Bassett: England Manager.*

Under fire as a gangster in *The 51st State* (2002).

Don't ask! From the film *Preaching to the Perverted* (1997).

On set with Robbie Carlyle and Samuel L. Jackson in *The 51st State*. Samuel struggled to believe I was a local sex symbol.

With comedian Johnny Vegas in *The Virgin of Liverpool* (2003).

Forty years on and I'm getting married again. Albert is still my best man, but now I have Clifton and Gareth to help him.

Among the guests were comedienne Faith Brown and Liz Dawn (Vera Duckworth).

With the gorgeous bride . . .

With Rita and my beautiful granddaughter Paige.

more than I could afford. Sure enough I fell behind and they were soon hounding me for money.

By now I had borrowed thirteen thousand pounds from my brother David and another four thousand from Freddie Grace, one of the regulars at the club. I owed another few thousand to Andy Lynch and four thousand to Mick McNally. On top of this I had borrowed twenty-eight thousand from ART to buy Chloe's cottage and the bank loan to pay Marlene.

Shuffling money around like deck chairs on the *Titanic*, I tried to keep the club and the agency afloat. Occasional acting jobs gave me some breathing space.

Chris Clough, a director on *Brookside*, gave me a lovely part as a womanising layabout on *The Bill*. He also wanted me to play an alien on *Doctor Who*, but I couldn't make the shoot so I suggested Scoggo for the role.

My biggest break came when the director Ken Loach rang ART wanting to audition about thirty working-class guys for a new film. I had never met Ken before, but I knew of his reputation as a film-maker. He reminded me of the gentle, quiet schoolmaster in *Goodbye, Mr Chips*. Laid back, but very sharp, he was passionate about movies, people and football.

He came to Liverpool three times, holding the auditions at the ART office, before finally choosing Jimmy Coleman and Georgie Moss, two lads I had worked with in the clubs. Jimmy is only about five foot five, with blond hair and a broad accent. He still does gigs as a cabaret singer, while Georgie Moss is a local comic.

As he was about to leave, Loachie said, 'If you fancy it, Rick, there's a part in this for you too.'

I was made up. Apart from needing the money, it would get me out of Liverpool for a while.

We started filming *Riff Raff* in June 1990 on a building site in north London. It is the story of Stevie (played by Robbie Carlyle), an ex-con from Scotland, who is trying to start a new life for himself. He takes a construction job and meets an odd bunch of fellas, who are all struggling to make ends meet. I play Larry, a trade unionist with high moral principles and political beliefs, which was pretty apt considering my background.

Robbie Carlyle was a total unknown from Glasgow when Loachie gave him his big break. I remember him arriving on set, a little bloke in jeans and a sweatshirt. He was quiet until I got to know him, but had a lovely nature and a strong social conscience.

What amazed me most was how he immersed himself completely in a role. He didn't just take on the accent and mannerisms – he 'became' the character and didn't stop until the final scene had been filmed.

I've worked with Robbie several times since then and each time it's like working with a completely different person. At the same time, he is incredibly generous. There are certain people in the acting profession who more or less just say their lines rather than perform them when the camera is doing a close-up on someone else. Robbie isn't like that. He always gives it everything.

Loachie did a brilliant job capturing the Thatcher era, when building workers were underpaid, exploited and working in dangerous conditions. Even the ineptness of the Labour Party comes through.

Much like Roland Joffe had done, Ken rarely lets his actors see a script. Instead he relies on setting up the scene and the tension between characters before letting the dialogue almost write itself. At other times he gives someone a piece of script with all the lines blacked out except their own so they have to ad-lib responses.

A typical example was a scene in *Riff Raff* where I'm in the bath. Ken told me I would hear a noise outside.

'From then on you just improvise,' he said.

'OK.'

I sat in the tub and sure enough heard a noise outside. Suddenly, three Muslim ladies walk in wearing the full garb. Loachie hadn't bothered telling these women I'd be naked. All hell broke loose. I jumped up and grabbed a bowler hat and covered my embarrassment. (A thimble would have done the job.)

The scene worked because the shock was genuine rather than contrived.

The shoot lasted five weeks and I had a great time living in a small hotel on Seven Sisters Road. Chloe came down with a friend to watch us filming and so did Scoggo who was doing a commercial in London. It was like an open house and people grabbed whatever bed was available.

Ken Loach entered *Riff Raff* in competition at the Berlin Film Festival. He called me up and asked if I fancied a few days in Germany. Robbie Carlyle couldn't make the trip and the organisers had requested me. I didn't fancy going on my own, so I asked if Jimmy Coleman and Georgie Moss could come with me.

It was my first film festival and I dusted off my dicky bow, ready for the red carpet. On the flight to Berlin each of us souvenired a lovely little knife, fork and spoon set which were kiddie size. Of course, this set off the metal detector at the airport and the customs officer asked us to empty our pockets.

He nodded and said, 'Knife, fork, spoon. OK.'

Two limousines were parked out front and cards were held up with our names: Mr Coleman. Mr Tomlinson. Mr Moss.

We all climbed in the back of a limo and the driver scratched his head.

'What's the matter?' I asked.

'This car is for you, Mr Tomlinson.'

'What about these lads?'

'They're in the other limousine.'

'Nah, we're all together.'

The accommodation was a lovely old hotel in the centre of the city, within a few minutes' walk of all the famous monuments and landmarks. Ben Kingsley and Terry Jones were staying in the same place. I spied Terry Jones on the first evening, but he turned and faced the other way, totally blanking me. I thought he was a rude bastard, but didn't think anything more of it.

The award ceremony wasn't until the next afternoon, so we had the morning in Berlin seeing the various sights. Getting ready for the show, I had a long bath until I looked like a basted turkey. Someone knocked at the door.

A heavy German accent asked for 'Mr Tomlinson'.

I thought it was Georgie Moss taking the piss.

'I have something for you,' said the voice.

'And I've got something for you and all,' I answered, flinging open the door still bollock-naked.

A hotel porter stood holding a bowl of fruit. His eyes went the size of oranges and he dropped the lot, before tearing up the corridor.

Ken Loach has a real aversion to dressing up unless it is absolutely necessary. All day he had asked me if I was going to wear my black tie to the award ceremony.

'Of course.'

'Are you sure?'

'Yeah.'

He didn't trust me.

We arranged to meet in the foyer of the hotel before going to the Marlene Dietrich Hall. Loachie came downstairs wearing a long coat that looked like an anorak. I could see him checking if we were all in black tie before he took it off. Otherwise he would have run upstairs and changed into casual clothes.

The award ceremony was a real eye-opener. I sat next to Ken and Sally Hibbin, the producer of *Riff Raff*. Shirley Bassey sang a couple of songs with a forty-piece orchestra.

I had been nominated for best supporting actor, but didn't have a speech prepared because I didn't give myself a chance. The award went to someone else, but I didn't mind. *Riff Raff* won best picture and we gave a huge cheer as Loachie went up on stage to collect the prize.

At the party afterwards, Terry Jones came over and apologised for having snubbed me earlier.

'I was one of the judges of the "Best Picture",' he explained. 'I didn't want to be seen talking to you guys, knowing that you'd won.'

Another big celebrity at the party was Glenn Close. I got a wonderful photograph of a few of us talking to her, which I had framed. Moments like that have to be savoured because you don't know when the next one will come along, if ever.

The money from *Riff Raff* barely made an impression on my debts. As my problems mounted, I became worn down by the constant worry of dodging bailiffs and making excuses. I was terrified of the postman because he brought more bills, final demands and threats.

At the cottage one day a bailiff caught me by surprise. I had no choice but to let him in. By then I had pretty much given up and figured he could take the lot. We stood in the dining area and he gave me his spiel about having a court order to seize my assets.

'There's nothing here, lad, but you take what you want,' I said.

He was ex-military – I could tell from his bearing. He wandered from room to room, looking for something he could seize. I had a table, two chairs, the jubilee sideboard, a mattress and a few old blankets.

'There's nothing here,' he said.

'What about the chairs?'

'I can't take those. I'm supposed to leave you something to sleep on and sit on.'

As I showed him to the front door, he wished me the best of luck. I thought he was going to give me a few shillings because he felt so sorry for me.

The lowest point came that Christmas. Diane had gone to stay with friends and I was at the cottage. I had no food in the fridge and the gas and electricity had been disconnected because of unpaid bills. I didn't have enough money to take presents to Clifton, Gareth and Kate.

Although I didn't realise it until later I was suffering a nervous breakdown. On Christmas Day I lay on a mattress in what used to be Kate's old room. I was ill, depressed, unable to move. I don't know how long I spent there. It might have been days. Maureen Singleton dropped by to see me and that's how she found me, wrapped in a blanket, shivering with sickness, hunger and cold.

She wouldn't let me stay in that place. She helped me get dressed and drove me to her house in Colwyn Bay. First she made me get in the shower because I stank. Meanwhile she washed my clothes and made me something warm to eat.

Maureen let me stay in her spare room and made sure I ate well and got plenty of rest. She would leave me during the day while she went off to work.

She asked me why I didn't seek help from my family and I told her I was too embarrassed. I didn't want them to see how far I had fallen.

Now I can understand why people contemplate suicide, but I didn't have the courage for that. There had always been something in me – even during the worst days in prison – that told me not to give up.

As someone once told me: the darkest hour of your life is only sixty minutes long.

I contemplated running away. I could just take off and start a new life somewhere else, perhaps with a new name and without any debts. In the end I couldn't do that because it would mean never seeing the kids again. And where would I run? Liverpool was the only place I knew.

The cottage was repossessed soon after that. The only thing I managed to save was the jubilee sideboard and a couple of banjos. Not long afterwards the bailiffs arrived at the club and someone made the mistake of opening the door to them. They took everything – the sideboard, the banjos and even the plaques I had been given for supporting the miners and post office workers.

The manager of Kerfoot's Campground phoned to say I owed the ground rent. I told him that I couldn't pay.

'Well, I'll have to take your caravan and sell it.'

'OK. That's fine.'

Next day there was a terrible storm and the caravan got washed away. Maybe that's what they mean by karma.

The casting agency was also a casualty. Ronny had already gone to work for my brother David and I didn't have the time to keep it running. Within days I also abandoned the

Limelight Club – doing a moonlight flit just ahead of the bankruptcy proceedings.

I owed David thirteen thousand pounds so I handed him the title deed to Chloe's beautiful cottage. The only thing I had left of any value was land at Summer Hill where the church had once stood. The drama school had been another financial casualty and I had made plans to build several houses on the site. I went to Marlene and explained the situation. I was going to sign the land over to her and hopefully, at some point in the future, we could build a few houses together.

I even suggested that Dennis, her brother, might build them for us. We could split the profit three ways. Marlene agreed and my solicitor made the arrangements.

Later, when I managed to stave off bankruptcy, I discovered that Marlene had already sold the site. I don't know what happened to the money. At some point it disappeared, along with her other assets, and she finished up living in a council house.

I could happily have stayed at Maureen's house, reading books, watching TV and getting my strength back. I was out of the way – in hiding. Diane had managed to get a secretarial job and had put down a deposit on a little two-up-two-down in Scorton Street. She came looking for me and convinced me to move back to Liverpool.

I began doing the occasional gig with a borrowed banjo, but I couldn't put my name about because I owed money to too many people.

The brewery launched the first of the bankruptcy proceedings. I owed about five grand. On the morning of the hearing I got Maureen to deliver a cheque to my solicitor.

'It's going to bounce all over Liverpool,' I told her, 'but

hopefully it will give me enough time to get some funds together.'

I took the view that the banks and major creditors could wait at the end of the queue. My main priority was to repay friends and family who had been kind enough to help me.

Unfortunately, not everyone was prepared to give me time. Mick McNally phoned me demanding his money.

'I haven't got it.'

'I need it today.'

'Believe me, Mick, I haven't got it. If I had the money I'd give it back to you.'

A few days later, I was home on a Saturday night when Diane had gone out with some friends. Someone hammered on the front door and began shouting, 'Come out, you bastard. Where's Mick McNally's money? He wants it back.'

My sphincter seized up and I lay on the floor, trying to pretend there was nobody home. Another voice sounded from the back door. There were two of them, trying to kick their way inside.

The old woman living next door started giving them an earful about making a racket. I could hear her telling them, 'I always said there was something queer about that fella.'

The boys were still kicking at the doors and shouting at me to come out. I decided to make a run for it. While they were at the front door I slipped out the back and very quietly took the padlock off the back gate. I peered up and down the entry. It was clear.

Closing the back door, I walked quickly down the entry until I reached the street.

'There he is, Dad,' one of them shouted. It must have been a father and son team. There's nothing like taking your kid to work with you.

The chase was on for young and old – and I was over fifty

and desperately unfit. I recognised the Dad. He used to be a professional boxer. Panting and heaving, I ran as fast as my legs could carry me. Ahead I saw a woman standing at her front door, showing a friend out. I turned the corner and ran straight into her house. Both women chased me inside, screaming, 'What's going on? Get out!'

I shut the door and turned the lock seconds before my pursuers threw their shoulders against it. They hammered on the door and the big picture window. I thought the whole thing would shatter.

'I've got a baby upstairs,' yelled the woman.

Her friend was hysterical. 'Get out! Get out!'

Thinking quickly, I told them I was being chased by crackpot fans. 'They want to kill Bobby Grant. Call the police!'

The women calmed down and made the call. Even before the Panda car arrived the father and son team had scarpered.

A policeman interviewed me in the kitchen over a cup of tea. I knew I couldn't tell them the truth about owing money to Mick McNally. Instead I told them that these two fellas had been taking the piss out of me because I'd been Bobby Grant on TV. When I answered them back they went mad.

The policeman took me back to Diane's house and checked that the doors and windows were secure. Even so, I barely slept that night. Was this the future?

A few days later Jimmy Coleman, who was in *Riff Raff*, came round and I told him about my unwelcome visitors.

'How much do you owe McNally?'

'Four grand.'

'Can you pay him?'

'Not yet.'

'Right,' said Jimmy, grabbing his hat and striding out the door. 'I'll sort this out.'

He went straight to the Fur and Feather, McNally's club, and found him sitting on a stool by the cash register. As always, he had a big cigar chomped between his teeth.

Jimmy let him have it. 'What's your fucking game, Mick? Why are you sending heavies around to Tomo's?' He laid it on thick. 'Don't you realise that he's got a heart condition? You coulda killed him . . .'

Mick was embarrassed and blustered about a misunderstanding. He claimed to have heard stories about me being cashed up. Someone had even told him that I'd bought myself another car.

'You ought to be ashamed of yourself,' said Jimmy. 'I remember when this club was bloody empty of a Saturday and a Sunday. Tomo came here and did some shows and packed the place. You couldn't move in here. You filled your pockets and this is how you treat him . . .'

'I was only going on what fellas told me . . .'

'Fuck them! Next time you talk to Tomo.'

Although grateful for what Jimmy did, it didn't alter the fact that I still owed Mick the money. He wouldn't wait forever.

17

The Red Triangle

Weddings are nothing but fuss and I'm staying well out of this one.
'Just tell me the time and the place and what I have to wear,' I tell
Rita.

The truth is I'm coming round to the idea of one of those pay and
display jobs they do in Las Vegas with an Elvis-lookalike as the
celebrant and complimentary photographs.

Rita gets a real gob on when I talk like that. She says I'm just too
lazy to get off my arse and help her with the arrangements. She says
it with true love in her eyes, so I know she's half joking. It's the other
half I have to worry about.

The only thing I've stipulated is that I want two dos. We can have
a fancy ceremony during the day, but afterwards I want an old-
fashioned knees-up.

'That's twice the work,' she says.

'Don't look at it that way, my little glow-worm. It'll be twice the
fun.'

She gives me the look and I opt for self-preservation. Best keep
out of the way.

I'm doing a film in town – The Virgin of Liverpool, *with Paul*
Barber, Imelda Staunton and the comedian Johnny Vegas. It's the
story of a twelve-year-old girl who rescues a statue of the Virgin

Mary that her local church has lashed out. It's the same statue that her grandmother had once seen crying.

The girl takes it home and puts it in her parents' front room, where it causes all sorts of problems for the family, including her adolescent brother who is desperately trying to get into his girlfriend's knickers.

I play Frank, the girl's father and a local bus driver and union steward. Imelda Staunton is my wife. In one of the last scenes we finish up in the Mersey trying to rescue the statue which is floating away. We have to be plucked from the water by a helicopter.

Although nervous because I can't swim, I have a lot of faith in the RAF guys, who are really professional. They show me how the harness is going to work and tell me I should relax when the winch begins hoisting me out of the water. We're filming where the river bed slopes down and I can just stand up. I have to go under three or four times, but there are frogmen all over the place just in case I don't come up again.

Doing my own stunts doesn't bother me. In that sense I'm a bit like Tom Cruise, although unlike Tom I don't use body doubles and screen nudity doesn't faze me. Strangely, I don't get many offers.

For nearly four years I had seen very little of my children. Occasionally, I saw the boys as I drove through the village and would pull over and chat to them, but they were very loyal to their Mum.

I missed Kate in particular because she had been the youngest when we divorced. I felt as though I was missing her childhood. Sometimes I drove down to the school and parked on the lane outside. I took a pair of binoculars with me and watched Kate in the playground. Someone must have reported me to the police one day because the village bobby came past in his car. His name was Trevor, a big lad with bushy sideburns. He recognised me and realised what was going on because he just kept driving.

Many times I considered picking up the phone and calling the school, but I knew the teachers wouldn't tell me anything. They were under instructions.

Every birthday and Christmas I delivered presents to the house, but was rarely allowed to see them. Eventually, Marlene's resolve softened and she began letting me visit on occasional weekends. I tried to give her what money I could to help with the household bills.

By then Kate was thirteen years old and in high school. Clifton and Gareth had left school at fifteen and drifted between different jobs, without ever settling down. Gareth was working for his Uncle Dennis, a master bricklayer. At seventeen he joined the Army, a decision that didn't thrill me, but I went to his passing-out parade and was suitably proud.

Just before Christmas in 1991 I had a call from Marlene asking for a favour. Somehow she had become involved in a property deal with my former partner, Pat O'Rourke. They had gone fifty-fifty buying a bungalow on a new estate. O'Rourke owed her a large sum of money and was supposed to pay her back in instalments, but had missed some of the payments. With Christmas and Kate's birthday coming up, she needed the money.

Clearly, there was very little love lost between myself and Pat O'Rourke. I was living with his stepdaughter and there were issues over the Limelight.

He and Agnes were now managing a pub called the Shipperies in Durning Road, Liverpool. I phoned and his stepdaughter Shirley answered. I told her that I was coming round to see Pat.

I grabbed my jacket and the keys to the car. As I was leaving I bumped into Jimmy Hackett, a local councillor and a long-time mate. I offered to give him a lift but told him I had to run an errand first. When I reached the pub he waited in the car while I went inside. Half a dozen lads were sitting around the bar. O'Rourke was serving.

'I need to have a word with you.'

'I'm busy, you'll have to wait,' he said.

'Marlene really needs that money, it being Christmas and all . . .'

'I said I'm busy.'

'OK, but if you don't mind I'll sit with these lads and tell them what you've been up to.'

Agnes lost her temper and started pushing me towards the door. I shouted to O'Rourke that I wanted the money. Suddenly, a stool came from behind me and whacked me across the back of the head. I stumbled and reached up with my hand to feel the blood.

Discretion being the better part of valour, I didn't hang around. Across the road at a little shop, I phoned the police. My glasses had been broken in the attack and I wanted to go back and get them.

'For God's sake, just get yourself to hospital,' said the policeman. 'I can call an ambulance.'

'It's OK, I've got me car. I'll make me own way.'

Holding a bloody towel to my head, I went to the Accident and Emergency department. A doctor had just finished stitching the wound when two detectives arrived. I told them the story of the money and the non-payment; how I went to talk to O'Rourke and finished up getting whacked.

I thought they'd come because of my 999 call, but it turned out they had come from the Shipperies. O'Rourke had phoned the police straight after me and made a complaint. It came down to my word against his, except he had his entire family singing off the same song sheet.

The next morning I had a call from the police asking me to come down to the station. I arrived thinking they must have charged O'Rourke, but instead found myself being arrested.

Roy Pybus, my solicitor, sat in on the interviews and tried to get me bail. They held me overnight and I appeared in court next morning charged with threatening to kill Pat O'Rourke.

Although it was a very serious charge, I couldn't take it seriously. Yes, I could be noisy, passionate and forthright, but I didn't threaten to kill anyone. I was the one who got whacked and I had eight stitches to prove it.

Because of adjournments and delays the court case wasn't due to be heard for almost twelve months. In the meantime I stayed out of harm's way, living with Diane. We had been together for more than three years and I had never expected it to last that long.

From the outset I had told Diane that she should find someone closer to her own age. I meant this, yet it came as a shock when she followed my advice. She announced suddenly that I had to move out.

'How long have I got?'

'A fortnight.'

'I don't know if I can move that soon.'

'You'll have to.'

I felt quite wounded even though I knew it was for the best. I also faced the prospect of being homeless until I bumped into Joe Curran who ran a boxing club called the Red Triangle in Everton Road, not far from where I grew up. The ground floor had a little social club that operated on weekends, but on the top storey, above the gym, there was a room for rent, with a pokey kitchen off to one side. I did a deal with Joe, who waived the rent because I agreed to play the banjo in the social club.

I stayed one more night at Diane's, not wanting to be alone and in the morning I packed the van with my few belongings. A woman who worked in the laundrette around the corner interrupted me, 'Have you seen the paper, Rick? There's a story about you.'

She opened the *Guardian* and revealed a photograph of me naked, with a bowler hat hiding my embarrassment. It was the scene from *Riff Raff* and the headline read: 'Have You Seen This Man?'

Ken Loach had turned to the newspapers when he couldn't find me through normal channels. He wanted me to set up an audition for his new film *Raining Stones* because he needed some rough, tough working-class guys. Although I didn't have the casting agency any more, I phoned some of the lads and we held the auditions at the Red Triangle.

Ken took over my room upstairs and must have realised right off that I was on the bones of my arse. Jackie Hamilton walked in, saw the bed and said, 'Jesus, Ken, I hope I don't have to sleep with you.'

Jimmy Coleman, Lee Brennan and Jackie all got chosen, along with a couple of the other lads. There was also a part for me, which I gratefully accepted.

A few weeks later I went to Manchester to be introduced to Bruce Jones, who played the lead. Loachie did his typical trick of getting us to improvise a scene together where Bruce had just bought a second-hand van.

'How much?' I asked.

'Four hundred.'

'Four hundred pound for that! He must have seen you coming. Who was the last owner? Ben Hur?'

'Money doesn't go far these days.'

'Neither will that van. It'll be lucky to get you home.'

This went on for a few minutes until Ken seemed satisfied.

He cast me as 'Tommy' and Bruce Jones played 'Bob'. We were two unemployed workers on the dole who were trying to make ends meet. Bob's little girl is making her first communion, but he doesn't have the money to buy her a new dress and shoes. Rather than disappoint her he takes every scrap of work possible and finally borrows money from a loan shark.

In the opening scene of the film, the two of us steal a stray sheep, but neither of us can bring ourselves to kill it. We take it to a local butcher who tells us we've caught worthless mutton and not lamb.

Every time I filmed the scene with Ronnie Ravey, who was playing the butcher, I changed the dialogue and he'd start laughing. We spent all afternoon trying to finish this one scene and had to come back the next morning. Most directors would have been furious, but Loachie shrugged it off. That's what I love about him. Spontaneity and realism are more important than his shooting schedule.

Jackie Hamilton, well known for liking a pint, was perfectly cast as a drunk in a pub scene. He arrived on set with a typically red face and a boozer's nose (not unlike mine).

Loachie commented to me, 'Bloody hell, make-up and wardrobe have done a brilliant job on Jackie.'

Then Jackie came over and said, 'Sorry I'm late, Ken. Where do I get made up?'

One particular scene was terrifying in its power and how closely it mirrored my own predicament. Bruce Jones's character had borrowed £260 from a loan shark and couldn't pay it back. The heavies were sent round to his flat and found his wife and daughter alone. The big fella playing the heavy was ideal for the role. Loachie took him to one side.

'Listen. This family owes you money. The wife is a real

hard case. She'll cry and get emotional, trying to make you feel sorry for her, but it's all an act. She's hard as nails. You won't frighten her no matter what you say.'

Then Ken went and spoke to Julie Brown, who was playing the wife.

'I want you to be careful,' he warned her. 'This guy can get carried away and we might have trouble stopping him. Just watch yourself.'

Julie was frightened before the cameras even rolled. The bloke stormed in bristling with aggression and threatening violence. He was terrifying and Julie burst into tears, while her 'daughter' crouched in the corner. The scene is among the most powerful in the film and yet another example of how Ken can draw amazing performances from people.

Jim Allen, an old-fashioned socialist from Manchester, had written *Raining Stones*. He had been a docker and a bus conductor, as well as working in the steel mills. Because of my past association with the National Front I worried a little that he might have problems working with me. I took him aside one day and said, 'Listen, Jim, you know about my past, don't you? I used to be a lot further to the right.'

He nodded and shrugged. 'Don't worry, lad. You've well served your time.'

I appreciated his honesty. I have always known that I can't shake my past and I have never hidden from what happened, but at the same time there are people who relish bringing it up. They know it is my Achilles heel, but as our Albert often says, 'What doesn't kill us makes us stronger.'

When the cheque arrived for *Raining Stones*, I didn't bother cashing it in. Instead I went straight to the Fur and Feather and signed it over to Mick McNally.

'There's your money. Thanks very much.'

The father and son 'heavies' were in the club watching.

Mick didn't know what to say. He had tears in his eyes, but it was too late to save our friendship. I didn't speak to him again from that day onwards.

The Red Triangle had a good reputation as a boxing club and Joe Curran was great with the young fighters. One of his lads had been national schoolboys' champion. During the week the boxing club opened from 6.30 p.m. to 9 p.m. After that I had the building to myself and kept an eye on the place.

I still had Joffe and of a morning I would take him down into the yard beside the Red Triangle so he could go for a bit of a run. All the kids walking to school would give him toast and biscuits through the iron railing fence.

During the day, if I had errands to run, I left him in the back yard, which had large padlocked gates. I came home one day and found the locks smashed and Joffe gone. Dogs like him were normally stolen for breeding purposes or to be turned into attack dogs. Joffe was so placid, he wouldn't have lasted five minutes.

I wasted no time. Getting hold of a local small-time villain I issued an ultimatum.

'I want me dog back tonight or tomorrow at the latest.'

'I don't know anything about it.'

'I don't care. I'm blaming you. You know everything that goes on around here.'

Early the next morning a young woman knocked on the door. She was holding Joffe on a leash.

'Sorry. We don't do this to our own,' she said, as she handed him over.

For the most part I didn't let anyone know where I was living. The lads at the boxing club were sworn to secrecy. I came in one day and discovered a woman had phoned asking for me. As instructed, the lads had never heard of me. The next day she called again.

'I had to get nasty with her,' said Joe Curran. 'I told her, "There's no Ricky Tomlinson here. Don't be ringing back."'

'What did she say?'

'She left a name and number. Said her name was Anne McCaffrey.'

I ignored the message and it wasn't until much later that I discovered that Anne McCaffrey was one of the biggest casting directors in Hollywood. When you're down nothing goes right for you!

My fall from grace had been pretty spectacular, but Mam and my brothers had no idea how bad things were. I wouldn't tell them. Only a few years earlier I'd been a TV celebrity and now I was hiding out from creditors and claiming social security.

My brothers are there when I need them, which is great, but they also knew it would embarrass me even more if they came offering handouts or a place to stay. Similarly, I would have slept on the street rather than knock on their door and ask for help. I know that sounds foolishly proud but that's the way I am. I had got myself into this mess and I would get myself out of it.

In July 1992 my luck began to change. After a charity gig at a pub called the Cabbage, I was packing up my gear and preparing to leave when Jimmy Coleman introduced me to a woman called Rita Cumiskey. She and her sister Mary had watched the show.

In her early forties, attractive, with a real twinkle in her eyes, Rita recognised me as Bobby Grant from *Brookside*. She had seen me a year earlier at the Limelight Club.

'You were carrying a crate of ale and wearing the same cardie that you wore in *Brookside*,' she joked.

I wanted to stay for a drink, but I lied about having to be somewhere else. The truth is I had no money and I was too embarrassed to let anyone know.

About three months later I was back at the Cabbage doing a gig and I saw Rita and Mary again. I still had no money to buy a round, but I told Rita I was working on *Raining Stones* and asked if she fancied coming to the wrap party.

If I imagined this was going to impress her I was sadly mistaken. She turned me down, opting instead for a night out with her mates at the Grafton.

Rita wasn't the sort of woman I normally went out with. She was politically aware, well educated and outspoken. She had a full-time job as a social worker, two grown-up children, and had recently separated from her husband of twenty-one years.

Her background was even poorer than mine – raised in a rough area of Bootle, in a two-up-two-down, with five brothers and two sisters. Her father had been a docker and all of his children grew up to be bright, confident and successful.

Rita was living with her sister in Sefton. Claire, her sixteen-year-old daughter, lived with her dad. Her son Tony, aged twenty, was at university. Once or twice a week I would drop round for a cup of tea and hopefully a spot of supper. For the first six visits I wore the same black tracksuit.

I didn't tell Rita I was living above the Red Triangle. Instead I tried to pretend I was doing OK. When I finally scraped together a few quid, I took her out to the Montrose, a local club. I arrived wearing a pair of cowboy boots that I had borrowed from Jimmy Coleman, which were two sizes too big, and an overcoat from the Oxfam shop. My hair was long and slicked back. When I took off the coat I revealed a woollen jumper, which had once been a polo neck, but now looked like a shapeless sack.

Rita was dressed to kill and she kept staring at me. I felt embarrassed.

From then on she began very subtly improving my wardrobe. She would say things like, 'I was out shopping for Tony today and they had this offer – two shirts for the price of one . . .'

I still hadn't told her where I lived, but she was starting to get suspicious.

'Are you married?'

'No.'

'Are you with someone?'

'No.'

'Why won't you tell me where you live?'

'I'm trying to sort a few things out. I'm not lying to you.'

I really liked Rita and I was frightened that once she knew about my debts and saw me living in the Red Triangle she'd run a mile. I should have given her more credit, of course.

She finally gave me an ultimatum and I had to tell her I was living above a boxing club.

'Can I see it?'

'If you want to.'

I tried to clean the place up, but probably should have had it fumigated. The bare boards were covered in dog hair and I spent two hours scrubbing one Venetian blind. The other stayed dirty. Having swept the floor, tidied the kitchen and made the bed, I bought a few things for supper.

Rita arrived, looking impeccable as usual. She stood in the centre of the room, as though worried about sitting down.

'Where are your clothes then?'

'In there.'

She glanced in the cupboard. I had a pair of trousers, my black tracksuit and two jumpers with big eagles on them, along with the things she had bought me.

I made a little scouse cooked on a single gas burner. If she'd seen the state of the kitchen she wouldn't have eaten anything. Afterwards, without saying a word about my accommodation, she said, 'You can come to ours, tomorrow.'

The thing about my relationship with Rita is how much we laughed. Sometimes I had tears running down my cheeks. We had various running jokes and mini-challenges. Rita would call me up and say, 'Right, who wrote this line: "It was the best of times, it was the worst of times"?'

Next day I would call her back and say, 'Charles Dickens, *A Tale of Two Cities*.'

Then it was her turn to get a question.

For months Rita thought I was so clever coming up with the answers. She didn't realise I had a writer friend, Frank Cottrell Boyce, who solved the problems for me.

Rita's sister Mary was doing an English literature degree and the two of them were demons when it came to competition. They refused to be beaten by the likes of me.

The British Council had invited me on a trade mission to Poland to publicise films like *Riff Raff*. I jumped at the offer. Here was a chance to stay in nice hotels and eat three meals a day for a few weeks. More importantly, it would get me out of Liverpool and away from my creditors.

'You don't have enough clothes,' said Rita.

'Yes, I do.'

She didn't believe me and bought me some sweatshirts. I phoned her almost every night and sent her postcards from Poland. I even managed to buy her a few small presents before I flew home, including a wooden jewellery box and 'Solidarity' badges from Gdansk.

I handed out the presents in Rita's kitchen. 'I don't want you to open this one now,' I told her.

'What is it?' asked Mary.

'It's for rolling pastry.'

'All right.'

'You should probably keep it in the fridge for a while.'

'OK.'

They popped the small parcel in the fridge and I went back to the Red Triangle. A couple of hours later they couldn't resist having a peek.

'Fancy bringing a bloody rolling pin back, what next?' said Rita.

She unwrapped the package and the two of them examined the contents.

'It doesn't look much like a rolling pin.'

'What do you reckon this button does?'

'Turn it on.'

Mary hit the switch and the two of them screamed so loudly they dropped the vibrator on the table, where it buzzed and bounced. They almost wet themselves with laughter.

Rita was astounded that I had the nerve to buy her that sort of present, but the two of us were always trying to wind each other up. One of her favourite tricks was to send me radical, feminist postcards and literature because she knew I was such a chauvinist.

My criminal trial began on 3 January 1993, more than a year after I had been charged with trying to kill Pat O'Rourke. Judge Portnoy told the jury, 'The fact that Mr Tomlinson appeared as Bobby Grant in *Brookside* does not make him any more or less likely to be guilty of the offence on which he is to be tried.'

The evidence against me was astonishing. Shirley O'Rourke claimed that on 17 December 1991 she had answered the phone at the Shipperies and recognised my voice.

'He said that if his ex-wife Marlene did not receive a thousand pounds by 1 p.m. he was going to come to the pub and throw a petrol bomb through the window and kill my dad.

'He wanted me to get my Mandy [her younger sister] out of the pub before he came with the petrol bomb. He said the dispute had nothing to do with her.'

Just before I apparently slammed the phone down, the tearful and distressed Shirley had invited the cleaner over and she, too, had heard me mention a petrol bomb.

She also claimed that I had been stalking her that morning while she was out shopping and had followed her back to the pub shortly before making the 'threatening' phone call.

Listening to evidence like this, I found it hard to maintain my composure. Why would I scare Shirley? I had no beef with her. My argument was with their stepdad.

During her evidence she had mentioned various shops that she had visited that morning. Roy Pybus went on a fact-finding mission and discovered that one of them wasn't even open on the day in question. My barrister also showed it was preposterous to suggest I could have followed Shirley through the shops and back to the Shipperies, then driven all the way to Diane's house to make the phone call five minutes later.

The prosecutor, John McDermott, suggested that I might have had an accomplice. I felt like shouting, 'Give me a break!'

The prosecution also fell apart when one of the detectives took the stand and was asked by my barrister if he had ever seen Pat O'Rourke before. He answered no.

'Are you sure?'

'Yes.'

'Isn't it a fact that you spoke to him only recently in relation to another case?'

The detective's face went the colour of claret and the admission sent the judge into overdrive. He pilloried the hapless plod and put the prosecution on the back foot. He even criticised the framing of charges and asked why I hadn't been charged with 'demanding money with menaces' rather than threatening to kill.

Marlene was called to give evidence and looked extremely nervous as she came into the courtroom. The Judge nodded to her and then nodded to the witness box. Marlene thought he was being polite, so she nodded back. He nodded again. She nodded back.

Eventually a court usher led her gently to the witness box. Although anxious, her answers were clear and definite. She had lent the O'Rourkes money, which had not been repaid. She had asked me if I could find out why. I hadn't sounded angry or threatening. I was just doing her a favour.

No amount of questioning from the prosecution could shake Marlene. She was straight as a Roman road.

The public gallery was packed with local showbusiness identities and old mates who had come down to show me their support. On the day of the verdict there wasn't a spare seat in the place. The Judge gave his final instructions to the jury and they adjourned to the jury room.

'We're breaking for lunch now, but don't go far,' he said. 'I don't think they'll be very long.'

Fifty minutes later they returned with a not guilty verdict. Newspaper reporters crowded around me as I walked down the steps.

'I am delighted and also extremely relieved because this case has been hanging over me for thirteen months. I am especially glad for my daughter, Kate, who was fifteen on Christmas Day. The verdict is a wonderful tonic for her and belated Christmas present for all of us.'

We all went out to celebrate, even old Eddie Ross, from Actors' Equity, who doesn't normally drink, but managed to get wasted on black rum and Coke.

Rita had ironed my shirts to go to court every day and was sitting at home waiting for news. Caught up in the celebrations, I totally forgot to call her and she heard the verdict on the radio.

She was furious. One of her mates called and told her where we were celebrating, but her response can't be printed here. Next morning, as I nursed a monumental hangover, she laid down the law to me.

'If you ever do that to me again then it's over between us.'

She was dead right. I was out of order.

Perhaps the most disappointing thing about the entire episode was the fact that my relationship with Diane became public knowledge. The *News of the World* did an 'exposé' about the soap star and the seventeen-year-old.

Hoping to limit the damage, I made a decision to cooperate and give them an interview. I also let the newspaper talk me into letting them take a photograph of me with Kate. This backfired, of course. The journalist wrote what he wanted and nobody came out of it well. Diane was so angry she marched into the Red Triangle and slapped me on the face.

Until then Rita had no idea about Diane. I hadn't told her. As a professional social worker who had worked with families and troubled children, she was shocked and upset. Where did it leave her values and beliefs?

I tried to explain that Diane had arrived at the lowest point in my life, when I was struggling with depression and mounting debts. She, too, was going through a difficult time and we helped each other survive. Maybe I was deluding myself. I know that Rita really struggled with the knowledge and it took her a long while to come to terms with it.

*

In the aftermath of the trial I couldn't just let the matter rest – not after copping a bar stool across my head. Some of my mates wanted to take matters into their own hands, but I calmed everyone down.

I took out civil proceedings against Pat O'Rourke, accusing him of assault. The case was heard in Liverpool Crown Court in July 1993 and this time it became even more personal, with allegations of vendettas and long-running feuds.

We subpoenaed witnesses who had been in the pub at the time of the attack, including members of O'Rourke's family, but none of them turned up at the hearing. Even so, we presented a strong case.

O'Rourke claimed that I had fallen drunkenly against a radiator, but it was only 10.30 in the morning which made that difficult to believe.

The defence barrister Anthony Barraclough brought up my previous convictions and claimed I had a history of violence and intimidation. When this failed to make an impression on the jury, he began to ask me about Diane. He made a big thing about her being 'only sixteen' when we met.

This had nothing to do with the case, of course; it was simply an attack on my character. I asked the woman Judge if I could say a few words and she nodded.

'This chap seems to be putting an awful lot of importance on a girl's age, saying that she was "only sixteen". That's not true. Diane was seventeen. Our relationship lasted nearly four years and we cared a lot about each other. When it ended neither of us had any regrets. I had refurbished a house for her and I wished her all the happiness in the world.

'I don't know why Mr Barraclough insists on mentioning Diane. She wasn't the reason I went to the Shipperies that day. And she knows nothing about the attack. Seems to me that the only reason she's being mentioned is because Mr Barraclough takes some sort of perverse pleasure out of it.'

His face went crimson and I could see him wanting to leap to his feet.

I thought the Judge was very fair in her summing up and she even went as far as saying, 'There is only one verdict here.' The outcome seemed like a foregone conclusion, but instead the jury couldn't reach a decision. It was hung in my favour, but there were no last-minute defections.

The Judge said something about a retrial, but the court costs already amounted to fifteen thousand pounds. I didn't have fifteen pence. Outside the court, the two barristers took me to one side and said the Judge had agreed that the court would pay my costs if I dropped the case rather than seek a retrial.

Reluctantly I agreed – a decision I still regret. The Judge directed that a not guilty verdict should be recorded against O'Rourke. That was the last I saw of him, although Marlene later threatened him with bankruptcy and I know he repaid her some, if not all, of the money.

18

Don't Go Stale on Me!

I have always loved those little campervans that you see trundling along country lanes and at seaside caravan sites. There's something wonderfully liberating about them – being able to just take off and explore the world.

I bought my first one a few years back, just after I met Rita. I found it advertised in Exchange & Mart and went to have a look. It was a lovely little campervan, with a fold-down bed, a table and chairs and curtains on the windows. I couldn't drive a column shift, so the chap took me for a ride around the block.

We agreed a price (it was probably my tax money) and that night he dropped it around to my place. His girlfriend had followed in her car.

'I want to thank you for buying this,' she said.

'Why's that? Is there something wrong with it?'

'No, not at all! You see we haven't had a weekend together in nearly eighteen months. He spends every bit of his spare time working on this bloody van. That's why I gave him the ultimatum. Either he gets rid of the van or he gets rid of me.'

First thing I did when I mastered the gears was to drive around to Mam's house, hoping to impress her. She was standing outside when I drove up.

'*What do you think?*' I yelled.

'*Give us two choc ices and a cornet,*' she said. Cheeky thing!

When Francesca Hunt, a lovely young actress, invited us to her wedding, we drove the campervan. It was a big society do in a beautiful part of the country near the Cheddar Gorge. A huge marquee had been erected on the lawn and lots of famous people turned up.

Late in the evening, Jimmy Cosmo, the Scottish actor, wandered over to our table and said, 'Excuse me, Ricky, have you got a wee campervan?'

'*Yeah.*'

'*Is it cream and white and parked by the toilets?*'

'*Yeah.*'

'*And the toilets are cream and white?*'

'*Yeah. Why?*'

'*Well, I think I just crapped in your glove compartment.*'

Rita thought I was too old for her at first, which is ironic considering Diane. There is eleven years' difference between us, which isn't much when you get to my age, although Rita might not agree.

I don't know exactly when I realised I was in love with her. The truth is I didn't *want* to be in love with anyone after going ten rounds with Marlene and losing on a technical knockout.

When I was younger saying 'I love you' was an easy thing to do, but not any more. I was older and wiser . . . more cautious. Rita was too.

I invited her to London for a British Film Council function – canapés and drinks at a fancy hotel. Rita drove and was terrified because she had never been to London, let alone driven on a motorway.

'I'm going to take you to this lovely place to eat,' I said as we headed south. 'The food is fabulous.'

'How much further? I'm starving.'

'It's just up here.'

We pulled off the motorway and I announced proudly, 'We're here.'

Rita's face fell. 'It's a friggin' transport caff.'

'Yeah. The food's great.'

She was not impressed.

Arriving at the party, we had to change in the car. Rita wore a plaid mini skirt, a little black jacket and a black polo neck jumper and black tights. She looked wonderful and seemed totally relaxed around film people. That night we stayed in Maida Vale with Keith Evans, who had been a director on *Brookside*.

Rita had taken a week off work and we spent the entire time together. Afterwards she sent a single rose to the Red Triangle to thank me for a wonderful time. No woman had ever sent me a flower.

About three months after we met, she moved out of her Mary's house and rented a small terrace in Walton. Her son Tony was still at university and Claire was now living with her. I started staying the odd night, putting Joffe in the back yard.

We used to have such lovely talks – sitting up until three in the morning. By the same token, we had some monumental arguments. Rita thought nothing of throwing me out (bin-bagging me, we called it). She would dump my gear in bags outside the front door.

'Right, that's it. I'm off,' I'd say. Four paces across the pavement, I unlocked the campervan and got my head down. At about two in the morning, Rita would normally cave in and come knocking on the door saying, 'Come in, you daft git.'

I had never known a woman who was so independent and who didn't need me. She had her own car, a good career, an education and tremendous self-confidence. By comparison, I could be childish, demanding and selfish. Sometimes I envied her strength and was frightened of losing her.

Still doing gigs at the Red Triangle, I had a little band including two lads on guitars. Halfway through the show I would interrupt proceedings to say that someone had sent me a letter during the week.

'If you don't mind, I'll read it out to you.'

The letters were total fabrications but gave me the chance to play agony aunt, dispensing advice about anything from romance to animal husbandry. One lad pulled Rita aside one night and gave her a letter – a real one, asking her to pass it on to me. He thought the whole routine was genuine.

If Rita came to the show I took her home afterwards and stayed over. Around midnight one night the phone rang.

'Is that you, Rick?'

'Yeah.'

'What time are you coming home?'

It was Joe Curran from the Red Triangle.

'I wasn't going to bother tonight.'

'Well, there's people casing the joint here. You're supposed to be here.'

'Hang on, Joe. I'm not the cocky watchman.'

'I want you back here.'

'Well, I'm sorry but I'm staying here tonight.'

'Well, you can get your stuff out by the weekend.'

Joe was totally out of order but I had no choice in the matter. A few days later I had a call from the boxing club.

'You better get around here, Rick. All your stuff is in the yard.'

Joe had tossed everything out in the rain – my bed, clothes, books, paintings and bits of paperwork. Most of it was ruined. It saddened me because he seemed to have forgotten all I had done for him. I had helped him raise money to buy the Red Triangle and organised to fix the leaking roof and have the place painted. None of this seemed to count.

I loaded anything I could salvage in the van and moved in with Rita. She was fine about that. Circumstances alter cases.

Rita never asked me for a penny for food or phone bills. I ate all my meals at her house, she washed my clothes and looked after me. My sole contribution every month was to cash in me Giro and take her out on a Saturday night.

Rita wouldn't let Joffe in the house, but I sneaked him in when she went to work and let him lie by the fire.

'I smell dog,' she'd say, when she got home.

'Nah, not in here.'

She had a roll of film developed and there were photographs of Joffe lying on the settee. She went mad.

Raining Stones had been entered in the Cannes Film Festival and Paralex Pictures and Channel 4, who had funded the film, were taking a party to the screening. Nobody does it better than the French. They out-American the Americans with film stars around every corner and topless beauties on every beach.

Rita took four days off work to come with me. Packing our suitcases, we took a crate of Pot Noodles, a little electric kettle, a few bags of crisps and dozens of teabags. We figured that we couldn't afford to eat at restaurants so we'd survive on Pot Noodles instead. For drinks we half filled bottles of cola with vodka. That way we could top up our glasses under the table saving money.

The steam iron I thought was a bit unnecessary.

'Why not bring the microwave?' I suggested. Rita gave me the look.

Bruce Jones had been invited, along with Ken Loach and

Jim Allen, the screenwriter. Jim turned up in Cannes wearing an old black coat with gravy stains, baggy trousers and crêpe-sole shoes with white stitching around the sides. He had a disposable razor in his top pocket and a plastic bag with dental glue for his dentures and Preparation H for his haemorrhoids.

Jim believed in travelling light, but unfortunately every morning without fail he would put his teeth in using the Preparation H and put the dental glue on his arse.

Raining Stones was due to be screened that evening. In the afternoon we all went to see the new Michael Douglas film *Falling Down* about a stressed businessman who suffers a nervous breakdown and goes on the rampage in Los Angeles. When it finished the audience gave a round of polite applause.

Back at the hotel we started getting ready. I wore my dicky bow and Rita had an outfit that she'd bought from Asda – a short black skirt and jacket with gold buttons.

Some of the girls from Paralex came knocking on the door asking Rita if they could borrow her steam iron. She shot me a glance that said, 'I told you so.'

Arriving at the theatre was an incredible experience – walking up the red carpet with cameras flashing and photographers calling our names. It was the first time I had seen *Raining Stones*. I don't mind watching myself on screen, but I am never entirely satisfied with any of my performances. I always wish I could do certain things again.

The movie was subtitled in French but people laughed in the right places and were quiet in the right places and shocked in the right places. In a scene where Bruce Jones curses the Pope there was a sharp intake of breath.

The movie ended and nothing. Not a sound. I remember thinking – maybe they didn't like it. Next thing they erupted, applauding wildly and shouting 'Bravo!' A spotlight criss-crossed the audience who rose to their feet and turned towards us. Loachie, an extremely humble man, was lost for words. Jim Allen looked as though he was at a rugby match.

The applause continued and eventually I had to say to Ken, 'Come on, we better move.'

'I can't move while they're still clapping.'

'But they're not going to *stop* clapping while you're still here.'

We edged our way along the seats and people followed us out of the theatre, shaking our hands and slapping our backs.

Michael Grade, the head of Channel 4, had flown into Cannes just to see the reaction to the film and was bowled over. Everyone seemed to want a piece of us and we were invited back to a swish black-tie dinner for the great and the good.

Jim Allen had nothing to wear so we scavenged bits and pieces. I had a spare bow tie and a cummerbund, while Bruce had a spare jacket. We could do nothing about his shoes.

Arriving at the dinner, we were seated at a table draped in white linen, with full silver service. There were only a hundred guests, mostly producers, directors, financiers and network executives – the people who make the deals.

The French champagne growers had sponsored the film festival and we could have washed our feet in the stuff (which Rita fancied doing). They didn't have any beer so I sipped water and soaked up the atmosphere. After two years living on the breadline it was surreal to be surrounded by such opulence.

As the food was served Jim took his teeth out and wrapped them in a napkin. This waiter put two carrots and two little pieces of green bean on the table in front of him.

'Where's the rest of the dinner?' Jim asked him.

'*Pardon?*'

'My dinner, where's the rest of it?'

There was an awkward silence. This was Jim's first experience of nouvelle cuisine and mine as well. I couldn't believe the size of the portions. It wouldn't feed a rabbit.

Rita had to leave early the next morning because we were booked on different flights. I said goodbye and put her in a taxi, before bumping into Jim, who came round the corner with a newspaper under his arm.

'You're up early,' I said.

'Always am – been to get me paper.'

Jim normally started writing at about eight in the morning and finished at lunchtime. Then he spent the rest of the day at the pub, timing his trips home to correspond with the police changing shifts so he didn't get pulled over.

'Fancy breakfast?'

'Yeah. OK.'

Waiters were laying the tables for the continental breakfast. We sat down and ordered pots of tea, then went to the buffet and loaded up our plates with beautiful boiled ham, pâté and pastries. Jim took out his teeth and wrapped them in a napkin before getting stuck in.

I can eat like a horse at the best of times and Jim had a similar appetite. We were just about finished when the chef came out and cried in alarm. The two of us had scoffed enough ham to feed the entire hotel.

Back in Liverpool Rita found a nice four-bedroom house that she wanted to buy. I didn't have any money to help her, but I took over the negotiations and managed to get the place for a few thousand less than the asking price. We moved in just before Christmas and had a proper tree with decorations.

With Rita at work every day, I spent my time doing up the place. I turned a washhouse into another bathroom and converted the shed in the yard into a kennel for Joffe.

Rita worked long hours and at night she spread her books out on the kitchen table doing her paperwork. By comparison, I had no prospects at all, so she certainly didn't want me for my money.

It took me a while before I told her how I really felt. At the same time I was leaving daft little notes around the house. Rita would open the dishwasher and find – 'We'll never be washed up.' In the bread bin – 'Don't go stale on me.' In the drier – 'I'm in a spin about you.'

Eventually I realised that I had better tell this person that I loved her, but at the same time I warned, 'Do you know what you're letting yourself in for? There are lots of skeletons in my cupboard.'

I didn't want Rita to be under any false illusions. We were likely to have loads of laugh and our fair share of heartache, but never be bored.

Not surprisingly, her family and friends worried about her. One friend told her, 'Do you know his politics?'

'Yeah.'

'No, do you *really* know his politics?'

'What d'ya mean?'

'Well, he's been further to the right than he has been to the left.'

Again, she was shocked, but we talked it through and I explained how my views had changed.

Rita is a battler, who thinks the world of her kids and is willing to give people the benefit of the doubt. Against many of her instincts she fell in love and stuck by me, helping me get back on my feet.

While still living in Rita's rented property in Walton, I had a phone call from an agent in Manchester called Patrick Nyland. Up until then I had never bothered with agents, but

Patrick seemed confident that he could find me work so I agreed to let him try.

Sure enough, within days a role came up in a new drama series, *Roughnecks*. Patrick took the credit and the usual commission. Years later I learned that Moira Williams from First Choice Productions had always wanted me for the part and had contacted various showbusiness people trying to get my phone number. She called Patrick because he represented Bruce Jones who I'd worked with on *Raining Stones*. According to Moira, Patrick knew about *Roughnecks* before he called me. This is how our working relationship began.

Set on an oil rig off the coast of Scotland, *Roughnecks* told the story of a group of riggers and their wives and girlfriends. I played Cinders, the oil rig chef who drove taxis part-time. Others in the cast included Liam Cunningham, an Irish actor, who later worked with Richard Gere and Sean Connery in *First Knight*, Jimmy Cosmo, who was in *Braveheart*; Hywel Simons, a young Welsh lad, and George Rossi, both now on *The Bill*, Paul Copley and also Bruce Jones.

Filming started in September 1993 on board an oil rig in the North Sea. We flew out on Monday morning and back on Friday night. Weekends were spent at a hotel in Edinburgh and Rita often came up to stay with me. Before we started all of the actors were sent on a special course that rig workers must undertake before being allowed at sea. Basically it dealt with emergencies such as a helicopter having to ditch into the ocean, a possibility that terrified me.

The training course had three final challenges. The first was to jump twenty feet into a pool wearing full safety gear, including dry-suits and life vests. This I managed without any problems. The second involved being strapped into what looked like a helicopter cabin, which was then submerged into water. We had to unbuckle our seat belts and scramble to the side of the sinking chopper. This was also OK.

The killer test was the third challenge. We were all strapped in the chopper in complete darkness as it was lowered upside down into the water. We had to release our harnesses, find the openings and swim outside.

No way. Not in a million years. My asthma meant I couldn't hold my breath for very long and the thought of being trapped terrified me.

'Come on, Rick, you can do it,' said Bruce Jones.

'I can't.'

'There are divers down there with you. They've got tanks.'

'Well, give me a bloody tank.'

In spite of this they still wanted me for *Roughnecks*. I signed an insurance waiver that gave the producers permission to let me drown in the event of a ditching.

The oil rig used for the filming had been decommissioned, but still had a team of maintenance engineers who kept everything in working order, as well as proper chefs and kitchen staff. Although no alcohol was allowed – too dangerous – it was still like a boys' trip away and we made our own entertainment, such as weekly quiz nights which became so popular that people would turn up an hour early to make sure they got a table.

Each team threw in a couple of quid as a prize for the eventual winners. I had the job of quizmaster and pinched the questions from a game of Trivial Pursuit. Some of the cheating was outrageous but that just added to the humour.

Another challenge consisted of a fishing contest off the main platform which must have been sixty feet above the water. We all put in a fiver with the money going to the first lad to catch a fish.

It was completely daft, of course. We needed these massive weights on the lines to take them from the platform into the water and then below. Every time we finished filming a scene we dashed outside to where we'd left the lines dangling in the ocean.

This went on for weeks and nobody had caught a thing. Finally I hatched a plan. A supply boat would come out mid-week with fresh fruit and veg as well as meat and bread. I got one of the crew to buy me a fish and when the boat pulled into the platform he hooked this thing on the end of my line.

Half an hour after the boat had gone, I was fishing with Bruce Jones.

'Hey! I've got something. I've got something,' I shouted.

I started winding it in and making sure this fish gave me a hell of a fight. Bruce was so excited he ran inside, shouting, 'Tomo's caught one. Tomo's caught one.'

The thing 'flapped' around in my hands as I pretended to give it a whack on the head. The lads were stunned. They'd all given up hope.

I pocketed the money and we gave up fishing after that. Nobody twigged except Jimmy Cosmo, who had a quiet word to me later.

'That's the first time I've seen a freshwater fish caught so far out to sea,' he said.

Practical jokes were an integral part of life on the rig. We were always finding new ways to wind each other up. One of the maintenance staff told us that a welder had lost his life when he fell into one of the giant legs of the rig. His body had never been recovered.

As we heard this story, I noticed Alex Westwood, a Scottish actor, give a little shudder. Bruce Jones noticed it as well. A couple of nights later we put a pair of welder's gloves on top of the locker in his cabin. The next morning, over breakfast, Alex told everyone in a hushed voice.

'Go away,' I said.

'Leave it off,' echoed Bruce.

We left it another few days and borrowed a welder's helmet from the maintenance shift. Again, we left it on his locker. This time Alex was truly spooked. We overheard him talking to the maintenance guys who told him how the welder's ghost had haunted the rig for years.

While Alex was shooting scenes that day, we organised one of the chippies to drill a tiny, almost invisible hole through the wall of his cabin. Then we threaded fishing line through the hole and tied it to a chair on castors, using a slipknot so it could be tugged off with a flick of the wrist.

At about two in the morning, when Alex had fallen asleep, Bruce and I tiptoed along the corridor and took hold of the fishing line. With a gentle pull, we sent the chair in his room rolling across the floor until it banged into the wall.

Alex's scream must have woken half the rig. We were away by then, legging it down the corridor and hiding in the shower. He came tearing out into the passageway, white-faced and trembling. In the morning he said nothing and has never mentioned it again from that day to this.

The final episode of the first series was a cliffhanger with a helicopter ditching into the ocean during a fierce storm. The disaster scene took days to set up and cost tens of thousands of pounds to film. A helicopter was turned upside down in the North Sea beside a quay and fire tenders had been organised to provide the 'rain'.

Beforehand the actors were taken on a safety course in Stonehaven. Our instructor was an amazing guy, who had trained Special Boat Service recruits and looked like a real action hero. He instilled me with enough confidence that I felt I could do anything.

'If ever you get in trouble, I'll come up and tap you on the shoulder,' he said. 'Then you'll know everything will be OK.'

On the evening of filming the director Sandy Johnson gathered the cast and crew together for a final talk on safety. He lectured us like a military commander with a whiteboard and pointer.

'Whatever happens we are not going to take risks. You can't mess about in the sea – not in these temperatures.'

As he finished, I piped up, 'Can I just say a few words, Sandy?'

He sat down and gave me the floor. A second unit camera crew had just arrived and didn't know me from Adam. I walked to the front carrying a plastic bag, which I put on the table.

'Right, chaps, we are here,' I pointed to the whiteboard. 'As some of you know I used to be in the SAS and you could drop me anywhere in the world and I'd be able to survive as long as there is a chip shop in the area.'

I took a kiddie's spade from the bag. 'I have gathered some useful tools for tonight's operation. We never want the enemy to know where we are, so if you go for a crap I want you to bury it with this. It may also be necessary to lie in shallow water to hide, so each of you will need one of these.' I produced a snorkel.

The second unit camera crew still wasn't sure if I was being serious.

'One last thing . . . desperate circumstances often require desperate measures. Should any of you be captured, you will need one of these . . .' I rummaged in the bag and they expected me to produce a suicide capsule. Instead, I held up a white flag.

Out on the water, fire hoses were spraying thousands of gallons into the air. Arc lights turned the sheets of water into silver. The water was bloody freezing, but all of us wore wet-suits and dry-suits as well as life vests.

Bobbing in the swell alongside Clive Russell and Theresa Banham, I hung on the side of the helicopter as the 'rain' teemed down. People were screaming and shouting in the aftermath of the crash. Every so often, I swallowed a mouthful of sea water.

Sandy Johnson yelled, 'Cut.' They dragged us out of the water and wrapped us in blankets. I clenched my teeth hard to stop them chattering. Unfortunately, the scene had to be set up again. The chopper had become exposed as the tide receded. Now it had to be dragged into deeper water.

We huddled on a barge, trying to get warm, but I could feel the cold leaking through the layers of protection into my core.

It took almost an hour to re-set the scene. Finally Sandy shouted, 'OK, let's do it again.'

I didn't want to go back in the water. Maybe it was the cold or having thought about it for too long. My confidence had deserted me. With water pouring into my eyes and up my nose, I couldn't see or breathe properly. Panic set in. I grabbed hold of Clive. He was a big man, but I was dragging him under. Theresa, God love her, got her arms around me, holding me up.

My heart raced and I sucked in each breath. Suddenly, I felt a hand on my shoulder. The instructor had reached me with a few powerful strokes.

'You're OK, Rick.'

I relaxed.

'You're coming out,' he said.

'No, I'll be OK now.'

'You're coming out.'

They brought in a rescue launch and dragged me out of the water.

'Lie still.'

'I'm OK.'

'Just lie still.'

The rest of the cast were taken back to shore. Filming was over. I felt terrible. I had cost them the scene. Tens of thousands of pounds had been wasted.

I needn't have worried. The next day, as they sat down to look at the rushes, they discovered that water had leaked into the cameras and not a single frame could be salvaged.

The disaster sequence had to be re-shot, but this time they didn't bother with an outdoor setting. We filmed at Pinewood Studios using a pool for the underwater shots and a larger tank with wind machines and a painted backdrop for the crash site. You couldn't tell the difference in the finished show.

As the second series of *Roughnecks* ended, I was disappointed they didn't commission a third. From a financial point of view it had lifted me out of a hole and most of those early cheques went straight to Rita. She still had no idea how deeply I was in debt.

Jimmy McGovern, who had written scripts for *Brookside*, was enjoying huge success with *Cracker* starring Robbie Coltrane as 'Fitz', a forensic psychologist. I was offered a day's work on the show, playing a tradesman.

Meanwhile, Christopher Eccleston, who played the part of DCI Bilborough in the series, had decided to leave so Jimmy and Paul Abbott, another of the writers, killed him off in the same episode.

A new character had been created to replace him, but at

the last minute the actor chosen to play the role couldn't commit to the series. An urgent replacement had to be found and Jimmy put my name forward.

Suddenly, I found myself in a smart suit, with short hair and a neatly trimmed beard. Instead of playing a tradesman, I became DCI Wise, the senior policeman.

How ironic to be playing a detective, after all my experiences with the police. Granada even sent me to a police station in Manchester to get acclimatised. I had to laugh. One of the detectives said to me, 'You won't be long will you, Rick?'

My first episode of *Cracker* featured Robbie Carlyle, who of course I already knew from *Riff Raff*. He played a skinhead, who sets out to avenge the deaths of Liverpool football fans in the Hillsborough Stadium disaster by killing an equal number of policemen.

Being a total perfectionist, Robbie once again steeped himself in the role. In this case he adopted a Scouse accent from the first day of filming whether in front of the camera or not.

I arrived late at the hotel in Manchester one night and realised that I didn't have a call sheet showing what scenes were being filmed the next day. It was two-thirty in the morning when I rang Robbie's room. He picked up the phone, groggy from sleep, and answered in a Scouse accent. Unbelievable! He kept this up until the very last scene and then slipped back into his own Glaswegian brogue.

I don't think actors give other actors the credit they are due. Lorcan Cranitch, an Irishman, played DS Beck in *Cracker* and he gave one of the finest performances I have ever seen as a grief-stricken detective, who blamed himself for his boss's murder. He should have won a BAFTA but wasn't even nominated.

The entire crew was a close-knit bunch and I loved going to work every morning. The make-up girls, Sue Milton and Anastasia Shirley, were a real laugh and Anastasia later married Robbie Carlyle after meeting him during the filming.

Robbie Coltrane is a huge man with a personality to match. The two of us would swap gags at 7 a.m. in the make-up trailer, getting the place rocking. Robbie could do wonderful voices and called himself the 'Wing Commander', giving the rest of us nicknames like 'Biffo' and 'Ginger'.

We filmed a two-part episode in Hong Kong, 'White Ghost', which had been written by Paul Abbott. Fitz has to investigate the motives behind the murder of a high-flying businessman and the disappearance of a young Chinese woman.

I have never been a confident traveller because I'm always getting lost and feel as though I need someone to hold my hand. People don't believe this, but I'm actually very shy. I have never walked into a pub on my own for a drink.

In Hong Kong Sue and Anastasia looked after me. They took me out sightseeing and would make lists for me to take to the supermarket. I went out with Robbie Coltrane one day and we came across a shop with carpenters busily sawing, hammering and gluing. These guys looked up, panic-stricken, and began motioning for us to get away.

I suddenly realised what was wrong. They were making coffins. Robbie is well over six foot and nineteen stone and I'm five foot nine and seventeen stone. There wasn't enough wood in all of Hong Kong to accommodate us.

For a long while I had managed to stay one step ahead of my creditors, but being part of a top-rating TV show isn't exactly conducive to keeping a low profile. Sure enough, the bailiffs and writ-servers began turning up on the set of *Cracker*.

The security lads on the show were very good, keeping them

away from me, but this couldn't last forever. A major bank waived my debt, but the new landlords of the Limelight building weren't so forgiving. They obtained a court order forcing Granada to garnishee my wages.

This was among my last debts and eventually I had repaid everyone. Some I had almost forgotten. When I was doing up the cottage in Coedpoeth I had ordered a lot of supplies from Minera Builders and the owner Derek Rennie had been really good to me. When things came crashing down I owed him something like two hundred quid. He had sent letters asking me to pay, which I ignored and later he took me to the small claims court.

I don't think Derek ever expected to see his money, but I was driving past Minera Builders one day and suddenly remembered the debt. Pulling into the yard, I took out every note I had in my wallet and walked into the office. Derek was serving a customer, but looked exactly the same, with a nice big red face and glasses. His wife was standing beside him, doing the books.

'I think I owe you some money.'

He nodded.

I gave him the handful of notes. 'I hope this covers it.'

'Thanks very much.'

As I walked out the door, I heard his wife say to him, 'Isn't that nice?'

I haven't seen Derek since then, but I'm glad I remembered him. I don't want to go through life owing people.

19

Does This Heart Match My Sleeve?

I'm at the Cannes International Film Festival again to promote Once Upon a Time in the Midlands *which I made last November with Robbie Carlyle and Kathy Burke. It's being shown as part of the Director's Fortnight, but isn't in competition.*

Last night I called a game of bingo on the beach at Cannes. The locals were totally flummoxed, but it was great for publicity. That's what festivals are all about as buyers and sellers network and negotiate distribution deals.

Ken Loach is here with his new film, Sweet Sixteen. *He invites me to the premiere and I get an amazing sense of* déjà vu *as I walk up the red carpet.*

The cast of Sweet Sixteen *are mainly teenagers who are all brand new to the game. They arrive at the theatre looking magnificent in full battledress of kilts, sashes and all the regalia. The crowd cheers for them and I can see the excitement in their eyes. It doesn't get any better than this.*

The film is brilliant. Set in Greenock, near Glasgow, it tells the story of a troubled teenager, Liam, who has pinned all his hopes on his life getting better when his junkie Mum gets out of prison on the same day that he turns sixteen.

It's a classic Loach film: angry, funny, heartbreaking and tender.

The audience rise as one in a standing ovation. It deserves to win the Palme d'or, but misses out to Roman Polanski's The Pianist. *As a consolation, Paul Laverty wins the award for best screenplay.*

After the screening, Ken asks if I want to join the cast for dinner. They aren't having a party because most of them are too young to drink. I tag along to the restaurant and have a great night telling stories and enjoying the enthusiasm of the youngsters. Just before midnight I say to Ken, 'I'm heading back. Thanks for the invite.'

'Hang on, I'll come with you,' he says. We're both staying at the same hotel. 'Just let me say goodbye to a few people.'

We leave the restaurant and turn along the boardwalk, with the beach on one side and the hotels and restaurants on the other. The shops are still open and the streets are crowded with people who are heading to parties or just enjoying a midnight stroll.

We haven't gone ten yards when a limousine slows and the power windows glide down.

'Bravo, Mr Loach! Bravo! Sweet Sixteen *is* magnifique. Bravo.'

Ken very modestly says thanks and we walk on. Another flash car pulls up.

'Mr Loach, Mr Loach. Magnifique. Sweet Sixteen . . .'

This continues the whole way back to the hotel as Ken gets stopped by women in evening dresses and men in designer suits. It seems as though everybody in Cannes wants to shake his hand and pat his back. Although embarrassed by all the attention, Ken is obviously pleased.

The interruptions continue and make the walk back to our hotel three times as long. About twenty-five yards from the front door we round a corner and come across a little hot-dog stand being worked by a scruffy-looking Frenchman, with a stubbly beard, slicked-back hair, a filthy T-shirt and a cigarette hanging out of his gob. His face lights up and he throws his arms out towards us. Here we go again, I think.

> *'Ah, Ricky Tomlinson. Bravo!' he cries.*
> *Ken and me fall about laughing.*

After two series of *Cracker*, Jimmy McGovern had decided to move on to other projects. We did the Hong Kong episode as a one-off special in 1996 and that was the last of DCI Wise.

By then I had known Rita for more than four years and she had helped turn my life around. I also owe enormous gratitude to my friends and family who stuck by me during the worst of times. They're the reason I love Liverpool so much. I'm proud of being a Scouser and I wear my heart on my sleeve. Sometimes this gets me into trouble, particularly from people who I don't feel are as passionate about their roots as I am.

Some celebrities can't wait to get out of Liverpool or become 'professional Scousers' trading on the accent and humour, but living elsewhere.

There's nothing wrong with this. People can live where they like. But at the same time I think it would be nice if some of the successful ones remembered where they came from and visited once in a while to do a charity gig, especially when you consider what a tough time Liverpool has had over the past twenty-five years. OK, things are better now, but this doesn't change the fact that people have gone AWOL when they were most needed.

I had a falling-out with Cilla Black many years ago at a function for Phil Redmond in Liverpool. I was working on *Brookside* and went to the do with most of the cast. Cilla was there with her husband Bobby Willis and the actor Gareth Hunt.

A local newspaper photographer asked if I could do him a favour and get the celebrities together so he could snap a quick photograph and then leave us in peace. I pulled the

Brookside crowd together and then said, 'Cilla, can you spare us a second?' I gently touched her arm and she spun to face me.

'Get your hand off this dress. It cost a lot of money,' she snapped.

I responded in kind. 'I wouldn't have thought so, the way it looks on you.'

Stony silence followed and she gritted her teeth through the photographs.

Since then relations have become even chillier. I mentioned the incident during an interview with a journalist a few years back and he later recounted the story to Cilla.

'Well, he's not even a Scouser,' she responded. 'He wasn't born in Liverpool.'

My response was 'I may have been away from Liverpool for the first three days of my life, but she's been away for the last forty years.'

The *Liverpool Echo* picked up on the story and went hard on the feud angle. They even offered readers the chance to vote on the person they believed to be the truest Scouser. Cilla got annihilated.

The Liverpool dock strike in 1995 was a time when some of these celebrities could have stood up to be counted. It was a long and bitterly fought union dispute, which ultimately ended in failure for the dockers who spent two and a half years on the picket line before being sold out by the union.

The dispute began when casual workers and trainees complained about their working conditions and five hundred dockers refused to cross their picket line and were locked out. The sackings were the final act in Liverpool's long history as a major seaport. In 1967 there had been sixteen thousand dockworkers in Liverpool. Within thirty years there were less than a hundred.

Having grown up with dockers, I have enormous respect for the dangers they faced and how hard most of them worked. And I was angry at the newspapers portraying them as militants and ratbags, when in reality they were good, solid, law-abiding family men, who wanted decent wages and conditions.

It must have been so hard for them, losing their jobs, going into debt and seeing their children go without. Some of them were heartbroken because their best mates had crossed the picket line. Lads they would never talk to again for the rest of their lives.

People don't realise the repercussions of a struggle such as this. It divided families. Little kids weren't allowed to play with other kids. The wives of scabs would band together and travel miles out of Liverpool to buy their weekly groceries, rather than risk bumping into striking dockers.

I spent some time on the picket lines, showing my solidarity. The incident that sticks in my mind happened one morning as we stood across the gateway to the dock. Nearby a couple of lads were warming their hands over a forty-gallon drum that had been turned into a brazier.

A car came along the road full of scabs. I don't know who was driving, but as they neared the entrance it accelerated and then swerved, ramming the brazier and putting one of the lads in hospital. The car didn't stop. It carried on through the gate.

The police had witnessed this entire scene. There were even camcorders recording the event, but they refused to get the driver's name. One of them actually said, 'All we'd do is warn him about a minor traffic offence.'

Under pressure, they finally investigated but took no action. The driver claimed something had been thrown at the car, which is why he swerved. This was a load of bollocks. I knew it, the police knew it and even the driver knew it, but nothing could be done.

It would have been nice to see Jimmy Tarbuck on the picket line because he made his start in show business telling jokes about the Liverpool dockers. And Cilla Black could also have come along because her Dad, Johnny White, had been a docker and a good bloke. Maybe they got past Birmingham and simply lost their way.

I know a lot of people who haven't forgiven Cilla for supporting Margaret Thatcher, a woman she described as having 'put the great back into Great Britain'. I don't know if she still feels the same way. Quite a few celebrities stood on the same platform as Thatcher and some of them even made grand statements about leaving the country if the Labour Party won power. That's why I have this persistent desire to visit Frank Bruno and Paul Daniels and ask them, 'How come you haven't left yet?'

I'm guessing they're still here because this Labour Government has done more for them than the Tories would have.

The dockers' strike was rich in drama and personal tragedy, which is why Jimmy McGovern decided to tell the story. But he was aware that often writers go to a location, pick people's brains, use their stories, pick up a BAFTA and are never seen again. He didn't want to do this so he decided to involve the dockers and their families in the production through every stage. He set up a writers' workshop and for a year and a half they tossed around ideas, wrote scenes and edited scripts.

Jimmy phoned me when the script for *Dockers* was finished.

'I want you to play this fella in it.'

'OK.'

'He's a scab.'

I went quiet for a few moments.

'Why?'

'Well, we don't want the stereotyped scab – the snivelling blackleg who sneaks in and out of the gate. We want someone who goes to work and has a reason and will stand and fight his corner.'

'I'm very flattered,' I told him, but my first reaction was to say no. Then I thought more about it and could see the benefits.

'OK, Jimmy, but if I do the part I want to play it to get everyone's sympathy.'

'That's what we want.'

The scene I remember best is a recreation of a typical morning on the picket line. I'm in a car about to run the gauntlet of the pickets for the first time. The director told me beforehand, 'When you go through the lads are going to be screaming and shouting abuse. I want you to do this . . . [he wagged his finger] and say, "No, no, I'm going in to work."'

We filmed the scene, which was incredibly powerful. Some of the dockers had tears in their eyes as we finished. One of them, a big guy called Larry, said it brought everything back to him. It had been his 'mate' who had crossed the picket line, waving his finger. The two had never spoken to each other again.

The story that emerged was one of betrayal: betrayal by their employers, betrayal by their unions and betrayal by the Labour Party. For example, the strike should have been over within two days of starting. A union official had been given a message to pass on to strikers that they should settle and return to work, but for some reason failed to do so.

And the most disappointing feature was how the TUC, having promised to march with the dockers to victory, sold them out. The Liverpool dockers had more support from unions overseas than they had from those in the UK.

The major problem with trade unions nowadays is the leadership. Many union bosses have become part of the Establishment and the unions are like corporations, always looking for takeover targets or mergers. The leadership act more like CEOs than shop stewards. They build fancy offices, have chauffeur-driven cars and forget about the rank and file who finance these lifestyles.

The dockers who wrote the script with Jimmy looked justifiably proud at the premiere of the film. And they gave me a wonderful compliment after the press screening. Jimmy McGovern was being interviewed and he was asked about his next project.

'I'm thinking of doing Mary Queen of Scots,' he said.

'Who's going to play Mary?' asked a journalist.

One of the dockers piped up, 'Ricky Tomlinson.'

I still see a lot of the lads today. With their redundancy packages, they put some money into buying a little social club in Hope Street, in between the Catholic and Anglican cathedrals. It has a bistro and a little concert room. I've been to cabaret nights at the club and the place was packed to the rafters. Some of the money also went into setting up the Initiative Factory, which has different creative schemes and its own little TV studio.

The lads who run the club and the factory don't take wages, only bus fares and meal money. They are still together; still having a go.

Elsewhere, many of the non-union men who took the Judas silver and crossed the picket lines now find themselves unemployed. They have learned the hard way that they sacrificed any job security when they signed rolling employment contracts to work on the docks. Ironically, some of them are now suing the union because the union won't accept them into its membership.

The rise and rise of personal rolling twelve-month contracts is a scandal in the workplace. No longer is there any job security and therefore no loyalty.

One of the reasons I admire Arthur Scargill is that he warned us all that this would happen. Even when Michael Heseltine said that thirty thousand miners were going to lose their jobs, Arthur said, 'Unless we stop this it won't be thirty thousand, it will be sixty thousand miners.'

Even Arthur underestimated the true number. Now we're importing coal mined by virtual slave labour in the Third World. It is an appalling situation.

My working relationship with Jimmy McGovern extended to another TV drama based on real-life events, which again shook Liverpool to its core. *Hillsborough* told the story of ninety-six Liverpool football fans who died in Sheffield on 15 April 1989.

I can still remember where I was when I heard the news. Driving along the East Lancashire Road, heading home, I turned on the radio and heard that the FA Cup semi-final had been abandoned because of crowd trouble.

A few minutes later the announcer mentioned that lives could have been lost – as many as six or eight. From then on the number kept climbing. My sense of trepidation and sadness grew into absolute devastation when the full scale of the tragedy became clear. A whole city united in its grief. Everton and Liverpool supporters stood arm in arm outside the Shankly Gates. The flowers and wreathes covered the pitch at Anfield.

The days that followed were full of terrible stories, lies and deceit. The authorities responsible for opening perimeter gates, and letting two thousand fans surge into an already crowded tunnel creating the crush, did their best to deflect the blame. They were aided and abetted by a whispering campaign, which blackened the names of ordinary fans.

Kelvin MacKenzie, editor of the *Sun*, launched an astonishing attack on the 'football hooligans' he claimed caused the tragedy. Under the headline 'THE TRUTH', the paper alleged that drunken fans had 'viciously attacked rescue workers trying to revive victims . . . picked the pockets of the dead . . . and urinated on brave cops . . .'

None of this was true and subsequent inquests and inquiries revealed that alcohol and hooliganism played absolutely no part in the tragedy. The *Sun* was boycotted on Merseyside and a lot of people in Liverpool, me among them, still refuse to buy a copy.

Jimmy McGovern wrote a wonderful script based on Hillsborough and the aftermath. The director Charles McDougal had actually been at the stadium that day and witnessed the tragedy. I played the part of John Glover, who in real life lived only about a mile away from me in Walton. He and his wife lost their son Ian at Hillsborough and their other two sons returned home different people. One of them, Joe, was so traumatised that he would sleep on his brother's grave.

Having agreed to play John, I met with him and was impressed by his quiet dignity and stillness. I knew I couldn't talk and act exactly the way John had done, so I asked if I could 'be myself' and hopefully I could bring across some of his strength and humility.

He and his wife Theresa came to see some of the filming. The inquest scenes were shot at Manchester Town Hall and I had to give a speech outside. John and Theresa couldn't bear to relive the moment and turned away. I have since heard that John has never managed to watch the drama right through until the end.

Not long after the drama-documentary, John asked if I'd help launch a new campaign for Hillsborough victims. A lot of people had become disenchanted with the existing Hillsborough Family Support Group, which they claimed was too authoritarian and non-inclusive.

The Hillsborough Justice Campaign started in a small shop not far from Anfield Stadium. I helped find the building and Albert and a few other mates did the refurbishment. I also guaranteed to pay the rent and rates, as well as any bills for the first year if the fundraising didn't cover them.

The Hillsborough Justice Campaign continues to lobby the Government and soccer authorities to hold a proper judicial inquiry into the disaster.

20

My Arse

I have this thing about women and tattoos. I'm not being sexist – I don't like them on men either. I try to picture someone like Melanie Chisholm – the most talented of the Spice Girls – as an old woman with black smudges all over her body. It won't be pretty (although I think she is).

Back in 1997 I sat next to a woman at a Royal Television Society Awards night in Manchester who had tattoos from the nape of her neck to the crack of her arse. It was one of those black-tie occasions with all the women in evening gowns and people six-deep at the bar. I first saw the tattooed lady at the buffet.

'My God, look at that,' I said to Rita. 'I hope I'm not sitting next to her.'

'Why?'

'In case anyone thinks I'm with her.'

Sure enough, we found ourselves seated next to each other. She turned out to be lovely and I've worked with her since on jobs where she's been employed as an extra.

Halfway through the evening I went to the bar and as I collected the drinks I backed into someone and apologised. It was Caroline Aherne, who I didn't know personally, but I had seen her on TV in The Fast Show *and* Mrs Merton.

'Oh hi ya,' she said. 'You're going to be me Dad, you know.'

Then she toddled off with her drink. I went back to the table and said to Rita, 'Caroline Aherne said I'm going to be her Dad. Do I know her Dad?'

We both shrugged and I put the whole incident down to too much champagne.

Early in 1998 I had a call from a BBC casting agent about a new comedy series written by Caroline, Henry Normal and Craig Cash. Invited to a reading, I arrived at the Granada Studios to find half a dozen chairs set up in a semi-circle. Caroline handed me a script. I sat next to Craig Cash and Sue Johnston. The others included Kathy Burke, Ralf Little and Liz Smith.

My character, Jim Royle, was a lazy, grumpy, unemployed father, who loves the TV remote control, hates parting with money, especially on household bills, and has trouble with his 'Rockford Files' (piles).

Sue Johnston played my long-suffering wife, Barb, who works at a bakery, smokes like a chimney and keeps trying to interest the family in mindless gossip.

Caroline was Denise, our bone-idle daughter, who had never done a day's work without complaining. And Ralf Little, the youngest member of the cast, was Anthony, a general dogsbody, who is picked on mercilessly by everyone.

Craig Cash sat next to Caroline for the read-through. He played Denise's boyfriend, Dave, who runs a mobile disco and already acts as though he's a part of the family. Next to him, Liz Smith was Barbara's dippy mother, Nana, who is always whingeing about her various ailments.

Complimenting this unlikely 'family' were Kathy Burke (the next-door neighbour Cheryl) and Geoff Hughes as 'Twiggy' (Jim Royle's best mate).

The read-through was filmed by a single camera, after which Caroline thanked us and sent us home. I didn't know what to make of the material. There were some wonderful asides and the characterisations were spot on, but nothing actually happened. It was all dialogue and long pauses that passed between a family sitting watching TV in a living room.

I said to Rita, 'This is either going to win all sorts of awards or we're gonna get jailed for twelve months.'

We assembled in Manchester again about a month later, only this time without Kathy Burke who had committed to another project. Fortunately, they managed to get Jessica Stevenson to play the role of Cheryl.

As we began filming the pilot, I still didn't understand what Caroline was trying to achieve. She didn't want to create a typical sitcom full of gags and pratfalls. It was almost the opposite. After spending a week filming the pilot, she still wasn't happy. Courageously, she threw the whole lot away and started again.

A different director was hired, Mark Mylod, who understood Caroline's vision of making the underlying humour as subtle as possible rather than in your face.

Battles still had to be fought. The programmers at BBC2 were frightened by the static nature of the sitcom and wanted to add things like a studio audience or canned laughter. Caroline fought against it.

The Royle Family went to air on 14 September 1998. Jim Royle sat slouched in an armchair, reading the phone bill.

'Ninety-eight quid! Ninety-eight quid! It's good to talk, my arse.'

And so it began . . .

Some of the critics were ecstatic. The *Evening Standard*

called the show 'windbreakingly funny', and *TV Quick* said it 'turns the mind-numbingly banal into a comedy classic'.

Others weren't so impressed. Some people couldn't appreciate that the magic of *The Royle Family* came from the perfect characterisation and dialogue. The long pauses between conversations, with people simply staring at the TV, simply added to the power of the show. Nobody had ever done this before.

The *Socialist Review* wrote: 'Why would anyone want to spend half an hour watching the idiosyncrasies of a family on television when probably we all know similar families to the Royles we can visit?'

My Mam wasn't the least bit impressed at seeing me swearing, nose-picking, farting, and taking the piss out of Barb and Anthony.

'And why don't you get your hair cut?' she asked.

'Mam, it's the part.'

'Don't be making excuses.'

'Mam, it is.'

'Your other brothers are dead smart, why can't you be like them?'

Caroline Aherne, Henry Normal and Craig Cash wrote the first series and I christened them the ANC. Henry went off to work with Steve Coogan after that and Caroline and Craig carried on the writing partnership. Ideas could strike at any time. The two of them would sit and talk it through, giggling like school kids as they came up with fresh dialogue. You could see how much they enjoyed the characters.

Each series of six episodes was filmed over six weeks, but it was more like a holiday than hard work. We were always getting into trouble for corpsing (laughing) during scenes and mucking about. Craig Cash is a real giggler and once he started he couldn't stop.

I was just as bad. We had this exchange of dialogue during one episode where Craig had to say, 'Oooh, that Helen Mirren, she doesn't mind flippin' her tits out.'

For some reason he changed it slightly and said, 'Oooh, that Helen Mirren, she doesn't mind flippin' them.'

It totally threw me. I broke up. The director yelled 'Cut' and we did another take. Craig looked at me with his big sad eyes and said, 'Oooh, that Helen Mirren, she doesn't mind flippin' them.'

I was lost. I laughed so much that we had to put off the scene and do something else.

In another episode Twiggy and Jim were stripping the wallpaper in the sitting room, while dancing to 'Mambo No. 5'. Geoff Hughes danced so hard that his trousers fell off to reveal a bloody big pair of old-fashioned Y-fronts. Both of us finished on the floor laughing.

The catering in Manchester was unbelievable, with everything you could possibly want on the menu. Caroline's mother used to turn up every so often, right about dinner.

'How is it that you just happen to be passing whenever we're having a feed?' I used to tease.

I swear to God, she was Mrs Merton without the glasses. She even used to cock up her sayings occasionally.

For the second series we moved to Ealing Studios in London, where they filmed the classic Ealing comedies. Staying in a nice hotel, I was picked up by a limousine every morning and dropped back at night. Rita often came down to stay.

If anything, the show got even funnier because we had grown more comfortable with our characters and could experiment. Jim grew a bit lazier and a bit grouchier. I took a deliberate decision not to cut my hair or trim my beard. Similarly, I wouldn't let wardrobe wash my clothes from one series to the next.

After working under lights they stank to high heaven, but I left them lying on the floor of the dressing room in a pile. The wardrobe guy used to force himself to look the other way.

Although I'm not what you might call a method actor, I felt I owed it to the writers and the character to 'become' Jim Royle – slob and couch potato. And as soon as I put on that striped shirt and those trousers that is exactly what happened. The transformation was instantaneous, although Marlene and Rita will probably tell you that I didn't need the clothes.

Sue Johnston had to seriously dress down to become 'Barb', stripping off her make-up, letting her hair go lank and wearing rumpled clothes. She'd walk on to the set looking like this and I'd say, 'I think they're waiting for you in make-up, Sue.'

She'd go mad.

At the end of each day's filming Sue and I had a routine. Back at the hotel we went to the seventh-floor bar, ordered a drink and read through our lines for the following day. It was strictly the two drinks and then back to our rooms for an early night.

Having worked with Sue so often before, we are like Pinky and Perky. She knows when I'm 'dry' (having forgotten my lines) and covers for me until I can pick up the thread of things.

Making a TV series is an odd sort of lifestyle. For six weeks you live in each other's pockets, sharing laughs, frustration and creative energy. Then you disappear home and don't see each other until the promotional campaign, or an award ceremony or maybe even the next series. It's like going on holiday, knowing you'll see the same friends every year.

Liz Smith is adorable and can make me laugh just by looking at her. I swear to God, all she had to do was knit to get the part of Nana.

She has embraced the Eastern art of feng shui, which as far as I can tell is an excuse for shifting furniture. Liz bought a carpet on condition that if it didn't fit with the feng shui of her flat the carpet company would change it for her. These poor fellas have been back and forth so many times up her stairs they're going to have to recarpet the stairwell.

Although I give him a hard time in the show, I have a lot of time for Ralf Little. This was his first big break into television and he achieved the sort of instant fame that most kids only dream about. Once or twice I had to pull him aside and give him advice. In particular, I told him that we could all piss about and have fun, but sometimes you simply have to put your head down and get the job done. He's going to have a very long and successful career.

Geoff Hughes and I are great mates. He was born in Liverpool and his family live just around the corner from our Albert. And years ago, when I had the Limelight Club, he used to come in and have a drink. In those days he was the most popular television character in the country – Eddie Yates in *Coronation Street*. Jim Royle had the same honour for a while, which is nice.

The lion's share of credit belongs to Caroline Aherne, who is entirely unselfish about giving away the best lines and letting others take the limelight. She was also generous with 'additional writing' credits if I suggested something that made the script.

Often, if a scene needed a good pay-off line, we all put our heads together. One example that sticks in my mind is when Nana was about to go to hospital to have a cataract operation. Craig and Caroline deliberated and we tossed around ideas.

'Here y'ar try this,' said Caroline, handing Liz Smith a sheet of paper.

Nana says to the family, 'The specialist says he's going to remove my cataract, but he's going to leave the twinkle in my eye.'

It was beautiful.

My favourite episode is when Denise goes into labour on Christmas Day in the bathroom. We were filming on a tiny set, with Denise sitting by the bath and me on the toilet. Memories of our Kate came flooding back to me – born on Christmas Day.

I don't think anyone could imagine the depths of emotion in the scene, especially when Jim tells Denise, 'You'll be the best Mum in the world', which was his way of saying I love you.

The director shouted 'Cut' and I looked up to see the entire crew had tears in their eyes. These were guys who did this sort of thing day in and day out.

Again the episode needed a pay-off line. There were dozens of suggestions, but nothing was quite right. I can't remember who came up with the eventual line, but it was brilliant. The whole family walks out of the house, following Denise and the ambulance to the hospital. Jim looks up and says, 'Taxi, follow that star.'

Caroline treated everyone from the set builders to the ensemble cast with equal kindness. Her attention to detail went beyond what happened in front of the cameras. At the start of every series, we arrived and found flowers and champagne in each dressing room. And each week, as we began a new episode, she would leave a greeting card or a small treat.

On Fridays when we finished filming, old-fashioned decorators' tables were set up at the edge of the studio with a couple of bottles of champagne, cans of lager, wine and soft drinks. She even sent out to get my cans of Sainsbury's Mild.

And if ever we had to work late she would order takeaways, getting a car to collect thirty portions of fish and chips, peas, pies or Chinese for the entire crew.

At the traditional wrap party, as well as free drinks and food, Caroline had these little miniature 'Oscars' made up. She and Craig did the presentations, taking the piss out of people for various stuff-ups and sins committed in the previous six weeks.

I have two of the statuettes in my sitting room. A third one belongs to Albert's grandson, Ryan, who fell in love with it one day when he came to visit. He treasures his as much as I treasure mine.

A lot of actors wait their whole lives to find a role that they were born to play. I love the character of Jim Royle and I feel very privileged and lucky to have played him. It doesn't bother me if I am typecast. He has helped to change my life and will always be a part of me.

I have often been asked why the show 'worked' and my answer is that everyone knew people like the Royle family. No matter where I travelled – whether it be Scotland, Spain or down south – people said the same things: 'You're just like my Dad ... or my Grandad ... or like the family next door ...'

There were so many memorable lines and most have been quoted back to me by people who can remember the scripts far better than I can.

'*Bloody hell, I paid a pound for these underpants and I've got fifty pence worth stuck up me arse.*'

Or Denise on parenthood: '*I'm only not smoking in front of baby David until he's old enough to get up and walk out of the room – then it's his choice.'*

Jim on Richard Branson: *'You can't get as rich as he is without being as tight as a camel's arse in a sandstorm, can you?'*

Jim on Elton John: *'He had a bloody wife and he still dropped anchor in poo bay.'*

Jim on foreign holidays: *'Them bloody travel agents are ripping every bugger off and mugs like him fall for it. There's nowt you can do abroad that you can't do here.'*

Barb: *'What about having a good time?'*

Jim: *'Having a good time, my arse! They spend half the bloody time on the khazi having the wild shites.'*

Jim on *Family Fortunes*: *'Most of these families are thick as pigshit. Les Dennis is no bloody better; if you put his brains in a bloody hazelnut they'd still rattle.'*

An example of just how popular the show became arose one night when I had a phone call from a mate of mine, Malcolm, who lived in Bolton. I had just walked in the door from work and he asked if I could do him a big favour.

'There are some young kids here who are supposed to get football awards and trophies. Someone from Bolton Football Club was going to come along but they've let us down. Can you do it for us?'

'Malcolm, I'm shattered. I haven't had a bath or anything to eat.'

'Oh, come on, Rick. Just this once.'

I arranged to meet him in an hour and in the meantime I washed my face, combed my hair and put on a fresh shirt. I drove to Bolton and arrived at a local hall. Instead of a handful of kids there must have been at least a hundred, all of them aged seven to fourteen. The coaches introduced each member of each team.

'This is Johnny Smith. Never missed a Saturday.'

I handed Johnny his trophy and shook his hand. 'Well done.'

He answered, 'My arse.'

'And this is Billy Davis, who plays his heart out in defence.'

'Well done Billy.' I shook his hand.

'My arse.'

I swear to God, every single one of these kids said 'My arse' to me. The catchphrase had entered the language of the playground and the workplace.

The third series of *The Royle Family* was switched from BBC2 to BBC1 because of its popularity. By then we had an audience of over ten million.

Back at Ealing Studios in west London, we were next door to another TV comedy production – *Bob Martin*, starring Michael Barrymore, Keith Allen and Denis Lawson. Barrymore was doing a straight dramatic role as a talk show host with a disastrous private life. Real guest stars were included every week, like Amanda Donohue, Johnny Briggs, Terry Wogan and Clive Anderson.

Ealing Studios has a pub on location, with a real nice grassy area and benches. We used to sit outside to have lunch and of a summer's evening, when work had finished, we often stayed behind for a drink.

It didn't matter if there were ten, fifteen or twenty people in the bar, Michael Barrymore would get the drinks in, standing at the bar to collect them rather than sending someone to do it for him. He made sure everyone had a drink before he sat down. He and Keith Allen were like a double act and had everyone in stitches.

Both productions had a catering crew and it became a

matter of pride about who had the best menu. Every lunch break we examined the blackboards.

'Hey, look, they're having roast beef, Yorkshire pud, strawberries and cream,' I said.

'And they've got pork chops and apple sauce,' added Craig. 'What are we having?'

'Lancashire hotpot or chicken in red wine.'

We finished up joining their queue and vice versa, if we fancied a meal on the other blackboard.

Sitting having lunch one day, I saw a face I recognised.

'Excuse me, are you Bernie Clifton?' I asked.

'I know who you are,' he said. 'I've watched your career – ever since you played the pubs and clubs.'

Bernie is a music hall legend – famous for his 'ostrich routine' where he rides Oswald, a shaggy orange ostrich, on to the stage. It's one of the funniest things you'll ever see. Back in the seventies, he was a huge star and did *The Royal Variety Show* in 1979, as well as his own TV specials.

Barrymore and Keith Allen came to our wrap party at the end of the series. Keith has a reputation as a bit of a hell-raiser, on and off the set. The night was hilarious and I still have photographs of Sue Johnston and Michael dancing the legs off each other.

Yet behind all the laughter and clowning around, I could see a vulnerable side to Michael. Like a lot of brilliantly talented funny men, he was desperate to be liked. I used to wonder what happened when the party ended and he went back to his hotel room. Did he stop smiling then?

In December 1999 *The Royle Family* swept the boards at the British Comedy Awards, winning four categories, including best comedy actress for Caroline and best comedy actor for me. The following year it picked up two BAFTAs for best sitcom and best comedy performance by Caroline.

After three series and three specials she decided to take a break. By then she had vowed never to appear on television again because she was sick of tabloid intrusion in her life. The press had given her a terrible time and paparazzi followed her on a holiday to Mauritius and took secret snaps of her by the pool.

When I see the crap that people have written about her it makes me angry. I can handle reading shit about me, but I hate seeing those close to me put through the wringer. In England we have a habit of trying to knock down anyone who is talented or different. And Caroline is one of the most talented and creative people we have. She is a beautiful human being, who is generous, unselfish and still the same working-class girl who came out of Manchester.

I adore her and if she phoned me up tomorrow and said 'I'm in the shit', I would drop everything to help her. And like a lot of her fans I hold out a secret hope that one day she might come back and write a few more episodes or one-off specials of *The Royle Family*. Jim's shirt and trousers should be really ripe by then.

21

Bricks and Balloons

OK! *magazine is offering to pay us for exclusive pictures of the wedding. My first reaction is to say no. I don't want some big fancy reception where people have cameras pointed constantly in their faces.*

Then I think about Rita. Her first wedding was in a little register office in Liverpool with only a few family and friends. Now she's looking forward to all the bells and whistles.

What are the pros and cons of selling the rights? Yes, there's a case to be made for privacy, but what chance do we have of an ordinary wedding without journalists and photographers trying to sneak in? They'll finish up selling grainy snapshots taken with long lenses or hidden cameras.

The magazines will give us picture approval and take care of the security. And I can spend the money making sure everyone has an unforgettable day. I want to pay for everything, including getting suits and shoes for all my mates, as well as taxis to pick everyone up and take them home. It won't cost anyone a single penny.

Our suits are getting fitted today. Albert comes along because he's the best man. He was beside me first time round and there's no question that he'll get the gig again.

We go to this warehouse in Warrington and they spend ages

*showing us lots of suits which are apparently different styles but I can
hardly tell the difference.*

'I can't be arsed with this,' I say.

Rita shoots me one of her looks.

'Don't you get a gob on.'

'You said I just had to turn up.'

*'And what are you gonna be wearing? I'm not marrying you in
those bloody old trousers with the elasticised waist.'*

I finish up sitting and watching while Albert does the modelling.

*'Are you sure you want to marry him?' he says to Rita. She rolls
her eyes and shoots me a wink.*

*They say it's bad luck to see the bride before the wedding. I'm
working on the principle that it's also bad luck to see the invitations,
menu, flowers, table arrangements, cake designs, hymns and
timetable.*

I must admit I do like the shoes.

In 1994, entirely out of the blue, I had a phone call from
Gareth.

'You're a grandad,' he said before hanging up.

What did he mean? Who?

I made some calls and discovered that Kate had given
birth to a girl, Paige. I had no idea she was even pregnant.
She was only seventeen and in my mind I still imagined her
with pigtails and wearing a school uniform.

I desperately wanted to see her, but ever since the court
case and the publicity about Diane I had been shunned by
Marlene and, in turn, the kids. Kate, in particular, had been
upset by the newspaper stories.

It was another fourteen months before I met my
granddaughter. By then Kate had her own little council house
in Minera. A mate of mine who does a bit of buying and
selling had some clothes and I thought Kate might like some

of them. We arranged to meet in the car park of the Five Crosses pub in Minera.

Little Paige was almost walking. She wore a denim bib and braces with a big pink hat and hung from the hands of Kate and Clifton. I only got to see her for a few minutes, but a week or so later I visited Kate at her council house. She held Paige in her arms as she stood waiting for me. Paige started crying and Clifton said, 'It's you, Dad. Your voice is loud. She's a bit scared.'

We had a cup of tea and I bounced Paige on my knee. It was marvellous. The hardest thing was holding back my tears. I am hopeless when it comes to family – I love them to bits.

Kate and Clifton were fine about the long separations. There were no recriminations and it wasn't a case of someone being right or wrong. Mistakes had been made – most of them mine – but I had never stopped thinking of them.

Now I wanted to be part of their lives and make up for lost time. The council house needed some work and I got my old mate Pat McMullen to decorate a few rooms for Kate. I also arranged to give her a little something so she could spoil herself and Paige occasionally.

Of all the kids, Gareth had stayed in touch the most. During his three years in the Army he would often ring me and sometimes come and stay with us when he was on leave. He did a couple of tours of Northern Ireland before being discharged. I suspect this was on medical grounds, but can't be sure.

None of the family realised he was ill. Only in hindsight were the signs apparent, but never obvious. I had started working on *The Royle Family* by then and Gareth had returned to live in North Wales with Marlene. He often phoned and sometimes came and stayed with us in Luxmore Road.

Once or twice he told me that he suffered from flashbacks and he also recounted how a couple of his mates had been killed on active duty in Northern Ireland. I had no reason to doubt him.

Over time his stories became more graphic and extreme. He talked about being in the SAS and going on secret missions that involved parachuting into hostile territory and building ice caves in the Arctic. I knew this couldn't be true. As much as I loved him, I knew Gareth wasn't exactly SAS material.

He had always been a great teller of stories. Even as a kid, when he went fishing with his mates, he used to come home of an evening and recount tales of 'the ones that got away'. He loved to romanticise about things and was always inventing games that involved shields and swords and daring rescues.

At one stage he spent almost six months with us in Liverpool and then announced one day that he was going home to Marlene's. Within a few weeks he was back again.

'I want to live in Liverpool,' he told me, 'but I really need my own flat.'

I arranged for him to rent a little house in the next street, Golden Grove. I gave him the deposit and helped him move in. We still saw him regularly. He would call in and spend hours chatting to Rita in the kitchen.

I dropped by his place one day and found loads of building supplies in the front hallway.

'What are you doing?'

'The landlord gave me some money to do the place up.'

I looked and saw that Gareth had started working in every room, ripping up floorboards, half painting a wall, putting up a bit of skirting board or dado rail. None of these tasks had been finished. He didn't have the skills.

'C'mon, Gags, let's get this sorted out.' Gags is his nickname.

'No, no, I'm gonna do it. I'll be fine.'

I could see him deteriorating. He couldn't focus on anything for more than a few minutes. He had also started going out late at night and sleeping in Stanley Park. He told Rita there were all sorts of rituals going on there and that he was going to marry a girl. He had no choice. He had to go.

At the park one night he was involved in a fight and had the top half of his ear bitten off. I phoned the local police who were tremendously supportive, searching the park for his attackers.

This didn't stop Gareth going back.

'What are you doing?' I asked.

'I'm waiting to get them.'

'Gareth, you don't know what you're playing with.'

Clearly he was ill but I didn't know what to do. I called doctors, social workers, even our local MP, desperate to get him some help.

Then I discovered that Gareth's problems had already been identified although not diagnosed. One of the reasons he had come to Liverpool was to escape from the mental health services in Wrexham, who had been sending a psychiatric nurse to visit him every month.

I arranged for Gareth to see a specialist who put him under 'assessment'. He was to come back in six months. In the meantime, I was given an emergency number of the community nurse.

Within days Gareth had done a midnight flit back to Wales, leaving the house in Golden Grove looking like a building site. Among the possessions he left behind I discovered martial arts equipment like fighting sticks and numbchucks. There was also a three-foot-long Samurai sword, which worried the hell out of me. I took it away for safekeeping.

I had no experience of dealing with mental illness and struggled to comprehend what was happening to Gareth. When somebody has a broken leg you can see what the problem is and sympathise, but when there is something wrong with his or her state of mind it is far harder to appreciate.

Saying that, most days Gareth seemed fine and just like his old self: chatty, good-humoured, eager to tag along with me. But on other days he was full of sinister conspiracy theories.

There are dozens of examples to show how his mind deteriorated. One afternoon at Luxmore Road, I answered a knock on the front door. A huge policeman stood outside.

'Are you Mr Tomlinson?'

'Yeah.'

'We've had a complaint off your son.'

'What about?'

'He says you won't let him have any access to his own money.'

'How do you mean?'

'He says you've got his bank account and you won't let him have any of his money.'

I looked at him in disbelief. 'Hang on. I'll just go and get Gareth. He's upstairs.'

The policeman realised something was wrong. I explained that mental health workers were assessing Gareth. He often made up fanciful stories.

'You can talk to him if you like.'

Suddenly nervous, he said, 'No. Thanks. I'm sorry to have troubled you.'

Another time Gareth told me, 'The thing is, Dad, if I get

an order to kill you, then I will kill you. A soldier has to follow orders.'

After a few months in Wales he returned to Liverpool. Again, he wanted his own place and had even seen a house just up the road which was up for auction.

'Are you sure this is what you want?'

'Yes, Dad.'

'And you'll look after the place?'

'Absolutely.'

It was a nice big terrace house, with a garage on one side. The owner had got permission to add a third storey but had never got round to it. The roof needed replacing and hundreds of birds were nesting in the loft.

With money from *The Royle Family* I bought the house for about fourteen grand. I paid someone to remove the birds and had a new roof built. Then I arranged to do the place up, decorating rooms, putting in a new bathroom and staircase.

In the meantime, Gareth spent his time either in Wales or living in Luxmore Road.

Every day he asked when he could move into the house.

'When it's finished.'

'What about tomorrow?'

'No, the staircase isn't done.'

Without warning or any explanation, he took off again. Here we go, I thought.

Work continued on the house, but Gareth never lived there. For years I left it empty, just in case he changed his mind.

I still saw him regularly and most days he was fine. Normally, he stayed in Wales and I heard he was seeing a girl in the village, but only just to say hello to.

While down in London filming the second series of *The Royle Family*, I had a frantic call from Kate saying that Gareth had a six-inch dagger and was heading to Liverpool on the train.

I called Rita to warn her, but Gareth had already been on the phone. He had told her, 'I am Gareth Tomlinson of Air Troop, 22 Squadron. My orders are to come and put your windows in. I'm coming now. I'm coming to get you.'

'Who gave you these orders?' Rita asked.

'A soldier has to follow orders.'

Although Rita tried to sound calm, I knew she was worried. For all she knew Gareth might be just around the corner. My mobile rang. It was Gareth.

'I know you're carrying on with my girlfriend,' he said.

'What do you mean?'

'I know you've been there. I've seen your golf clubs in the front hallway.'

I did once have a set of clubs. I played one game and gave them away.

'Listen, Gags, I don't even know your girlfriend . . .'

'Don't lie to me! You're seeing her.'

I couldn't make him listen to me. His mind was in another place.

Within minutes he phoned Rita again.

'There's a helicopter circling. There's a helicopter circling. Your house is getting it . . . I'm coming to do it. I have my orders . . .'

Sitting in a London hotel room, I had never felt so helpless. Rita had called the police who didn't seem interested. I also phoned but they dismissed the warnings as a domestic disturbance.

Gareth reached Luxmore Road and hammered on the front door. Rita was on the phone to me and I heard the front window smashing.

'He's coming round the back. He's trying to get in . . . I can see his face. He looks terrifying.'

I knew that if Gareth got inside there was no way Rita could fight him off. He had done martial arts. He had a knife! Where were the police?

Rita called 999. I could hear her screaming down the phone, 'Hear this! He's getting in the house. He's smashing the windows . . .'

I phoned Albert and told him to get to the house. Then I called Colin Walker, hoping he might be even closer. When Albert arrived Gareth had already gone. Two policemen had turned up and searched the surrounding streets without finding him.

As Colin drove to Luxmore Road he spied Gareth in a phone box a couple of streets away.

'I know where he is. I've just passed him,' Colin told the police.

The senior officer shrugged and said, 'I haven't eaten all day. I'm not going there now.'

I went ballistic. A mentally disturbed young man was on the loose with a six-inch knife and this copper was more interested in getting a pie and chips. Later this became the subject of an official complaint about police inaction.

While Albert sorted out the broken windows and made sure Rita was OK, Colin went looking for Gareth. He had cleared out, but I had a good idea that he'd be heading back to Wrexham. The last train would have just left Lime Street Station in Liverpool.

I phoned the British Transport police who put me through to the station. I kept telling people it was a matter of life and death. Somehow I managed to get patched through to the driver of the train.

'Look, I don't want anyone to panic,' I said, explaining who I was. 'Can you ask your guard to go through the train. See if there's a young lad in his early twenties. He's got blond hair and he's wearing a big white quilted coat. For God's sake don't approach him, just let me know if he's there.'

He came back. 'Yeah, he's on the train.'

'OK, just keep your eye on him. Don't go near him. He has a knife. I'm going to phone the Wrexham police and they'll hopefully meet the train.'

'OK.'

I called the police and told them what had happened. I gave them a description of Gareth and details of when the train was arriving. Then I stayed in touch with the guard until Gareth reached Wrexham. When he stepped on to the platform there were no police waiting for him. I don't know why. He walked home and went to bed.

Sadly, there were other similar incidents over the following year. Gareth would make threats and hurl accusations. I could handle this, but it was tough on Rita. Gareth would often threaten her because he knew it was the perfect way to get to me.

He began living in a little flat in Queen's Park, Wrexham, which didn't please me because it was too isolated and in a rough area. Growing progressively worse, he had stuck bin liners over the windows, turning the flat into a cave.

One day he phoned and said, 'I've got a gun. I'm gonna use it.'

I drove like a madman to his flat and discovered the weapon behind the washing machine. It was loaded with three bullets that Gareth said were blanks.

'But what are you doing with a gun?'

He shrugged and didn't answer. By then he was getting proper mental health services at Wrexham, with a psych nurse visiting him regularly, but sometimes he wouldn't unlock the door when the health worker arrived.

I wanted him taken into care, but couldn't get anything

done. I had talked to the police and the local MP for Wrexham, as well as the health authority. What were they waiting for? Did Gareth have to hurt someone first?

The constant worry and distraction was affecting the entire family. Marlene was almost in denial and I couldn't talk to her about what was happening. It reached a point where I seriously considered giving up acting. I discussed this with Rita. Maybe I could set up a house and live with Gareth to look after him. I owed him that much. At the very least, I wanted to take on less work and spend more time with him.

You could almost see in Gareth's eyes when his mind was slipping out of control. He certainly couldn't hold down a job, yet he had almost too much time on his hands to uncover 'conspiracies'. Almost daily he visited Wrexham police station, full of wild stories. They treated him like a harmless loony and the desk sergeant got quite angry with me when I suggested he should take some action.

Not surprisingly this attitude changed dramatically when Gareth phoned and claimed to have a bomb. He made no specific threat against anyone, but the police had no option but to act. A SWAT team was sent to his flat, wearing flak jackets and carrying shields. Gareth was arrested and taken to the psych ward of Wrexham Maelor General Hospital. Thank God, I thought. Now they're going to help him.

The sectioning order only lasted for twenty-eight days after which Gareth's case came up for review. He was diagnosed as a paranoid schizophrenic and given an on-going course of medication, which would change over the months as the experts experimented to find the right drugs and dosage.

Despite the tremendous help he received, Gareth was his own worst enemy because he hated being medicated and having sessions with psychiatrists and counsellors. For this reason, he could never be relied upon to keep appointments or open his door to health visitors.

At the same time, whenever he faced a crucial assessment, Gareth would present wonderfully. He knew exactly what the experts wanted to see and hear. This happened time and again as he managed to avoid greater supervision.

Just before Christmas in 1999, Rita and I moved from Luxmore Road into a dockside apartment in a converted warehouse. Although we really loved the terrace house, it had proved to be impractical, particularly after the success of *The Royle Family*. At least twice a day we were getting kids knocking on the door and saying 'my arse'. It was also a nightmare on Everton match days because the surrounding streets were blocked off and parking bans were put in place.

At first I thought the idea of a waterside apartment with intercoms and extra security was a bit flash for the likes of me. I worried that some people might think I was betraying my class.

Rita laughed and told me not to be so daft. 'You're less than a mile from where you grew up. You're not selling out. You're moving house.'

I was again away in London filming when Gareth took a turn for the worse. He phoned Rita.

'You think my dad's in London, don't you? He's not. He's here. He's having an affair with my girlfriend. He's shaved off his beard, but I know it's him . . . I'm looking at Dad's van right now. It's parked outside her house. My dad is here . . .'

In the next breath he became convinced that I wasn't his dad. The real me had either been replaced or I had never been his biological father.

Determined to discover the truth, he went to the births, deaths and marriages office in Wrexham to look for his birth certificate. The office was closed and he smashed the glass door as he tried to get in.

By the time the police arrived Gareth had gone. By then he was on his way to Liverpool. He phoned me on my mobile and began making threats.

'Let's talk about this, Gags. Come over. We'll meet at the flat.'

In the meantime Rita spoke to the police in Wrexham CID and told them where Gareth would be. They put a call through to St Anne's CID in Liverpool and passed on the address.

Half an hour later I phoned. 'Did you pick him up?'

'We've sent two lads around there in a squad car.'

'A police car! If he spots that you won't see him for dust. He's been in the Army. He'll take off and go to ground.'

The squad car was recalled and two plain-clothes policemen were sent to the flat. Sure enough, Gareth turned up and they arrested him.

'How is he?' I asked, when I called the station.

'He's not well, is he, Rick?' said a woman police constable.

'No, but do me a favour. If he kicks off, don't let the lads hurt him. He's a lovely kid.'

She promised me that Gareth would be looked after and was true to her word. Shortly afterwards he was transferred to Wrexham and charged with criminal damage. He was held overnight until he could appear in Mold Crown Court the following morning.

I drove back from London and made sure I arrived early at the court. It was a Saturday morning and there was virtually nobody at the courthouse except for a couple of security guards. They directed me towards one of the smaller courts. I took a seat in the empty public gallery and stood when the magistrates made their entrance.

The only other people in the room were the prosecutor, a clerk and the duty solicitor. Gareth was led through the doors and placed in the dock. My heart felt like breaking when I saw him. His head was shaved and his cheeks were sunken. He had a cut on his lip and a black eye. His trousers were dirty and his polo neck woollen jumper was miles too big for him.

Gareth had always prided himself on his appearance and been very neat and well groomed. I put that down to his time in the Army. Now he looked dishevelled and dull-eyed, as though he'd given up trying.

He turned and saw me.

'Get him out of here!' he yelled.

A policeman told him to be quiet.

'Get him out of here!'

He seemed to calm down and the prosecutor outlined the facts of the case. Then the court-appointed solicitor made a short submission. I stood and asked if I could address the court. The magistrates conferred and agreed.

'You don't know how difficult this is for me,' I said, trying to stop my voice breaking. 'This is my lad and I love him. Anyone can see just by looking at him that something is wrong. He's a mess. He's dirty. Look at that black eye. He needs proper treatment . . .'

One of the magistrates lowered his head.

'. . . When you're a parent you love your children through thick and thin; the good and the bad times. You forgive them things. You're their biggest fans and harshest critics. I love my son. I know he's done wrong, but I want to help him. That's why I'm asking you. No, I'm begging you to make sure he gets treatment. He's a good lad and his family love him.'

The magistrates went into recess and came back twenty

minutes later. They asked for a psych report and medical records to be made available. At the same time they dropped some of the charges. The cost of the criminal damage was put at fifty pounds for new glass in the door.

'I'll pay for that now,' I said, writing a cheque.

Gareth was remanded in custody until Monday morning. I hated the idea that he would spend his weekend in jail, but I had no choice. At least I knew he was safe.

Unfortunately, the next morning the story was splashed all over the Sunday papers. A local newspaper reporter had written a piece saying that I had Gareth arrested and 'flung into jail'.

I knew the reporter involved. I had known his father for thirty years but this counted for nothing because he wanted to impress the nationals by getting a big scoop.

I couldn't be in court on Monday. Marlene watched as the magistrates ordered Gareth to be detained in a psychiatric hospital for assessment and treatment. I felt tremendously relieved.

Once on his medication the change was amazing. Within a week or two he was back home and happily calling me every few days for a chat. He was never going to have a completely normal life, but the future could still be OK.

Since then we've had some ups and downs, but more good than bad. Gareth can sometimes be a bit scatterbrained and his attention span is nil, but he is such a charmer that everyone develops a soft spot for him.

He can be his own worst enemy by not taking his medication. I don't know why. Either he forgets or he doesn't like the way it makes him feel. Marlene is too soft and forgives him everything, but I'm just as guilty at making allowances.

I spoil him, just as I spoil all my children. Perhaps I'm making up for all those lost years. Or maybe I just realise that when you get to my age you have to keep telling people that you love them just in case you're not around tomorrow.

22

Are You Lookin' at Me?

Clifton hasn't been himself lately. He's lost nearly three stone in weight and isn't looking after himself. I've asked Kate if he's OK and she says he's on a bit of a downer.

Clifton is a big lad, over six foot. I've always worried about him because I know the divorce affected him more than the others. There's a lot of me in Clifton. He loves to dance and I once found a book of his poetry after Marlene had moved out of the cottage. He had obviously kept it hidden just like I did all those years ago.

Despite all his talent, Clifton has been a bit of a lost soul. I'm hoping that he'll discover a new direction. It's never too late – just look at me! I came out of jail and stumbled into acting.

He has a girlfriend in Coedpoeth and some really good mates, but everyone is worried about him. I've heard a few little rumours about drugs, but I haven't wanted to believe them. Clifton wouldn't be that foolish.

Then Marlene tells me there might be a problem. She doesn't know for sure, but has her suspicions. I go to visit Clifton at his little house in Wrexham. He's doing the place up bit by bit and I give him a hand when I'm not too busy. We're sitting in the kitchen having a cup of tea and I ask him straight out, 'Are you using drugs?'

He looks me right in the eye. 'No, Dad.'

'OK. I had to ask.'

'I understand.'

A week later I go to see him about something else and he comes clean.

'Look, you asked me the other day about drugs. I lied to you. I'm using. I'm sorry. I want to come off.'

'What are you using?'

'Heroin.'

'How long has it been going on?'

'Six to eight months.'

I thought I'd rant and rave because I'm so anti-drugs, but instead I tell him, 'I can't understand why, but I'm glad you told me.'

Years ago I was watching this documentary on TV about Joss Ackland, a wonderful actor, who recounted the story of how his eldest son had died of a drug overdose. He talked of how proud he was of his son, which I found very strange.

I wrote to him anonymously, via the TV programme, saying, 'I understand that you love your son – which is great – but how can you say you are proud of him for dying of a drug overdose?'

I couldn't get my head around that but now I understand what he was trying to say. Addiction is sometimes hard to comprehend, but when it takes hold of a person it takes a lot of courage to say that you have a problem and to try to change things. Clifton has done just that.

As I try to work out what to do I remember seeing an advert in the Liverpool Echo for a private clinic in Harrogate, north Yorkshire. I get Rita to phone and they have a vacancy for the following week. First we need a doctor's note confirming that Clifton is healthy enough to go through the process.

This is arranged and I clear my diary so I can drive him up to the clinic on Monday.

Over the weekend I get a call from Albert.

'*Have you seen the papers?*'

'*No.*'

'*Get a copy of the* Sunday Mirror.'

HEROIN AND BOOZE HELL OF RICKY'S SON

Ricky Tomlinson's eldest son is battling heroin addiction and drink problems. Jobless Cliff Tomlinson, 31, is due to begin five days of detox at a private clinic tomorrow.

Royle Family star Ricky, 61, arranged the treatment and agreed to pay the £2,950 bill after a crisis family meeting last week.

How on earth did the press find out? I can't blame the clinic because Clifton hasn't even started there so they must have got their information from closer to home.

Clifton phones me when he sees the story.

'*I'm just so sorry, Dad.*'

Instead of being worried for himself, he's concerned for Marlene and me. He thinks he's embarrassed us, but I tell him it's not his fault. If it weren't for me the newspapers wouldn't have run the story. He'd have gone into rehab and out again without having his picture splashed all over the papers.

On Monday I drive him up to Yorkshire, along with Marlene. He seems relaxed and happy. For the next five days he's on his own, with no visitors or phone calls allowed.

When he comes out he's a different person. It's like someone put the spark back into his eyes and the music in his laugh. As we drive home I think about all those parents who can't afford a private clinic for their kids. The NHS is swamped with drug cases and can't deal with the numbers needing treatment. Maybe it suits the politicians not to fix the problem. Maybe it suits them because these kids are so wasted on drugs they have no time to fight back against a system that has no jobs for them and gives them no hope. Some of them leave school and go to their grave never having had a decent job. What sort of society is that?

I know you can never say never, but I really think things are going to be OK for Clifton.

I still don't regard myself as an actor. I have worked with people who had been to drama school and done stints with famous repertoire companies and they deserve to give themselves the title, but for me it has never seemed like a proper job. It's still like a game.

Some actors take an interest in both sides of the camera and will ask questions like, 'Will I stand this way? Is that the cutting point? Are you going to edit there?'

I have never really understood the dynamics of what makes a scene work so I don't want to know these things. As long as the director tells me what I'm supposed to do and yells 'Cut' when it's over, then I'm happy to bumble along.

People often ask me if I have a favourite role, but I've enjoyed them all. If really pressed I tell them the performance that gave me the most satisfaction was in a black comedy called *Nasty Neighbours*. The writer, director and producer Debbie Isitt was an absolute dynamo who refused to give up on the project despite numerous setbacks – most notably the budget, which was virtually non-existent. Halfway through we took up a collection to buy more film.

I played the part of Harold Peach, a frustrated salesman, who lives in suburbia with his wife Jean (Marion Bailey). Like a lot of Englishmen, Harold's house is his castle and he looks upon the cul-de-sac as part of his shared kingdom. Everyone brings out their bins on Thursday morning at precisely the same time, walking down the drive, plonking them on the pavement and turning around with military precision. This is all down to Harold, holding things together.

Suddenly, his life begins falling apart. Bills are piling up and his wife is having a nervous breakdown. The couple next door, their best friends, move to Australia to live and are replaced by a horrible couple, the Chapmans, who rip out the fittings in the old semi-detached house and throw late-night parties.

Harold wages a relentless war against them and wishes his old neighbours would come home.

Phil Daniels plays the flashy cockney who moves in next door. In one memorable scene we fight each other and in the lead-up I said to Phil, 'We'll have to go hard at this. You can't fake it.'

The stunt coordinator looked petrified.

'I'll choreograph it,' he said.

'No, you can't do that. It won't look real. It'll finish up like one of them Western bar-room brawls where everyone can see the punches are missing.'

Against all his instincts he agreed, but insisted we wear knee and elbow pads beneath our clothes.

They left the camera rolling and we went for each other. Phil was a young man and much fitter than me. Eventually we wrestled to the ground, he turned me over, smacked me in the head and started shoving soil down my throat.

Debbie Isitt yelled 'Cut' and we broke the clinch. I had a mouthful of dirt and bruises all over me, but I knew the scene had worked.

The film has dream sequences set in Australia because Harold keeps fantasising about his former neighbours and wishing they'd come back to England. Because of the tight budget Debbie wanted to fly in to Sydney, do two days' work, and fly out again. Rita said, 'No way. He's too bloody old for that.'

Instead, we spent a fortnight in Sydney, which gave me time to recover from the jetlag and do a bit of sightseeing. The crew hadn't bothered getting permission to film anywhere just in case this meant paying fees to the local council or tourist board. Instead we did lightning raids; setting up the cameras, doing the shot and then piling into the cars again.

One of the final scenes was shot on an isolated beach in Mount Ku-Ring-Gai National Park on the northern outskirts of Sydney. We carried all the equipment through the bush and climbed down a narrow path from the cliff tops. I was roasting in my full suit.

The scene involved me jumping into the sea, holding myself under for a few seconds and then bursting out of the water as if re-born. Apart from not being able to swim, I had visions of white pointer sharks eyeing me up from offshore thinking all their Christmases had come at once.

They had a fella behind the rocks making sure I didn't drown, and I wouldn't go in the water without my glasses so Rita found a piece of elastic to tie them on. We did half a dozen takes before I waded ashore like a drowned rat. Rita thought I was dead brave.

I had no change of clothes and there were no proper towels to wrap me in. The crew packed up their gear and started walking back up the path.

'There's no way Rick can walk out of here,' Rita told the director.

'It's the only way up.'

'You'll have to get a boat to pick him up.'

They called a water taxi but the driver was nervous about getting too close to the shore because of the rocks. Three people had to wade out with me, making sure I didn't drown. The water came up to my chin, but I managed to hoist myself into the boat and was still waterlogged that night.

Back in England, Debbie and her partner Nick worked around the clock to edit *Nasty Neighbours* and get it ready for the 1999 Venice Film Festival.

They turned up at Heathrow for the flight with plastic carrier bags bulging with film canisters. It was the only copy so they couldn't risk putting the film through the X-ray machines. Each reel had to be examined by hand.

Arriving in Venice, we were walking down the steps from the plane when one of the carrier bags burst and canisters of film went rolling across the tarmac with people trying to chase them down.

Debbie and Nick had just enough money left to get a couple of hotel rooms. Rita and I managed to sleep, but Debbie and Nick were up all night putting subtitles on the film.

It was shown in competition the next day and received a standing ovation. People actually applauded in the middle of the movie after the fight scene. And afterwards they followed us down the street, offering congratulations.

We were invited to one of those swish American parties with Harvey Keitel as the guest of honour, but I was so exhausted I went back to the hotel and crashed.

Rita still thinks *Nasty Neighbours* is the finest thing I have ever done and she might be right. Maybe it's the closest I've ever come to 'acting'. It won me the best actor prize at the Stockholm International Film Festival, but the credit belongs to Debbie Isitt.

My first big American film, *The 51st State*, had a budget that would have paid for *Nasty Neighbours* fifty times over. Samuel

L. Jackson was the undoubted star, but the supporting cast included Sean Pertwee, Rhys Ifans, Emily Mortimer and my old mate Robbie Carlyle.

The basic plot revolved around a new designer drug fifty-one times stronger than any other. Samuel plays Elmo McElroy, a kilt-wearing, golf-obsessed illegal chemist who comes to Liverpool to clinch a multimillion dollar drug deal. Sean Pertwee is a bent copper, Robbie Carlyle a small-time hood and I play an effeminate local gangster with haemorrhoids.

I only worked for a day or two with Samuel, who was very nice, but I was amazed by the size of his entourage. He had his own hairdresser and make-up artist, as well as a personal assistant and a companion.

The Winebagos were enormous. Samuel had one about the size of Yorkshire; Robbie's was the size of Lancashire and mine dwarfed Liverpool Town Hall. It had two separate lounge areas, a dining room, bedroom and a bathroom with a flush toilet.

At one point we were filming in central Liverpool and the facilities trucks had parked at the back of Alison's Theatre Club. The parking area backed on to a girls' school and at lunchtime they all came out of the classrooms and stood at the fence chanting, 'We want Jim! We want Jim!'

Samuel L. Jackson must have looked out of the window of his Winebago at all these screaming girls and thought, 'Who the hell is Jim?'

I came out of my trailer and started signing autographs for the girls. Of course, they were shouting, 'My arse.'

Later, Samuel noticed some of the crew asking for signed photographs and I explained to him, 'You have to understand that I'm a local sex symbol.'

I could see him thinking to himself, 'Thank Christ I'm American.'

The director, Ronny Yu, a Hong Kong Chinese, had cut his teeth on action films. We worked well together and I think he appreciated my asking him how he wanted me to play particular scenes. Should I go for laughs or was it meant to be more serious?

Ronny used to sit me down on the settee and explain exactly what he wanted. I got the impression that he didn't get asked very often.

My big scene in the movie ended with me getting crushed to death beneath a huge shipping container. I had to go to London and get a reinforced fibroglass cast made of my torso, which acted like body armour. My clothes went over the top and steel wires were used to attach me to the base of the container. The make-up department gave me a couple of weeping bullet holes and blood ran out of my nose.

The container was then hoisted into the air by a crane with me suspended underneath. Meanwhile, Sean Pertwee's character poked at my bullet holes with his walking stick, torturing me to get information. It was bloody uncomfortable and nobody expected me to last more than twenty minutes at any one time in the body armour. I persevered for more than an hour because I knew how long it took to set up.

Eventually, the container drops and I get crushed underneath. The body armour was designed to save my life, but it meant putting enormous faith in the stunt coordinators.

On the final day of filming Ronny Yu gave me a golden Chinese good luck charm as a keepsake, which was a lovely gesture.

Although I enjoyed my taste of big-budget film-making, I regard myself as having been spoilt because I've worked with directors like Loachie and Joffe who make films that *mean* something.

The same is true of Wolfgang Becker, an enigmatic German, who directed *Life is All You Get*. Becker had been carrying a photograph of me around in his wallet since seeing *Riff Raff*, hoping to find a German actor who looked and sounded the same. Eventually he approached me, but had to talk me into doing the film. For starters, I couldn't speak a word of German.

The deal breaker was allowing me to do my lines in English and having them dubbed into German afterwards, although it still meant responding to dialogue that I didn't understand.

The film is basically a series of stories following the lives of a handful of Berliners, who are each searching for something better amid the chaos of street riots, unemployment and single parenthood. It was shot in a non-glamorous industrial wasteland not far from where the Berlin Wall once stood.

I play Buddy, an abattoir worker obsessed with Buddy Holly to the point of wearing fancy coats and sporting sideboards. I even got to do a bit of jiving.

Most of the cast could speak English and made me feel welcome. And I loved some of the distinctly German touches like the piping hot sausages served up in the middle of the shoot and the head massages that put me to sleep while I was getting made-up.

The success of *The Royle Family* seemed to trigger a rush of offers and I had never been so busy. One script that appealed to my sense of humour and love of sport was *Mike Bassett: England Manager*.

Done in a spoof documentary style, the premise of the

film is that England has only three games left to qualify for the World Cup in Brazil but disaster strikes and their manager suffers a near-fatal heart attack. Oddly enough, nobody else seems to want the job so football's top brass turn in desperation to Mike Bassett, the manager of lowly Norwich City.

Calling him an old-school manager is probably unfair on old schools. At one point, as he writes his team on the back of a cigarette packet, he finishes up selecting both Benson and Hedges in one of his squads.

Although people cringe at Mike's ineptness, they also want him to succeed. And movie audiences could relate to him because, like all good satire, he wasn't far removed from reality.

With past managers like Graham Taylor, Glenn Hoddle and Kevin Keegan, it's clear that tactical naivety, poor press relations and outrageous excuses are job specifications for the England management.

Wembley had been decommissioned when we came to do the filming. The pitch had been ripped up, but the film-makers spent sixty thousand pounds relaying new turf so we could play the 'international'. We filled one part of the stands with spectators and used technology to generate the rest, making it look as though a hundred thousand had packed Wembley.

This has created a wonderful piece of sporting trivia. Next time you meet a two-legged football almanac, ask them: who was the last manager to take an England team to Wembley?

The answer is Mike Bassett.

The World Cup scenes were filmed in Brazil and we were given permission to use the Maracana Stadium, the biggest on earth, and the scene of the 1950 World Cup Final.

Initially we hoped Pelé would do a little cameo appearance

but his minders said he wasn't available. Even after he agreed they insisted on no autographs or photographs. Pelé arrived, ignored the instructions and happily signed shirts and smiled for photographs.

His scene in the film is set in a bar as the England campaign is self-destructing. The team captain has been arrested and my star player is having a fling with a beautiful woman . . . who turns out to be a man. The press are baying for my blood, so I drown my sorrows and finish up dancing on a bar wearing just my underpants.

At this point Pelé was supposed to walk in, take one look at me and say, 'Oh no, not the English.' Instead he burst out laughing as I fell off the end of the bar.

We also wanted to get the Great Train Robber, Ronnie Biggs, to make a guest appearance, playing a bartender or club owner. Having got the address of his bar, I went along with Phil Jackson. There was no sign of Biggsie and the regulars were very protective of his privacy. Eventually, I wrote a letter and gave it to a woman who said she could get it to him. I offered her a few quid, but she refused to accept the money.

Biggsie didn't get in touch, but I discovered later that his health had declined rapidly and he was negotiating a return to Britain, courtesy of the *Sun*.

The premiere of *Mike Bassett: England Manager* had all the trimmings: the big chauffeur-driven limo, VIP lounge and loads of celebrities. I loved seeing Albert's face as he spotted the likes of Andy Gray, Bob Geldof and Sir Richard Branson. Our Ronny and all his soccer mates from the Thirlmere pub came too. I cut my teeth as a manager carrying the bucket and magic sponge for pub teams like this.

One of the best remembered scenes in the movie is where I give a dressing room talk to the players just before they go out and play Argentina. It's a rousing, Land-of-Hope-and-Glory speech, which inspires them to score a goal although they still lose the game.

Ever since then I've had numerous requests to give pre-game talks – geeing up the players. I also get invitations to be a guest commentator, as though I'm some sort of expert. Truth is, I can only name about half the players in the Liverpool side.

I stopped going to The Kop years ago. In the old days I was really passionate about the game and when Liverpool got beat it used to affect me deeply. This can't be right, I thought. Football is a great game, but it's not the end of the world. That's when I stopped taking it so seriously.

Strange as it may seem, I don't get many offers to do love scenes. I figure people would probably pay good money to avoid that. Even so, I've been lucky enough to work with some wonderful actresses like Sue Johnston, Marion Bailey, Kate Fitzgerald, Brigit Forsyth, Joan Kempson, Amanda Redmond, Imelda Staunton and Kathy Burke, to name just a few.

My only real love scene was in an episode of *Clocking Off*, with a wonderful actress called Denise Black who has been in *Coronation Street*. In this particular episode I play a man whose wife (Kate Fitzgerald) suffers from a degenerative disease and needs constant care. Although I've been a loving husband, I decide to snatch a brief bit of happiness by having an affair with my wife's nurse.

The director Tom Shankland cleared the set for the love scene. (Notice I use the term 'love' and not 'sex', because the sex scenes you see portrayed on screen bear absolutely no relation to reality most of the time.)

Denise crawled under the sheets and I joined her. Only

Tom, a cameraman and a sound engineer were in the room.

'I want you to make lots of bonking noises,' said Tom. 'Just imagine we're not here.'

Not much chance of that.

Of course we both got a fit of the giggles and the situation soon deteriorated into helpless laughter. Denise was great fun and a real old pro, which made things easier. I wasn't even bothered about suffering from the embarrassing erection syndrome. I'm grateful to get one any time and Rita even more so.

Although I'm destined never to be a romantic lead, there is something rather nice about being a character actor because I get to play lots of quirky roles or provide the comic relief in more serious dramas.

In November 2001 I did *Once Upon a Time in the Midlands*, directed by Shane Meadows, who has done three films, including *TwentyFourSeven*, which I had turned down a few years earlier. This time I didn't hesitate. Shane wanted me to play a plumber who calls himself Charlie Nashville and moonlights as a guitar-playing country-and-western singer doing 'One Night Only' gigs every Saturday. Kathy Burke plays my wife and we look hilarious together, her in her shell suit and me wearing cowboy gear.

Kathy is a lovely girl, tough on the outside and tender-hearted underneath. She had a troubled childhood and turned her life around. I've heard someone call her the 'patron saint of the British underdog', which is a great description.

Once Upon a Time in the Midlands is the sort of film I really love – full of humour and real people. It contains about three different love stories but the main one is a love triangle between Rhys Ifans, Shirley Henderson and Robbie Carlyle.

My character Charlie Nashville was easy to play because I know at least twenty guys exactly like him. For instance, there's a smashing country-and-western singer in Liverpool called Lee Brennan and as soon as he puts on a stetson he starts talking in an American accent. I swear, if he takes the hat off in mid-song he goes back to Scouse. He doesn't know he's doing it.

Towards the end of filming, Shane Meadows asked if I would go down to London to record a song for the movie.

My mate Les Bather drove me down, but the traffic was so horrendous I began to panic. I knew the recording studio had only been booked for three hours at great expense and I didn't want to be late. We arrived with five minutes to spare and I walked into the studios, which were owned by George Martin, the legendary producer of The Beatles.

'We're not quite ready for you,' said one of the production staff. 'There's a café in the building. Order what you like.'

We had a pot of tea and at twenty past three someone fetched me to the studio. I was introduced to Guy Chambers, but I had no idea he was the song-writing partner of Robbie Williams.

'These are the songs we want you to record,' he said.

'Songs?'

'There are two of them.'

The first one is about six verses long, with eight lines to a verse and the second was eight verses long with four lines to a verse, not counting the choruses.

'Do you want to listen to the music a couple of times?' he asked.

'Why?'

'We're going to record the two of them now.'

'How long have we got the studio?'

'Three hours.'

'Start the car,' I said to Les, which is an old showbiz expression.

'What do you mean? What's wrong?' asked Guy.

'I can't do this.'

'Why?'

'How long does it take Robbie Williams to make an album?'

'About twelve months.'

'And you want me to do two songs in three fucking hours, when I've just seen the lyrics and never heard the music?'

Les and I walked out the door, got into the car and drove back to Nottingham. Meanwhile, there was murder. Phone calls flew back and forth and the producer of the film phoned me on my mobile while we were still on the motorway.

'They're bleating about how much it cost for the studio,' he said.

'That's show business. I'm not a singer. You can't expect me to just turn up and record two songs that I've never heard before.'

I talked to Shane Meadows who I have enormous respect for. He's a good, working-class lad, with no airs and graces.

'I'm awful sorry,' I told him.

'That's fair enough,' he said. 'We'll write a couple of songs ourselves.'

'That suits me.'

Totally independent of the film, I had just finished recording some songs for an album. My old mate Colin Walker (my foe in many twenty-four-hour Scrabble marathons and poker schools) had met a record producer in the New Year and they hatched the idea of me recording a song.

My first reaction was to laugh. Sure I love playing the banjo and belting out songs in the pub, but that doesn't make me good enough to record anything.

The producer already had a song in mind – 'Are You Lookin' at Me?' – an Irish tune by The Popes, who were a breakaway group formed by Shane MacGowan after he left The Pogues.

I agreed to listen to the track and was completely sold on the idea, particularly when he said I could work with anyone I wanted to. I got hold of former Slade frontman Noddy Holder through his agent. We struck a deal. He'd do the song with me if I gave him twelve quid, a bacon sandwich and use of my caravan for a week.

I wanted to use Noddy because I loved his style and his voice, which was very powerful and raucous. I also roped in Geoff Hughes and Michael Starke, who played Sinbad in *Brookside*.

We had great fun in the studio and the result surprised everyone, particularly myself. The publicity turned out to be the hardest part of the process. I finished up touring the country doing chat shows and performing the song. We did *Parkinson* and the crowd went wild. I can remember these two women in the front row who were yelling for an encore. One of them was Parky's wife, Mary, who came up and introduced herself afterwards.

'Are You Lookin' at Me?' entered the UK charts at number twenty-eight, which just goes to show that there's no accounting for public taste. Suddenly songs were being sent to me and there was talk of doing an album. Against my better judgement I agreed, but I couldn't really devote the time and energy necessary. The subsequent album, *Music My Arse*, was a reasonable effort, but I had no real desire to be a recording artist.

It did, however, help solve the problem of what to do about the songs for *Once Upon a Time in the Midlands*. I had written a couple of songs on the album with Colin Walker and a real Liverpool character, 'Woodsy', who reckons he's the best welder in the world (according to legend he can weld two pieces of paper together). The tracks had a real country-and-western flavour so I played them to Shane Meadows.

'They're absolutely perfect,' he said.

One of them finished up playing over the credits at the end of the film.

23

Saying Goodbye

Rita calls me 'drop it and hop it' because I drop things wherever I am and hop off to do whatever I'm doing. Meanwhile, she has to pick everything up. Although she's probably right, I'm not conceding anything. I know the thin end of a wedge when I see one.

It is Christmas and I'm doing a public appearance at Alder Hey Hospital in Liverpool. Some of the kids have devastated limbs and terminal diseases. There is a lovely Christmas tree and someone tells me that every light represents a child who has died. Yet these kids keep fighting and smiling. It's a humbling experience.

This is the first Christmas without Mam and I spend all day thinking about her. I can still picture her sitting in the armchair, looking out the doors to the water, with a half glass of champagne beside her.

I call Kate to wish her Happy Birthday and Merry Christmas. Paige gets on the phone and tells me excitedly what she found under the tree.

'I've still got a present for you,' I tell her.

'Have you, what is it?'

'I can't tell you. You'll have to wait.'

'Just tell me what it's like,' she says.

'No, I can't do that either.'

Then there's a pause. 'Are you coming over today, Grandad?'

I laugh. 'Not today, but I'll see you tomorrow.'

The lads are coming over on Boxing Day and they're both in good form. Clifton looks really healthy and I truly believe his problems are behind him. One positive aspect of the whole thing is that I'm spending a lot more time with him. The same is true of Gareth who calls me about six times a day.

I love all my kids. I might scream and shout and I haven't always been there for them, but I would die for them.

My relationship with Marlene is up and down. I'm the lightning rod if anything goes wrong and she can sometimes be vindictive, but I wish her all the happiness in the world.

The wedding is a week on Saturday. It's been planned to within an inch of its life and I won't be surprised if David Dimbleby and Angela Rippon are doing the bloody commentary.

Rita is having her hen night on Saturday. She and loads of girls are going to Ma Boyle's, a little jazz club in town. I've decided to have my stag night after the wedding, which is unconventional but probably safer considering some of the stuff my mates are likely to plan. It also means I can invite loads of people who I couldn't ask to the wedding.

I don't know how I'm going to choose – we'll end up inviting half of Liverpool at this rate. Friends have been coming up to me in the street saying, 'I haven't received my invitation yet, Rick.'

'Is that right? I don't know what's happened. Maybe it got lost in the post.'

I didn't think Mam would make it through the winter. Towards the end, in the bungalow, she wasn't going to bed. Instead she sat up in her easy chair, which was higher off the ground so she didn't have to lift herself up.

She had always been a big woman, but she seemed to be shrinking . . . disappearing.

She was really fond of Rita and now and again she would stay overnight with us. Rita decided to give her a bath one day and wash her hair. Everything was fine until it came time to get Mam out of the tub. She was too heavy for Rita to lift so they needed my help.

Mam was embarrassed about me seeing her naked so Rita drained the water out of the bath and draped a huge bath towel round her. I took off my shoes and socks and stood in the bath in front of Mam, while Rita stood behind. I put my arms around her and lifted. She was laughing hysterically by then and soon she had Rita going.

I helped her get one leg over the bath on to a footstool and then the next leg. She was laughing so hard she quivered like a jelly. We were all as bad as each other.

On 22 April 2002, Rita and me went on a Mediterranean cruise. Mam had seemed a bit stronger when we left. We were three days out of port when Ronny phoned.

'Mam's bad. She's gone into hospital.'

The next port of call was Parma in Italy, three days away. Mam had suffered a stroke and her condition was serious but stable. They were the longest days of my life until we reached land and caught the first flight to England. From the airport we went straight to the Royal Liverpool Teaching Hospital.

Mam looked awful and she had little awareness of people. They were swabbing her mouth with a sponge. The stroke had partially paralysed her face and lots of tubes were sticking out of her.

All four of her sons were there. The specialist asked if we wanted Mam resuscitated in the event of another stroke. He was sort of saying, 'I don't think it's a good idea given the condition of her heart. It would only do more damage.'

Without even having to talk about it, we all said, 'No, don't revive her.' She was eighty-six years old and she was burnt out. I just wanted her to go peacefully.

At first she was in the assessment ward, which had about six beds, with no privacy and gaping holes in the walls. Later they moved her upstairs to a lovely room that was spotlessly clean, but still showing signs of decay.

Talking to a big blonde nurse, she explained that each stroke patient is graded according to certain parameters. Fifteen points means their brain is still sound. Mam arrived with eleven points and had slipped down to six. I could almost see her deteriorating.

'She'll be moved out of this room and be taken back to Broadgreen or to the previous ward.'

Our David was having none of it. 'She's not going back there.'

None of our anger was directed at the staff. The nurses and doctors had been marvellous and deserved to be called 'angels'.

Of all the kids, Gareth was probably closest to his Gran and would phone her most days. I took him in to hospital and he stayed with her for perhaps an hour. By then she'd fallen into a coma and she couldn't see his tears.

On Monday 7 May, Ronny phoned me at home at six in the morning.

'We have to get to the hospital. Mam is getting worse.'

I arrived a few minutes after him and then came Albert and our David who lived furthest away. Mam was still in a coma. I kept saying under my breath, 'Please God, don't let her breathe any longer.'

Now and again she gave a strangled sigh and at one point she came round for a split second and uttered Gareth's name. It was the last word she spoke.

After a few hours I said to the others that we should sit

with her in shifts. Two of us should stay and the others could get off. Like with Dad, we wanted to make sure there was someone with her.

Ronny insisted that David and I go home for a few hours' rest. He and Albert stayed at the hospital. I had barely walked in the door when the phone rang. I raced back to the hospital, but she had already gone. She lay on the bed with her eyes closed. I kissed her forehead and squeezed her hand. Ronny was still fussing over her, smoothing her hair, closing her mouth and trying to straighten her paralysed lips. Honest to God, I don't know how he did it, but I was glad that he took over.

24

The Queue Starts Here

Saturday 4 January 2003

Waking up with a hangover on the morning of my wedding wasn't the plan. We were going to have an early night but the neighbours turned up with a bottle or two for a quiet pre-wedding drink. There is no such thing as a quiet drink under those circumstances.

I have never seen them so excited. They've spent a fortune on clothes and hats and stuff like that. It's all they've talked about for weeks. The buzz is infectious and I find myself getting caught up in the spirit of things.

Rita left at eight o'clock this morning. She and the bridesmaids, Claire, Kate and Paige, are getting ready at the Liverpool Marina and Harbourside Club. That's where we're having the ceremony and the reception.

I was still writing my speech when she left. We wished each other luck and that was it. Unless she gets cold feet I'll be seeing her soon enough.

The wedding is at one o'clock. I spend most of the morning in front of the TV, letting Albert fuss over our suits and whether the knots on the ties are too big. When it comes to sartorial decisions I always defer to Albert. Rita's son, Tony, is getting ready with us. He's giving Rita away.

A great big limo was initially going to take us to the yacht club, but I think that's over the top. Instead, Les Bather is going to drive us in his car, which is smart enough for the likes of me.

As we drive through the gates, reporters and cameramen jostle to get photographs and footage. *OK!* and *Hello!* have hired a team of local bouncers to stop any uninvited guests getting inside. These guys are bloody huge, but dressed real smart in white collar and tie. And they're really polite, opening car doors, ushering people inside, showing them where to go.

As I get out of the car all the reporters and photographers are yelling questions to me. I'm wearing a raincoat over my suit and an Aussie hat with corks bobbing around the edge. I go over and give them a few minutes.

'Why are you wearing that hat?' one of them asks.

'I'm going to Australia for me honeymoon,' I explain. 'I might even get a game for the England cricket side. The lads haven't been doing so well.'

I wave goodbye and turn back towards the club. For the first time I find myself getting nervous, but I only have to look at Albert and I feel much better. Nobody could be more nervous than he is.

Walking between the rows of seats I stop and say hello to loads of family and friends like Sue Johnston, Frank Carson, Stan Boardman, Ken Dodd, Liz Dawn, Faith Brown, Norman Collier, Eddie Archer and Noddy Holder. Gareth and Clifton look dead smart and really happy for me.

It takes me ages to reach the front where the registrar is waiting. Classical music is playing and the place looks like the inside of a florist shop. I keep fidgeting with my white waistcoat and glancing over my shoulder. Rita is always bloody late.

The music changes and then I see her on Tony's arm. She looks fabulous. It's like some magician has cast a spell.

The wedding gown (her description, not mine) is ivory silk crepe with gold inlet and a floor-length organza coat bordered with tiny gold beads to match the gold lace. And she's wearing a little tiara like Princess Diana.

'That's sound, that is, Rita,' I tell her when she reaches my side.

She has this huge smile and I can't tell if it's from the happiness or the champagne she and Claire have been drinking.

The registrar welcomes everyone and starts her spiel. She reaches the part where she asks if anyone present can give any reason why these two people should not be joined together . . .

I turn around and say, 'Come on, Doddy, help me out here?'

He replies, 'The queue starts here.'

From then on the entire ceremony is punctuated by one-liners and asides. The registrar eventually reminds the hecklers, 'This is Ricky and Rita's show.'

Sue Johnston gives a special reading, reminding everyone that she has played my wife twice (in *Brookside* and *The Royle Family*) which makes her well qualified to give advice to Rita.

Then she quotes from a *Woman and Home* article published in 1952 advising wives on how to care for their husband when he comes home after a hard day's work.

'Arrange his pillow and offer to take off his shoes. Speak in a low, soft, soothing and pleasant voice. Allow him to relax and unwind. Listen to him. Let him talk first . . . Never complain if he doesn't take you out to dinner, instead try to understand his world of stress and pressure . . .'

Sue ends by saying, 'Rita, I'm sure you know these things already and I'm also sure you know exactly where to put this advice.'

Everything passes so quickly that I want to slow things down so I can remember them better. Vows are exchanged and then the rings and the essential kiss. During the formalities of signing the register, I say to Rita, 'She's here, you know. Mam is looking down making sure everything is going all right.'

'Yeah, I know,' she says, giving my hand a squeeze.

While we pose for a thousand photographs all the guests get to drink champagne and start the party. The only people who haven't arrived are Sir John Mills, who is ill; Geoff Hughes and his wife, who are snowed in; Les Dennis, who is in South Africa, and Arthur Scargill, who is out of the country but does manage to get a message to us.

Frank Carson and Doddy have bookings tonight, but can stay for the reception, which is rowdy with loads of humour and spectacular food.

Of all the speeches (and there were lots of them) Tony makes the finest. You can see he's nervous. It must be daunting knowing that people like Frank Carson and Doddy are going to follow you.

'I don't want to get all cheesy or anything like that,' he says, and every woman in the place lets out a sigh. 'My Mum will always be a large rum and Diet Coke sort of person and that's because in her own immortal words, "Who could be arsed with a single?"

'The thing I like most about Rick is that he was only a celebrity until I met him. And then he was just Ricky, which to me is his best quality. He is the celebrity who drives me into town when I am drinking with me mates. And he's the celebrity that comes round and fixes the light switch at Claire's place – the same light switch he fitted, mind you.'

Tony gets choked up a couple of times, but everyone wills him to get through. His speech receives the biggest cheer of the day and he looks relieved.

Doddy and Frank are suitably irreverent when they come to speak and, of course, I'm the prime target. At one point Ken asks what possessed Rita to marry me. 'Had you run out of options or something? Do you ever fantasise that he's George Clooney? Or Bernard Manning?'

People don't want to leave and a lot of them finish up tagging along to the evening do at the Provincial, a local working men's club. We've planned for a hundred and eighty, but the more the merrier.

This is the do I've most wanted to have – all me old mates from the clubs and building sites, some I haven't seen for years. The lads from the Hi-Fi Three are here, including Scoggo and Tommy Scully. Tommy has a heart condition, but he brings the house down by getting up and singing.

Teddy Prescott, seventy-eight years old, plays the ukulele and gets so out of breath that he seems to be competing with Scully to have the first heart attack of the night. Cyl Con, at seventy-four, does a few ballads and Marie Rose breaks a tooth when she falls off the stage during her turn.

Halfway through the evening, we stop proceedings for a game of stand-up bingo. Everyone buys a bingo ticket and if the caller yells out a number on your ticket you have to sit down. The last one standing wins the prize.

Everyone comments on the food. There's ham, roast beef, salmon, trifles, meringues . . . I bet they don't have catering as good at Buckingham Palace. There's so much left over that I tell the manager to let the staff take it home.

'Let them have the biggest doggy bag they can carry and put some in the fridge for the cleaners in the morning.' It would have been a tragedy to waste it. We also take up a collection for the bar staff and raise £188 for tips.

I've given Billy Owens, the manager, a cheque and told him to make sure every glass stays full. Nobody abuses the privilege and I'll settle the bill in the morning.

In the same spirit, we haven't bothered with wedding presents. There's nothing we need. Instead we ask everyone for a five quid donation which we'll put towards a Sunshine Coach for underprivileged kids.

Paige is still dancing. She hasn't stopped all night.

'Where did you learn to dance like that?' I ask her.

'From watching *Dirty Dancing* on video,' she replies, bunching up her dress at her hips and twirling away from me. Later, when it's well past her bedtime, she stops dancing for just long enough to ask Rita, 'Can you get married again tomorrow?'

I don't know when the last person leaves, but the lads who have looked after security all day escort every last one of them into a taxi and make sure they get safely home.

I'm exhausted, but over the moon. There are so many people I didn't manage to invite, but I'm thrilled with the people who came. Kate, Paige, Gareth and Clifton are staying at a hotel around the corner from us. They're coming to ours in the morning for breakfast, along with Tony and Claire.

It's quite ironic that we chose the Provincial for the party. It's just a few hundred yards from where Mam's funeral procession passed and further along Everton Road is the Red Triangle. I can't get away from my past, it's all around me.

Mam always used to say to me, 'If you died tomorrow, Ricky Tomo, you'd have had three lives.'

She's right. People say I started with very little, but that's not true. I started with everything. I started with a loving mother and father who would have done anything for their kids. I wish they were here now. Dad would be on the dance floor while Mam would be sitting at a table, the star of the whole show.

Who'd have thought when I was living above the Red Triangle, without a penny in my pocket or arse in me kecks, that I'd finish up being married to Rita and on the front cover of *Hello!* and *OK!*?

Mam was right when she told me that I'd lived three lives, but even she might have miscounted. Maybe the fourth life is just beginning.

Epilogue

Oh, Lucky Man!

A very good friend of mine once told me that life is made up of bricks and balloons. When we die there is a scale that weighs our achievements. Each good thing earns us a balloon on one side of the scale while each bad thing puts a brick on the other. You need to do a lot more good things to balance it all out.

I don't have any other great theories on life or pearls of wisdom. Basically, I believe in keeping things simple and enjoying the everyday things like bacon sandwiches, live music, dogs with sad eyes, quiz nights and three channels of sport on satellite TV. More people should play the banjo and take up painting as a hobby. Diets should be made easier. Emile Heskey should be taught to remain on his feet and football should be returned to the people. Every kid deserves to have a job; trade unions should be treasured and not demonised; rolling contracts should be outlawed and New Labour should stop masquerading as a party for the workers.

I firmly believe that opportunity knocks every single day, but not everyone opens the door or makes it welcome. With a lot of luck, the right breaks and a bit of talent, then even someone like me can succeed. There are actors out there who are so good that I don't deserve to lick their boots. Some have never been discovered because they haven't been given the chance or maybe don't believe enough in themselves.

Why did it happen for me? I honestly don't know, but I thank Roland Joffe every day. I suppose I'm a bossy bastard. I gee people up, organise things and make things happen. Maybe my face just seems to fit, which is a pretty scary thought.

If a letter came through my letterbox tomorrow morning and said, 'Sorry, your career is finished', I wouldn't shed a tear. I have had a wonderful time. I have made a few quid. I have given a few quid away and I've made a few people laugh along the way.

I have filmed in Hong Kong, Germany, Australia and Brazil. I've even made a record that climbed into the charts. That'll do me. I'll happily step aside and let someone else have a go.

Years ago when I worked on *Brookside* a small part came up and the casting department offered it to a great old British actor called Ian Hendry. I remember being really excited about meeting him because Ian Hendry was a screen legend. In 1960 he starred in *Police Surgeon* and also in the original *Avengers* series as Dr David Keel, the first partner of Patrick McNee before Honor Blackman and Diana Rigg came on the scene. Later he made dozens of films including *Children of the Damned* and *Get Carter* with Michael Caine, which won him a BAFTA.

Hendry had been one of the most handsome actors of his generation. He married an actress, Janet Munro, and they were always being photographed by society magazines and showbiz papers.

This is the man I expected to meet, but the one who arrived on set that first day looked awful. Someone said that he'd recovered from throat cancer and I know he suffered from problems with alcohol.

He was staying at the Adelphi Hotel and someone picked him up every morning and brought him to the set to make sure he arrived on time. He must have ached inside when he realised how far he had fallen. From being a huge star he had become a bit-part actor in a soap opera.

I don't put myself in anywhere near the same class as Ian Hendry. He was a *real* actor. But if the roles dry up tomorrow, I know I can always make a living playing the banjo and putting on little variety shows. Ian Hendry didn't have that luxury. Acting is all he knew.

I still have the same circle of friends that I've had since I was a teenager. I live less than a mile from where I grew up; I still play Scrabble twice a week with Eddie Ross. We have our own set of rules about using abbreviations and if anyone loses a challenge they get docked twenty-five points. The rivalry is terrifying.

I have a wonderful wife, three great kids, my grandchildren and my brothers. Although both of them are gone now, I also feel that Mam and Dad are still with me. I can hear their voices in my head, telling me when I've done them proud or if I could have tried harder. I miss them dreadfully.

Although I'm satisfied with what I've achieved, it doesn't mean I'm going to rest on my laurels or retire to feed the ducks. There are lots of things I still want to do.

For the past forty years I've dreamed of getting a comedy show band together with lots of great musicians and personalities. I want to call it Colonel Bogy's Ex-Servicemen's Military Musical Ensemble as a tribute to the 'crippled' veterans and chancers who I used to see playing in the streets after the war.

I would happily do another series of *The Royle Family* and I fancy working in Hollywood at least once. A few years back I had a call about doing a buddy film with Brad Pitt, but the casting director had assumed I was younger and slimmer.

I don't think I would ever do another TV soap unless it was extra special. If I did go back I think it would be at the end of my career. There are some great actors working on these shows and I think we underestimate some of them.

I would love to create a TV show and have written a script for the pilot of a series that the BBC is considering. Called *Tomo, Dick and Harry*, it's about three guys who do a bit of plastering and building during the day and spend their nights in pubs and clubs. Tomo is a compere, Dick plays guitar and Harry is the pot man collecting the glasses.

I'm also working on a kids' show, *Rusty and Dusty*, and me and Eddie Ross are always coming up with ideas for game shows during our Scrabble marathons.

Apart from that, I have only one other ambition. It has been nurtured for nearly thirty years – not just for me, but for Dezzie, who is crippled with Parkinson's disease and doing it tough. I know I can't turn back the clock and reclaim the years we spent in jail. Nor can I alter the effects of the liquid cosh and give him back his health. I can, however, try to restore his reputation by seeking to overturn our convictions and have us declared not guilty.

I want to see justice done. It's never too late for that.

Acknowledgements

A lot of people have helped me with this book; so many that I can't begin to thank them all here. They know who they are, and how much I appreciate all their support. But I would like to give a special mention to Michael Robotham, who has worked tirelessly to help me get my story into shape, and who has become a good friend in the process.

Picture Credits

Plate 1: 1–14 from author's private collection; 15–17 (on release from prison and at TUC conference) © PA Photos Ltd; 18 (Right to Work rally) © Getty Images. Plate 2: 1, 17 (The Grants; with Caroline Aherne) © UPPA; 2, 7, 10, 11 from author's private collection; 3 (Roland Joffe) © Kobal Collection; 4, 5, (*Riff Raff* with Robert Carlyle; in bath) © Parallax/Courtesy Kobal Collection; 6 (with Ken Loach) © Steve Finn, Alpha; 8 (*Raining Stones* with Bruce Jones) © Parallax/Channel 4/Courtesy Kobal Collection; 9 (Limelight bar) © *Liverpool Echo*; 12 (scene from *Cracker*) © Granada Television; 13 (*Dockers*) © Channel 4; 14–16 (*The Royle Family*) © BBC. Plate 3: 1, 2, 4–6, 10, 11, 13, 14, 16, 17 from author's private collection; 3 (with Doddy and Mam) © Doug McKenzie; 7 (with Arthur Scargill) © John Powell; 8 (with Rita) © Trevor Owen; 9, 12 (Jim Royle playing the banjo; on *Parkinson*) © BBC; 13 (with Ally McCoist) © John Daly Show; 15 (as Mike Bassett) © Artists Ind. Network Flash Film

Council/Courtesy Kobal Collection; 18 (with Robert Carlyle and Samuel L. Jackson, *The 51st State*) © UPPA; 19 (with Johnny Vegas, *The Virgin of Liverpool*) © Mob Film company; 20–23 (wedding) © *OK!* magazine.

Index

SERIOUS

The Autobiography

The Number One International Bestseller

John McEnroe

John McEnroe made waves from his very first Wimbledon in 1977. An eighteen-year-old qualifier from Queens, New York, he stunned the tennis world by reaching the semi–finals, and shocked it with his on court behaviour. What followed was a double act of technique and temperament that set the sport alight: SuperMac, the sublime, unorthodox genius, who won seven Grand Slams and seventy-seven singles titles; Superbrat, the foul-mouthed fireball, furiously yelling at officials, fans, players and himself alike.

John McEnroe can be serious. He can also be humorous, impassioned, controversial and painfully honest. This is his autobiography; a book as enthralling and as straight-talking as the great man himself.

'McEnroe emerges as a funny, wise and articulate raconteur, acutely aware of his foibles . . . *Serious* is an antidote to the anodyne dross contained in most sporting autobiographies' *The Times*

'Frank and engrossing' *Daily Telegraph*

'An ace' *Sunday Express*

'A fascinating insight into the mind of a true legend' *The Times*

GREAVSIE

The Autobiography

Jimmy Greaves

A goalscoring legend. One of the game's great characters. A man who faced down the demons. A top television pundit and columnist. This is the story of James Peter 'Jimmy' Greaves, one of the all-time greats of English football.

Greavsie is a gripping and truthful autobiography, the story of a remarkable life laced with Jimmy's trademark wit. It is a fascinating account of the golden era of football, the characters who populated it, and the goalscoring machine at the centre of it all.

'Top-notch autobiography . . . An inspiring story of a hero who earned his right to a second chance' *Sunday Times*

'Candid and poignant' *Independent on Sunday*

Other bestselling Time Warner Paperback titles available by mail:

The prices shown above are correct at time of going to press. However, the publishers reserve the right to increase prices on covers from those previously advertised, without further notice.

――――――――――――― **timewarner** ―――――――――――――
paperbacks

TIME WARNER PAPERBACKS
PO Box 121, Kettering, Northants NN14 4ZQ
Tel: 01832 737525, Fax: 01832 733076
Email: aspenhouse@FSBDial.co.uk

POST AND PACKING:
Payments can be made as follows: cheque, postal order (payable to Time Warner Books) or by credit cards. Do not send cash or currency.
All UK Orders   **FREE OF CHARGE**
EC & Overseas   25% of order value

Name (BLOCK LETTERS) . . . .

Address . . . .

. . . .

Post/zip code: . . . .

☐ Please keep me in touch with future Time Warner publications

☐ I enclose my remittance £ . . . .

☐ I wish to pay by Visa/Access/Mastercard/Eurocard

Card Expiry Date
